CHANGE EVERYTHING AT ONCE!

The Tavistock Institute's Guide to Developing Teamwork in Manufacturing

Jean E. Neumann, Richard Holti
and
Hilary Standing

First published in 1995 by Management Books 2000 Ltd
125A The Broadway, Didcot, Oxfordshire OX11 8AW
Tel. 01235-815544. Fax. 01235-817188

Printed and bound in Great Britain by WBC Book Manufacturers, Bridgend

British Library Cataloguing in Publication Data is available

ISBN 1-85251-128-1

Foreword

Throughout my career in Personnel and Industrial Relations people have talked about teamwork. This was usually defined in very general terms, using phrases like 'pulling together' and 'support for colleagues'. In recent years teamwork has taken on an altogether sharper edge. In many companies it has meant a complete change in the way work is organised, with employees being divided into self-contained groups with greater responsibility for their own output and the way their work is prioritised and performed. This in turn has led us to rethink the need for supervision, to redefine the role of managers and ultimately to make changes, some of them dramatic, in our management structures. Frequently the move towards teamworking has been further complicated by the need for companies to cut costs and reduce the size of their workforce in order to maintain competitiveness.

ACAS has monitored these changes and observed their effect on industrial relations and we were pleased to join The Tavistock Institute in the Teamwork in Manufacturing project. This book follows two years' intensive research into six core companies and a wider network of interested organisations. The changes within these organisations, especially those involving people, were complex and did not lend themselves to simple analysis or conclusions. *Change Everything at Once!* will help organisations to analyse the issues and dilemmas involved and provides methods for developing and reinforcing teamwork across a wide range of circumstances.

John Hougham
Chairman, Advisory Conciliation and Arbitration Service

Contents

1

Introduction

The title of this book, *Change Everything at Once!*, captures a feeling widely reported by people inside today's organisations. They feel overwhelmed with the volume of change with which they have to cope. It seems to them that everything within their workplace is changing: the jobs they do, the rules that guide their behaviour, the way they are paid, the technology with which they work, their boss's behaviour, and the criteria for judging whether they are doing a good job. Even the very definition of what is inside and what is outside their organisation is being challenged. It looks as if all aspects of the organisation as they have known it have been, or are being, changed. Their bosses warn them that even more will have to change as soon as possible if their organisation is to survive.

Such feelings are common during comprehensive organisational change, especially those in which business strategy and product development, along with new technologies, often play a major role. Employees experience such comprehensive change as too much to cope with, too fast. By definition, comprehensive changes usually involve realignment of organisational structure (including flow of business processes), work design, decision-making processes, communication procedures, and assertion of new norms as to how employees should think and behave. These changes are sometimes also referred to as 'cultural' because nearly all significant aspects of the organisation are implicated.

Organisational leaders face the seemingly impossible challenge of managing the many, simultaneous and sequential initiatives necessary for bringing about comprehensive developments and change. The subtitle of this book, *The Tavistock Institute's Guide To Developing Teamwork in Manufacturing*, indicates that we at The Tavistock Institute consider 'teamwork' to be just such a genuinely comprehensive change. This book summarises what we have been able to learn that might help others to meet the challenge of making this particular type of change, within this particular industrial sector.

The TIM Project

For nearly 50 years, the Institute has concerned itself with 'semi-autonomous work groups' and other forms of job and organisational design which attempt to address both social and technical issues. In fact, The Tavistock Institute's original 1950s work on 'socio-technical systems' has played a significant role in the history behind the current wave of teamwork throughout the industrialised world. Developments in both Scandinavia and North America from the 1960s to the 1980s often involved members of the Institute in projects which were destined to become influential.

However, not all of the developments in teamwork are ones which the current staff at The Tavistock Institute would point to with pride. Innovations in the 1960s and 70s, under the rubric of 'quality of working life', were designed to make a contribution both to employee satisfaction and to productivity. Overcoming work alienation and retaining good employees were typical motivations. But innovations in the 1980s and 90s have not always combined these values.

Major redundancies and a decrease in trade union influence have often accompanied so-called 'empowerment' and teamwork programmes. Workers can feel coerced into 'enriched jobs' and 'flexibility'. Executives and senior managers feel swept up into teamwork as the direction in which they too must take their companies in order to remain competitive, cut costs and increase responsiveness to customer demands. Managers who argued against employee participation in the late 1960s find themselves being dragged into training on how to be a 'coach' or a participative manager in a dramatically flatter organisation.

It was the desire to try to address just these sorts of tensions and contradictions that motivated staff within the Institute's Organisational Change and Technological Innovation programme (OCTI) to undertake research and development on approaches and methods for encouraging workplace innovations that address satisfactorily both business rationales and the needs of employees. For over 20 years, OCTI staff have engaged in action research projects with individual companies developing such innovations. More recently, they have undertaken larger projects with many companies involved.

The 'teamwork in manufacturing' (TIM) project was one such major project. Funded in part by the UK government's Department of Trade and Industry (DTI) from 1992 to 1994, it fell under their 'Manufacturing, Organisation, People and Systems' (MOPS) programme. This book is one outcome of the TIM project: designed to provide methods for introducing, developing and reinforcing teamwork in manufacturing.

The TIM project was a three-way collaboration between social scientists, manufacturing companies, and industrial relations specialists. Social scientists from The Tavistock Institute (Richard Holti, Jean Neumann, Hilary Standing and – until July 1994 – Mark Stein) provided expertise on the management of comprehensive changes and relevant research methodology. Virginia Rounding administered the project. Senior industrial relations officers and quality of working life advisers from ACAS (the Advisory, Conciliation and Arbitration Service) provided expertise on both the content and process of integrating industrial relations issues into comprehensive changes.

Including ACAS in the TIM project was a conscious choice, precisely because inadequate attention to industrial relations typically plagues teamwork-related changes. Campbell Ford, from the ACAS Head Office, led a team composed of Joyce Ashcroft (for the duration of the TIM project), Frank Price and Brian Chaney (for the second year), and Ian Hodge and Norman Bannatyne (for the first year). Within the UK, ACAS are available to provide advice on industrial relations issues connected to teamworking. Addresses of their regional offices can be found in local telephone directories.

Six core companies participated in research and development activities over the two-year period between 1992 and 1994. Each site had a project leader and key actors who met in a monthly project meeting to review actions and emerging issues, and to plan next steps. Representatives from the core companies met quarterly to study issues they had in common. At some points in this book, case material from core companies is presented with the relevant company's name appearing in bold letters. Examples illustrating themes from more than one core company appear with pseudonyms. The core companies and key actors were:

- **Acco-Rexel Ltd**, Llangeinor, produces metal and plastic-based stapling and tacking machines, staplers and paper clips for home and industrial purposes; part of a US multi-national corporation. (Trevor Hoskins and Tom Fitzgerald.)
- **BICC Cables**, Blackley, produces metallic telecommunications cables for an international market; part of a British multinational corporation. (Keith Bott and Jo Young.)
- **Britax Vega Ltd**, Droitwich, produces lighting and electrical components for the automotive industry; part of a British multinational corporation. (Tom Wilkins and Maureen Nightingale.)
- **Leyland Trucks Manufacturing Ltd**, Leyland near Preston, designs and produces light and medium-sized trucks for European and international markets; formerly owned by DAF and now an independent British company. (Stewart Pierce and Alan Tonge.)
- **Rover Group Ltd**, Longbridge near Birmingham, designs, produces and markets small, medium and executive class cars; formerly owned by British Aerospace and now owned by BMW. The purchasing department was involved in TIM. (Richard Boorne, Diane Rance and Keith Day.)
- **Tucker Fasteners Ltd**, Birmingham, produces various types of metal rivets and similar fasteners; part of a US multinational corporation. (Mike Cunniffe and John Morgan.)

In addition to these six core companies, another 20 companies participated in a TIM network for the duration of the TIM project. These companies sent representatives to quarterly working conferences at which special topics were examined. The network companies also provided valuable additional data about their own change projects, and especially data about change initiatives in particular areas. When case material from a network company is presented, the company's name has been changed to a pseudonym to protect their confidentiality.

Even though this book is an outcome of the TIM project, data from other organisations has been included. This is because The Tavistock Institute has a rich store of accumulated experience from consulting to manufacturing companies over the years. Through these consultations, it has been possible to explore some change initiatives not covered during the TIM project. When a client organisation's case material is presented, a pseudonym has been used.

The Complexity of Teamwork

In *Change Everything at Once!* scientific staff from The Tavistock Institute report the results of the TIM project, and relevant consultations, in a way that we hope organisational leaders will find useful. By organisational leaders we mean executives, senior managers, middle managers, technical specialists and employee representatives – in short, those people inside the organisation who find themselves in the position of planning and implementing changes related to teamwork. Consultants to those inside organisations might also find the book useful.

In its most expansive and hopeful meaning, a teamwork-oriented organisation uses the principle of 'autonomy, in the context of responsibility, linked to organisation-wide influence' (Neumann, 1989). This can be applied to individual, group, sub-unit and organisation-wide activities. At an individual level, this usually means that one's job tends to require more discretion, to use both manual and mental skills, to demand more psychological attention, to combine elements that previously were located in several jobs, to attract more direct accountability for outcomes, and to necessitate a high degree of cooperation with peers, managers and people from other groups. Flexibility, job enrichment, job enlargement, and empowerment are typical words or phrases used to describe such changes to jobs.

At a group level, teamwork takes many different forms

[13]

indicated by such labels as 'semi-autonomous work groups', 'production cells', 'customer teams', and 'naturally occurring working groups'. Regardless of the form, however, group-based work involves a set of individuals taking mutual responsibility for a section of a production process, a particular function or a particular issue. Often, some managerial tasks or service tasks are also given to the group.

Depending on the size of the 'team' and the sub-unit of which it is a part, teamwork may also involve individuals and groups taking part in product or process improvement activities. *Ad hoc* problem-solving groups, 'quality or customer improvement teams' and 'cross-functional project teams' are examples. Similarly, individuals and groups may be required to send representatives to organisation-wide bodies for solving problems, planning changes and negotiating with other sections of the organisation. Factory-wide 'improvement groups', joint 'cross-functional' review and planning teams, works councils, employee associations, and co-determination often complement the individual, group and sub-unit elements of teamwork.

In order to introduce, develop and reinforce teamwork in manufacturing, organisational leaders must practise the craft of implementing specific changes that lie within the authority of traditional functions as well as addressing the interconnections amongst these more functional changes. Typically, many different methods are used within a manufacturing organisation – both advantageous and disadvantageous – in order to make teamwork-related changes. The motivations for making changes in one area are often different from the motivation for making changes in another.

However, organisational leaders often do not perceive or understand that changes within a particular function – accounting or production planning, for example – have anything to do with teamwork. Only in retrospect does it become apparent that a change in one section of the organisation is connected to a change in another. A teamwork organisation is created by making alterations, simultaneously and sequentially, both within individual functions and in ways that cut across the entire organisation.

The TIM Book

Change Everything at Once! is written with the needs in mind both to implement specific changes and to address overall interconnections. Chapters 2 and 3 describe the history, context and types of teamwork. Chapters 5 to 9 discuss issues in making changes specific to the five particular aspects of organisation implicated in creating a teamwork organisation:

- Business and organisational strategy
- Work design and related training developments
- Quality, manufacturing and engineering systems
- Business planning and accounting systems
- Industrial relations and personnel practices.

In each chapter, a number of methods are described for carrying out changes, and their relevance to teamwork explored, usually through case studies. Chapters 4, 10 and 11 address the difficulty of changing one aspect of organisation without working with the interconnections with other aspects that are changing or need change as well. We argue for the importance of planning and sequencing many simultaneous and sequential change initiatives. Chapter 4 provides a framework for thinking about comprehensive changes as they develop over a long period of time. Different aspects of organisation are changed at different times, sometimes alongside each other and sometimes following on from one another. Chapter 10 offers a model for development of teams over time – a development possible only through comprehensive change.

Chapter 11 presents a methodology for reviewing the multiple issues that need to be addressed during a comprehensive change, and for planning how to schedule and sequence the changes needed. The purpose of the methodology is to help organisational leaders find a way to manage specific functional changes simultaneously with managing the interconnections and uncertainties inherent in comprehensive change. Hopefully, the methodology, the framework and the options for change contained in this book will also help decrease the feeling of being overwhelmed at everything changing at once.

How to Use this Book

The main point of *Change Everything at Once!* can be stated simply: in order to succeed at introducing, developing and reinforcing teamwork in manufacturing, executives and senior managers need to bring about changes to specific aspects of their organisation and, at the same time, pay attention to the interconnections between those changes. A certain degree of complementarity must be achieved so that consistent messages are being sent to employees about the role behaviours required of them.

This book has been written in a way to facilitate this dual attention to specific changes and their interconnections. Chapters 5-9 describe methods useful for changing specific aspects of organisation. Thus, people within the relevant functions and occupational groups may benefit from reading these chapters.

Those executives, senior managers and specialists concerned with the overall direction of the teamwork and with managing multiple change initiatives may benefit from studying Chapters 4, 10 and 11. These chapters focus specifically on the importance of interconnections.

Personnel unfamiliar with teamwork may benefit from reading Chapters 2 and 3. The history and context of teamwork provide a good introduction to the motives of organisational leaders committed to introducing teamwork. Chapter 3 might help clarify some of the confusion about the many types of teamwork being used by companies.

Like any field of practice, practitioners of organisational change and technological innovation have a tendency to create their own jargon. New terms and phrases appear on the consultancy market every year in an attempt to capture the minds and pocket books of potential converts. Even The Tavistock Institute has been guilty of adding to the jargon of organisational change. In this book, however, we try to speak in as straightforward a language as possible. This isn't always easy as we are describing aspects of human behaviour in workplaces and under conditions of change. We do refer to popular methodologies by their most common names, using single quotation marks to indicate their status as jargon the first time they occur in the book.

Further Reading

Neumann, J. E. 1989. Why people don't participate in organizational change. In Pasmore W.A. and R.W. Woodman (Eds.), *Research in Organization Change and Development*, Volume 3. Greenwich, CT: JAI Press, pp. 181-212.

2

Teamwork in Organisations: History and Context

Teamworking is an old idea experiencing renewal in many contemporary enterprises. Bookshops are full of titles exhorting managers to 'take the teamworking road'. At the same time, those who are already travelling on this road are well aware that it is not an instant solution or quick fix, but a lengthy, complex process involving many areas of organisational change. Further, each organisation will experience the process in a distinctively different way. Step-by-step prescriptions are of limited value in the messy, real world of organisational change.

In this chapter, we look briefly at the background to the current interest in teamworking in organisations and why organisations are showing so much interest in it. This forms a context for the following chapter which considers the kinds of teams that might be introduced and developed in relation to particular organisational aims.

A History of Ideas about Teamworking

Teamworking seems like a new idea to many people, but as a mode of workplace organisation it has a long history in Europe, the USA and Japan. Interest in the theory and practice of group-based work stretches back several decades. Many different historical strands can be traced. In the US, pioneering studies of industrial work organisation and workers' motivation were carried out from the late 1920s by Elton Mayo and his associates under what became characterised as the 'human relations' school of industrial relations (Blumberg, 1968). A central finding of this school emphasised the impact on productivity of positive attention from managers.

The work of the social psychologist, Kurt Lewin, and his colleagues in the 1930s and 40s laid the groundwork for extensive study of groups in their own right. Lewin's work on group dynamics and leadership derived partly from his industrial experiences and partly from his desire to prevent a repetition of Nazism. He was the first researcher to distinguish participative leadership from authoritarian leadership. From field and laboratory experiments, Lewin conceptualised groups as configurations of forces which derived from the wider environment as well as from the individual. He thus raised questions about the power of groups to influence the behaviour of their members. Crucial to the history of teams, he demonstrated the usefulness of a democratic leader on the creativity and effectiveness of the group.

Common to this early work is a set of concerns with how individuals relate to groups in a work setting and how groups affect the behaviour of individuals. Researchers and practitioners were searching for an approach to work organisation that would produce a more satisfying working life and hence greater commitment and motivation within the workforce. The importance of a participative style of management dominated US thinking on this topic for years.

In Britain, however, a more structural approach was emerging. Early post-war work at The Tavistock Institute became the foundation for much of the thinking about the quality of working life in Europe and, then eventually, in the US. The 'socio-technical' systems approach derived originally from research on the effects of the introduction of new technology on working practices in the British coalmining industry (Trist and Bamforth, 1951). With mechanisation, small groups of workers who had been responsible for a whole task were replaced by large groups of 40-50, working on fractions of a task. Sickness rates increased and productivity declined. Tavistock Institute researchers established that the new technology only delivered production gains when combined with a return to smaller self-regulatory work groups, coordinating with each other across shifts. Both group effectiveness and individual motivation improved dramatically. Additional research – for example, that undertaken in an Indian textile factory (Miller and Rice, 1967) – contributed to the development of the concept of the 'semi-autonomous work group'. Nearly three decades later, many teams are structured along principles developed from this research.

The significance of this work has been very wide-ranging. From the point of view of thinking about work teams, it provided a conceptual framework for linking the social and psychological needs of individuals in the workplace to specific kinds of work organisation. An important set of assumptions stemming from this empirical work (and supported by some psychological findings) concerns individual and group needs for autonomy and responsibility in relation to the work performed. Autonomy may be defined broadly as a high degree of self-direction and self-control in determining the performance of work tasks and in achieving their coordination. The associated hypothesis is that workers with greater autonomy and responsibility will be more committed and motivated to achieve better performance.

Concern with increasing workforce motivation and commitment underlies the many approaches which come together under the rubric of the Quality of Work Life (QWL) movement. In the late 1960s and early 1970s (perhaps significantly at a time of high employment and still expanding industrial economies in the Northern Hemisphere) increasing attention began to be paid to the conditions of working life, particularly in automated systems of production.

According to some organisational theorists, the emergence of QWL in the US was a response both to the need for greater employee well-being, which was part of the wider democratic movement for citizens' rights, and a concern with declining productivity. The problem of what became known as the alienated or dissociated workforce, as manifest in high rates of absenteeism and labour turnover and poor product quality, was linked to low job satisfaction.

Researchers and practitioners blamed scientific management, with its routinised, fragmented tasks on automated production lines, for low job satisfaction and the resulting poor productivity and rising absenteeism. A few significant trade unions and influential social scientists used QWL principles to insist that work should be redesigned in such a way that it met both organisational objectives and the social and psychological needs of employees. Job design emerges during this period as an important way of developing group-based working.

Early versions of QWL in the US focused on individual job enrichment, an approach pioneered by the psychologist Frederick Herzberg. Later versions, in both the US and Europe, were influenced strongly by socio-technical systems theory in recognising the need to make more fundamental changes in the whole organisation, and notably in the role of management. QWL programmes thus became associated with a wide range of measures to improve job satisfaction which focused on the workplace as a whole, such as employee involvement, decentralised authority, participative forms of management, job redesign and semi-autonomous work groups. Their significance varied. Scandinavian countries adopted QWL strategies as part of a comprehensive commitment to industrial democracy. In Britain, on the other hand, QWL programmes have achieved little formal recognition from the state and have not been high on the agenda of the trade unions. However, the publicly funded Work Research Unit (under the auspices of the Department of Employment) actively promoted QWL ideas until its closure in 1993.

Interest in the work group or team from the 1950s to the 1970s thus shows a certain continuity. Work groups were a means of returning autonomy and control to workers involved in automated production. They accomplished this through making groups responsible for a whole product or process and for the tasks involved in coordinating production. Work groups were linked to an improved quality of working life by giving individuals meaningful and varied tasks to perform and enabling them to exercise greater control and choice over

[21]

the conditions under which they carried out their work. Such changes were expected, in turn, to be reflected in a greater commitment to work and improved productivity. The problem of the alienated or dissociated workforce was seen essentially as a motivational one. Autonomous or self-regulating work groups were an effective route to increasing motivation.

Post-war Japan has been the other significant arena for the development of ideas about group-based work. Japan's manufacturing success was built up out of conditions of acute scarcity which required a rethinking of every aspect of the manufacturing process (as exemplified in the concept of 'lean production'). Many of these ideas and practices have been borrowed or adapted by European and North American firms, and Japanese manufacturing practices have become the standard to which leading manufacturers aspire. In fact, many aspects of Japanese management, such as employee suggestion schemes, quality circles and other quality control techniques, arguably originated in Europe and the US but were incorporated and improved upon by the Japanese as part of a comprehensive restructuring of their manufacturing industries.

This restructuring addressed, most prominently, the need to improve quality through the lean and efficient use of all resources. While the European and North American traditions of group-based work were rooted in a much wider debate about participative models of management and employee involvement, Japanese models are not primarily concerned with individual employee involvement and autonomy, but with harnessing employees' capabilities to collective goals of quality, efficiency and customer service.

Current models of teamwork represent something of a hybrid of the different traditions. As we shall see below, teamwork may be driven by hard-headed concerns about efficiency and quality but it can also be understood and represented differently by different stakeholders.

Trade union representations of teamwork vary considerably. Some unions consider teamwork to be a barely disguised way of intensifying workloads and attacking carefully protected skill differentials. For others, it appears to offer developmental opportunities to employees whose training requirements and working conditions have long been neglected. Similarly, for managers, teamwork can be an exciting challenge in changing the 'culture' of an organisation, or a threat to their own jobs and status. Such differences caution against the almost unlimited optimism manifest in some current literature on teamwork in which 'everyone is a winner'.

In summary, the concept of working in a group or team has been fairly consistently associated with ideas about improving motivation and commitment, productivity and the quality of people's working lives. In particular, the semi-autonomous work group has provided, for nearly half a century, an influential alternative way of thinking about work organisation. Teamwork has been considered a viable alternative to the principles of Taylorism, or scientific management. More recently, concepts coming out of Japan emphasise efficient use of all resources, including human, and management of the workforce to make a total contribution to the achievement of quality and productivity goals.

The reasons for the recent, more mainstream interest in teamwork are somewhat different from the underlying concerns of earlier decades. The primary concern for improved motivation and commitment has given way to a direct concern for improved performance on cost, quality and innovation. Even so, some threads of continuity can be found.

Teamwork for Responding to Global Competition

Why have so many organisations begun to introduce teamworking or to develop their existing teams further? The answers to this question lie very much in the changed conditions of world markets and in the potential created by new manufacturing concepts and techniques. Commercial pressures of a global nature have led executives and senior managers to search for an approach to work organisation that would mobilise the workforce to meet these pressures. This motivation accounts for the remarkable spread of teamworking into manufacturing organisations.

During the 1980s, the Japanese and other Pacific Rim manufacturers increasingly posed a serious competitive threat to European and North American firms. They were able to capture world markets through new or improved quality products, produced at lower cost. The Japanese succeeded through 'putting the customer first'. Success in world markets was won through driving down costs and producing products or services which were distinctive – sometimes in design, usually in reliability, and often both. Design distinctiveness may be in terms of quality or innovation, or in the ability to customise products for particular consumer groups.

These competitive pressures have forced Western manufacturers to develop new business strategies. Whether firms decide to compete on cost, product, quality or product innovation, they face the need to rethink and restructure their organisations to cope with changing demands. A positive assessment of teamwork has emerged in this context.

Different kinds of teamwork can help managers to achieve the competitive advantages they seek. Overall labour costs can be reduced by introducing self-directed shop floor teams. This results in flatter hierarchies and pushes responsibilities downwards. It increases labour flexibility through multi-skilling and reduces the number of functional and support staff required.

Quality control and continuous improvement programmes are also linked to teamworking. On a technical basis, multi-skilled teams can take responsibility for quality control and waste reduction and can operate with lower inventory. Socially, self-directed work teams may be more motivated to take on continuous improvement activities and solve production and quality problems.

Firms seeking to innovate with new products may find cross-functional teams the best way to bring production and design staff closer together. Such teams enable greater collaboration and communication across the organisation. The need to develop a 'customer-driven' organisation has prompted organisations to develop relationships with suppliers and customers which stress inter-organisational teamworking.

Teamworking and New Manufacturing Techniques

Changes in production technology, particularly the availability of information technology, enable production to be much more flexibly organised. Small batches and non-standardised products can be produced more easily. Consumer choice can be increased. At the same time, new production processes require changes to the way work is organised. This means a move away from standard mass production. Mass production and scientific management have grown up together: a very detailed division of labour with strict job descriptions combined with little interplay between different stages of production.

Instead, a more flexible, teamwork-based organisation becomes possible. This involves multi-skilling, cooperation across conventional hierarchical and functional divisions and devolved responsibility for monitoring and improving quality. Information technology plays an important role in enabling shop floor employees to take on this responsibility. Conventional distinctions within the workforce become blurred as work becomes increasingly focused on the product or process.

Many researchers and practitioners have seen these new organisational concepts as stemming from information technology. However, in many branches of manufacturing, these changes have come about through the influence of Japanese production concepts which have very little to do with information technology. Some researchers and practitioners consider these to be the most important set of techniques driving change. Lean production, which emphasises the much more economical and flexible use of all factors of production, technical and human, emerged out of the Japanese car industry (Womack et al., 1990). It has diffused, in the West, both through competition and collaboration with Japanese companies.

Similarly, the notion of 'world class manufacturing' (Schonberger, 1986) applies Japanese style production methods developed out of manufacturing systems engineering. 'Just-in-time' (JIT) production scheduling and cellular production layouts keep inventory to a minimum and improve materials handling. In human and organisational terms, this goes along with product-focused manufacturing cells. Cells contain teams of operators who take responsibility for quality, maintaining work schedules and product or process improvement.

[25]

Teamworking and Motivational Goals

In earlier decades, an important link was made between group-based work, increased motivation and commitment among the workforce and the quality of employees' working lives.

With the development of flexibly organised production and the need to devolve responsibility to the shop floor, the importance of the 'people factor' in achieving organisational success is becoming much more appreciated. Teamwork is being seen as an important way of harnessing people's brains, and hence commitment, to the greater efficiency and competitiveness of the organisation. Teams are repositories of knowledge which is critical to organisational effectiveness.

Teamwork can also provide a challenge to traditionally adversarial management-labour relations if it is sensitively introduced. By giving greater control and responsibility to groups of employees who normally have little of either, conflict and lack of trust can be reduced. Instead of defining the interests and needs of owners and employees as in opposition, recent developments in teamworking tend to emphasise 'being all in the same global competition boat together'.

The language of teamwork increasingly serves an important motivating purpose in many organisations. The use of the term 'team' (as compared, for instance, to the earlier, more common term 'work group') is a rich metaphorical source of exhortations taken, in particular, from the sporting arena. It conveys desired personal attributes ('good team player', 'team discipline', 'all pulling together', 'playing the same game', etc.) in a way which mirrors the desired attributes of the contemporary organisation. Instead of the traditional military style hierarchies and chains of command, team metaphors suggest flat organisations with strong lateral communication and a unity of purpose based on competing with like organisations. The pervasiveness of the sports metaphor in contemporary manufacturing companies suggests that it offers a powerful unifier which – at least for male employees – crosses status divisions.

Why Introduce, Reinforce or Develop Teamwork?

As this discussion has shown, there are a number of compelling reasons why organisations are turning to teamwork. The need to adjust business strategy to increasingly competitive world markets, changes in production engineering techniques and the necessity to develop the knowledge, skills and commitment of the workforce have all contributed to the rise in teamwork-based organisations. For some companies, the decision to move to teams has appeared essential to survival. For others, it has been a definite choice, and for yet others, it has been a gamble.

Executives and senior managers who are thinking about introducing teamwork should ask themselves whether they can achieve their organisational goals equally well through other means. Once on the teamwork road, it can be difficult to stop or turn round without damaging credibility and trust. Teams need continual reinforcement and development if they are to work in an optimal way. Once formed, a team does not stand still. It is dynamic and requires new challenges to remain motivated and productive.

The needs of the organisation also change, and teams need to be able to respond to these. The process of introducing, reinforcing and developing teamwork is one which, as shall become apparent through the rest of this book, involves people from all parts of the organisation as agents of change. Anything less than determined commitment to the ideas of teamworking will result in a less than satisfactory outcome.

Further Reading

Blumberg, P. 1968. *Industrial Democracy: The Sociology of Participation.* London: Constable.

Cummings, T.G. and Huse, E.F. 1989. *Organisation Development and Change.* St. Paul, MN: West Publishing Company.

Miller, E.J. and Rice, A.K. 1967. *Systems of Organization: The Control of Task and Sentient Boundaries.* London: Tavistock Publications.

[27]

Pearce, J.A. and Ravlin, E.C. 1987. The design and activation of self-regulating work groups. *Human Relations*, 40 (11), pp. 751-782.

Schonberger, R.J. 1986. *World Class Manufacturing: The Lessons of Simplicity Applied*. New York: The Free Press.

Trist, E. and Bamforth, K. 1951. Some social and psychological consequences of the longwall method of coal-getting. *Human Relations*, 4, pp. 3-38.

Womack, J.P., Jones, D.T. and Roos, D. 1990. *The Machine that Changed the World*. New York: Macmillan.

3

Team Structures and Boundaries

The term 'teamwork' can be confusing. These days, just about every grouping of individuals in an organisation gets called a team, regardless of how that group actually works together. This indiscriminate use of the term actually damages efforts to introduce proper teamwork. Proper teamwork means the introduction, development and reinforcement of new forms of work organisation. Instead of simply exhorting employees to behave like 'team players', top managers need to recognise that strategy, work design, production systems, control systems and personnel practices have to be formed into a dynamic, new whole. This complex of changes results in an organisation that sends consistent messages to employees about behaving with increased autonomy, in the context of a group engaged in common tasks, and linked through to some mechanism for departmental or organisational influence.

Many goals motivate a move towards teamwork. It is not unusual for top management to attempt to achieve one goal without having to make the necessary organisational and technical changes. Chapter 2 on history and context describes these motives in more detail, but a brief list of managers' typical goals might help in the clarification of team structures and boundaries:

* Increasing employee self-direction
* Introducing greater flexibility through multi-skilling
* Devolving responsibility for quality
* Creating links across functions and organisational boundaries, and
* Gaining greater employee commitment.

But it eventually becomes apparent in any half-hearted application of teamwork that picking and choosing from the goals doesn't always work, or doesn't work for very long. Progress on any one of these typical goals establishes the potential and expectations for making progress on others. Organisations tend to revert back to scientific management in order to avoid this progress or to move forward towards greater development of teams.

That said, three varieties of teamwork can be seen in action in manufacturing organisations today: operational teams, service teams and cross-functional task teams. Companies emphasise the development of one type of team at a time, although it is not unusual to find all three types of teams in a company well down the teamwork road,

The reasons for choosing one form of teamwork over another can be traced to the particular strategy being pursued by the top management, and also to the history of organisational and technological developments in the company. The starting point for teams will have as much to do with the nature of the product as it will with the particular influence of one occupational group within the company. This argument is examined more fully elsewhere in Chapter 11 on planning and sequencing comprehensive changes.

What Kinds of Teams Are There?

The three types of teamwork differ in terms of functional location, degree of shared tasks and the proportion of time spent in the team. Here we describe the main types of teams, the key characteristics which make them an identifiable team, and

[30]

where they are likely to be put in place within an organisation. It should be noted that the location in any case partly defines the kind of teamwork which can be introduced.

- **Operational teams** consist mainly of production operatives but, especially in their more developed forms, may incorporate maintenance and quality personnel. They are permanent, full-time teams based around a chunk of the production process. Individual members will have some degree of cross-training in technical and, possibly, coordinating tasks that had historically been the responsibility of a line manager. Some alternative labels or variants may be: shop floor teams, cellular teams, self-managed teams, self-directed teams, self-regulating teams, semi-autonomous work groups, primary work groups. With the exception of the first two labels, all the others could theoretically refer as well to service teams.
- **Service teams** may be either support teams for production areas, or based on a product or a client brief, as in commercial services. Employees tend to be assigned to permanent teams consisting of other technical and administrative personnel. If structured primarily as a support team, their members divide the work by being assigned, full-time or part-time, to a section of the shop floor or a group of operational teams. These are understood to be dedicated service teams. They could be located near the shop floor, although it is just as common to find them still integrated with a central function. Centralised functions themselves may be structured into self-managing teams focusing full-time on, for example, all the products sold within a geographical area or all the services to a cluster of customers. Within manufacturing, service teams have been underdeveloped.
- **Cross-functional task teams** have a membership drawn from different functions and areas of the organisation. Cross-functional teams are more likely to consist mainly of white-collar, professional or managerial staff, although specially skilled operators and technicians might be selected for solving a particular problem. These teams tend to be permanent or semi-permanent, but part-time. They concern themselves with intra-organisational and, sometimes, inter-organisational coordination tasks, such as supplier develop-

[31]

ment or customer service. Temporary cross-functional task teams bring people together to work on a specific project, such as scrap reduction or developing a new product, after which the team disbands and members return to their function of origin. These teams have been referred to by many names: project teams, product development, process improvement teams and so on.

Of these three types or categories of teams, operational teams and self-managing service teams are the most complex and generally require the greatest organisational resources to put into place and develop. These teams require the degree of multiple change initiative emphasised in this book. Within a manufacturing context, cross-functional task teams and dedicated service teams contribute positively to an environment which reinforces operational teams and encourages their development.

In some types of service enterprises, a slightly different form of teamwork-based organisation is emerging. It is possible to find organisational structures which consist, effectively, of cross-functional task teams organised on a matrix basis. Employees report to both a functional boss and a project boss. 'High tech' firms involved in the design and manufacture of new information technology, construction management firms and other service organisations working on a project management basis illustrate this trend. Retail financial service companies, local government and some parts of the NHS are experimenting with teamwork-based structures that redesign their operational work into service teams requiring permanent assignments by customer or by product.

Operational Teams

Operational teams are organised around a segment of a production process or into product-based cells. In terms of team structure and boundaries, three key interrelated concerns need to be addressed in setting up an operational team. The first is how jobs are designed. The second is the degree of self-direction given to, or expected of, the team. The third is the kind of leadership chosen. These will, in turn, influence or determine the relationship between the team and the rest of the organisation.

Teams can take different forms, depending on the kind of production process and organisational requirements. It is possible to set up a team with a fairly modest degree of self-direction, but which will fulfil a need for greater cross-skilling among production workers and improve quality standards at the point of assembly or manufacture. Alternatively, team-

An Example of Operational Teams

Food Factory Ltd, a food-processing factory, introduced teams into its production areas in 1990. The company had been bought by a multinational group which invested a very large amount of money in modernising the plant. At the same time the workforce was reduced by a third through a programme of voluntary redundancies. Teamwork was seen as a way to make this investment pay off and to succeed with a much leaner workforce.

Each team is organised around a self-contained section of the production process. The aim of teamwork is to have multi-skilled, interchangeable team members who can operate all the equipment used in that section and perform all the tasks associated with that process. Each team comprises 6-12 members. They are expected to perform quality checks and carry out first line maintenance. Teams are also expected to deal with routine production problem-solving before calling in maintenance staff. Teams organise their own work in whichever way they wish. Craft workers are incorporated into teams operating the most complex technologies, where full multi-skilling is impractical.

Teamworking was also brought into the maintenance department and an agreement with the unions enabled the company to introduce cross-skilling between electricians and mechanics. Permanent team leaders were selected from existing employees, who were all eligible to apply. All applicants went through a four-day training and assessment process before final selections were made. Alongside teamworking, a TQM programme was begun, starting with problem-solving techniques and followed up by the development of personal improvement programmes for each employee. The company introduced a new skill-based pay structure and harmonised working hours for manual and staff employees.

[33]

working may be treated as a developmental objective for the whole organisation, starting with some basic redesign of the production process and working in the longer term towards optimal self-direction for teams. This will involve much more comprehensive changes in strategy, work design, production systems, control systems and personnel practices.

Top managers need to be clear about what they want to achieve by introducing teamwork. There are questions of time-scale and resources. Highly self-directed teams can take several years to establish fully. And although they may result in important cost savings in relation to staffing levels, efficiency, improved quality, etc., they will also require resources in terms of training and organisational development.

An Example of Operational Teams

EngineCo plc, an engineering and assembly firm, introduced self-managing work teams in the late 1980s. This was part of the company's drive for greater efficiency and came alongside the introduction of JIT and an MRPII system. The company was reorganised into business units, and cellular teams were set up in each unit. The number of management layers was cut from seven to three. Distinctions between different grades of operator were removed and generic jobs were created.

Supervisory positions were abolished and much of the supervisory decision-taking was devolved to the work teams. The teams have no official team leaders. Teams are expected to decide among themselves how to coordinate their tasks and manage their boundaries. The introduction of self-managing teams has meant major changes in selection procedures, payment and grading systems, training, appraisal systems and managerial roles.

The two examples above give some flavour of the kinds of environment into which teamwork is being introduced and the kinds of changes which accompany even limited forms of teamwork. It may be noted that in neither case were maintenance or other support staff brought directly into the operational teams. In Food Factory Ltd the emphasis was on having flexible, multi-skilled teams to cope with the reduced numbers of employees. At the same time, craft distinctions were broadly retained, both within some production teams and among maintenance staff. Although all levels of the organisation had lost staff, the main impact of teamwork was on first line management, as team leaders took over some of this role. The introduction of teamwork necessitated changes to the payment system and to traditional differences in the working hours of manual and non-manual employees.

In EngineCo plc teamwork was introduced mainly as a response to developments in manufacturing systems engineering and inventory control. These production technologies favour cell-based work design where jobs are grouped based on materials flow. In this company, far-reaching organisational changes took place alongside the move to teamwork. Reorganisation into business units devolved financial management and accountability downwards. De-layering and the abolition of supervisors pushed many previously managerial tasks down to the work teams. The development of a high degree of self-management among team members has required comprehensive investment in selection and training. Payment and grading systems have had to be completely revised.

These examples also begin to suggest something of the variety of people within an organisation who might be involved in introducing, reinforcing and developing teamwork. Teamwork is not the preserve of human resources managers only, although they will generally play a critical role. The people involved, aptly described as 'change agents' in this book, may come from finance, production engineering, quality, information systems or personnel. They may also be designated as internal organisational development consultants responsible for managing the types of changes which teamwork entails. Both examples also begin to suggest the issue of sequence: what comes first, who initiates which changes and in which order?

Basic Characteristics of Operational Teams

Each company's operational teams have some qualities that make them unique to that organisation. Regardless of this uniqueness, operational teams can always be described in terms of three key aspects of structure and boundaries: job design, degree of self-direction and leadership. Introducing, developing and reinforcing operational teams involves paying attention to these characteristics.

Job design concerns the boundaries of the operational team and the nature of jobs inside those team boundaries. Chapter 6 on methods for changing work design considers the relationship between job design as a technical activity and teamwork in more detail. At this point, it is important to note that the boundaries of production teams are drawn around a relationship between technology (e.g. machines), a physical space, a task or set of tasks and human activity.

Any serious attempt at introducing teamwork will require rethinking these relationships between people, machines, space and tasks. At minimum, teams must be organised around a complete process and a set of tasks which make sense as a technical and social whole. It is not sufficient simply to divide up, say, the machines on the assembly line at every tenth operator and call the divisions 'teams'. Here, the link with self-direction must be noted. A basic aim of most operational teamwork is to give team members greater control and responsibility for their area of work. This requires that the work tasks are meaningful, contain variety and offer a sense of completeness.

Rotation of tasks, either routinely or in order to provide cover, is often an intrinsic element of team organisation. Identification with others working in a team around an area of the production process, and its associated machines and necessary technical skills, can be facilitated tremendously by modifications in the physical layout of the production area. This can vary from a minimum of moving machines closer together, through cellular reorganisation, to designing the technology around the work teams (although it is rare for this to be undertaken in brownfield sites).

Restructuring into operational teams also has implications for the design of support staff areas. Whether support staff are co-opted into the teams or remain as a separate group, it is preferable that they be readily accessible to teams. The degree to which teams must rely on managers to request technical support is the degree to which they lack self-direction. In many cases, this has meant physically locating support functions so

[36]

that technicians are adjacent to the teams they service.

Whether teams are structured around processes or products will depend to a large extent on the type of production involved. Process-based teams tend to be more linear in form, grouping team members along a line or lines of machines. Product-based teams are more likely to be cellular, grouping machines in more circular or square shapes. Decisions about structure and boundaries essentially comprise these related concerns about space, machines and people.

An Example of Operational Teams

Cable Plant, manufacturers of high-performance cables for the defence, marine and aerospace industries, reorganised its manufacturing operations from a process-based operation to a dedicated product layout. In the old layout, machines which performed similar operations were grouped together, resulting in long distances between one process and the next and time-consuming materials handling. Materials flow was poor. In the new layout, the product range was split into four product families and the machines were laid out in four discrete product-based cells. JIT and teamworking were introduced at the same time. Team boundaries coincide with cell boundaries and there is one permanent team for each of the three shifts. Cells vary in size and teams contain between four and nine members with interchangeable skills. The small group of craft workers remains outside the cellular teams and services all four cells.

To be both motivational and efficient, operational teams must be structured around a segment of the production process. Ideally, the team boundary will be drawn around a complete process or product. The team, then, consists of individuals who have particular roles in production but who are cross-trained on at least basic tasks and can potentially take on coordinating tasks. If the boundaries are so drawn, multi-skilling can develop through cross-training within the team, along with a significant delegation of coordination. Different configurations are possible, ranging from relatively restricted degrees of rotation where members retain some functional identity (such as engineers or maintenance staff), to complete interchangeability of tasks. The latter is generally associated with advanced forms of self-directed teams. The degree to which coordinating tasks are devolved to teams, as well as the type of leadership, are a matter of organisational choice, coupled with the training and experience of teams.

All these factors will determine the optimal size of a team. For instance, the more tasks there are, the greater the number of members required for meaningful cross-skilling and task rotation to occur. At the same time, if teams become too large they can also become difficult to manage and may develop counterproductive dynamics: over about fifteen, there is a tendency for subgroups to emerge, sometimes in conflict with or opposition to other subgroups. Below about six, there is likely to be an absence of the social and intellectual diversity which is a major factor in team effectiveness and productivity. Small teams also run the risk of being more dominated by powerful personalities.

The most successful teams seem to operate within the range of six to fifteen. However, there are examples of smaller and larger teams working effectively. Training for teamworking will need to take account of the implications of size and associated interpersonal complexity for team functioning.

The degree of self-direction of a team (also sometimes called self-management or self-regulation) means the capacity of the group and its members to operate effectively, both internally and externally, with minimal or no managerial or other outside hierarchical supervision. Self-direction is essentially a developmental issue for teams. It cannot simply be put in place but requires developing over time and in the context of wider decisions about organisational restructuring.

Fully self-directed teams (also called semi-autonomous working groups) have major implications for levels of hierarchy, managerial roles and industrial relations. While this notion of teamwork has been confined to operational teams, there is no practical reason why self-directed teams could not be developed for service and cross-functional teams. Three basic dimensions of self-direction are relevant for teamwork: internal self-direction, self-direction in relation to the interfaces with other similar teams, and self-direction at the interface with the wider organisation.

[38]

The first dimension of self-direction is internal to the team. This encompasses the degree of self-motivation and responsibility of individual team members and how effectively the team operates as a whole. It also concerns the extent to which team members are able to cover each others' jobs and the range and distribution of specialist skills through the team. Some degree of multi-skilling is generally a prerequisite for operational teams. This may vary from individual competence in some or most of the basic operational tasks performed within the team to full responsibility for operations, maintenance, quality and improvement activities. Team members may also have individual specialist skills and/or maintenance and other technical personnel may be integrated into operational teams to enable them to manage the full range of associated technical and coordinating tasks.

The second dimension of self-direction is the interface between the team and other teams of a similar kind or involved with other operational tasks. Self-directed teams will have at least some minimal capacity to operate without managerial involvement in administration and coordination, and to deal directly with other teams carrying out similar or interdependent tasks. For example, teams along an assembly line will each be engaged in a different part of the assembly process: interfacing with each other may be useful in addressing quality problems or working through mutual difficulties. Associated with this is an appropriate degree of technical self-reliance in maintaining operational standards.

The third dimension of self-direction is the team's interface with the wider organisation. This is about the capacity of the group to manage its own interfaces, both with service teams and with the rest of the organisation. Self-direction also involves being able to respond flexibly and appropriately to changes in the external environment and the ability to initiate and carry through improvements in working methods.

In developing self-direction as a process over time, there are likely to be significant changes in each of these dimensions. In the beginning, it will be important to decide on some basic requirements for self-direction for work teams; for instance, the minimum level of cross-skilling necessary to enable the team to function as such, what aspects of task coordination accrue to the team and the level of external supervision

[39]

required. The process of developing self-direction is considered in depth in Chapter 10 on continuously developing teams.

Leadership is the third key aspect of the structure and boundaries of operational teams. Again, decisions about leadership will be importantly connected to decisions about the degree of self-direction. As with self-direction, leadership roles also have a developmental dimension, and this is considered further in Chapter 6 on work design. The question of team leadership, which is very much about managing boundaries, is inseparably linked to that of the role of first line management, if there is to be any.

The content of a team leader's role differs significantly from that of a supervisor or first line manager in a conventional chain of command. The team leader's primary concerns will be in activities geared to ensuring that the team can operate effectively. This amounts to managing various boundaries: between individuals within the team, between the team and other teams, and between teams and management. These may include taking responsibility for assessing training and developmental needs within the team and facilitating technical and administrative problem-solving. In some cases, the team leader also works as a member of the team, carrying out both routine and specialised tasks.

The team leader's role can thus be very demanding, requiring a combination of interpersonal, social and technical skills. This points to the importance of selection processes and of appropriate training. Because of the need to ensure the efficient performance of tasks, technical skills are often given the greatest emphasis in selection. Many companies have learned the hard way that the most technically skilled do not necessarily have sufficient 'people skills'.

The need for 'people skills' is not, however, solely an issue for team leaders. Introducing operational teams, in however modest a way initially, has implications for the roles and styles of middle and senior management. Modest operational teamwork usually retains line managers in some form. Developing self-direction among team members and facilitative styles of managing among team leaders will be at odds with an unreformed, directive style of middle or senior management.

What are the options for leadership of operational teams? There are a number of possibilities. In practice, a company may be constrained in choice by factors such as the availability of suitable personnel, the need for particular technical expertise in a position of authority and the need to accommodate existing managerial capacity to the emergent team structure. As such, the team leader role may be an adaptation from existing positions (as in the case of redefining supervisors into team leaders). Many organisations opt for removing supervisors and creating an entirely new position, located hierarchically somewhere between operator and supervisor. Provided they have adequate training and development, teams can operate without a formally designated leader, but this is a more challenging option.

It is important to think about leadership roles for operational teams as a developmental issue. The degree of self-direction and the initial job design of a team strongly affects the kind of leadership which a team will need. As teams develop greater skill flexibility and self-management, leadership roles will need to be modified to take account of their increased competence. Otherwise, the teams will turn their frustration inwards on themselves and productivity and quality will suffer.

Service Teams

Service teams can take a number of different forms. In manufacturing industry, they tend to be set up to support production areas along one of three models: business unit teams, dedicated service teams or self-managing teams. Here, maintenance, administrative and clerical staff, separately or in combination, are likely to form the basis of service teams. In commercial and service organisations, they are generally defined around a particular client service or product brief. Setting up service teams raises some of the issues discussed in relation to operational teams, but there are also some distinctive issues.

Business unit teams are made up of the line managers, middle managers and technical specialists concerned with a particular business, defined in terms of products or customers.

They move out of functional departments and into the business, usually onto or near where the actual production takes place. These are permanent, full-time assignments reporting to a middle or senior manager in charge of that particular business.

Dedicated service teams remain under the chain of command of a centralised service function. However, personnel are assigned prime responsibility for providing service to a set of operational teams or to a particular product

---

An Example of Service Teams

Digital Equipment Company (UK) introduced what it calls 'high-performance work groups' into its manufacturing plant in Ayr. It reorganised its support staff into teams in and around the production area to facilitate communication, particularly the sharing of information. The support teams cover all aspects of materials management for a particular commodity or group of commodities, including procurement, forecasting and master-scheduling.

The aim has been to develop as many multi-skilled support staff as possible. Some success has been achieved in integrating planning and buying, but materials sourcing proved less amenable to integration as it required the person to be off-site for long periods. The company also found there were limits to multi-skilling. For example, routine engineering skills were transferable, but there was a need to retain highly specialist skills. It was not cost-effective to try to pass these skills on to non-engineers. The company also faced more difficulty in defining a bounded task than it did with production areas. For instance, a particular process of materials acquisition may take two years, thereby making spatial or temporal boundaries appear more arbitrary than in operational teams.

This organisation's overall experience has been that teamwork in support areas has greatly improved communications, decision-making, action and relationships between support and production staff. In support areas, by bringing critical functions together, general understanding of how the business works and of the interdependence of functions has greatly increased.

From D.A.Buchanan and S. McCalman (1989)

An Example of Service Teams

ElectronComm plc, a telecommunications company, implemented what it described as self-managing teams (SMTs) in several of its customer service functions. In the Sales Development Centre 70 employees, the majority of whom are customer service representatives, are organised into seven sections, which are known as 'directed autonomy' teams, as they have supervisors. Team members sit at adjacent desks. A centralised computer routes customer calls automatically to any member of a section. Teamwork has increased the sharing of information and the degree to which representatives help each other with unusual requests. Each team has a small amount of discretion to set up their own operational procedures and are able, for instance, to credit a customer's account up to a certain amount without a manager's approval.

Installation and maintenance crew are organised into teams, each of which is responsible for servicing customers over a particular geographical area. All team members are skilled in all of the tasks required. Each team meets briefly each morning to assign the work; then members work largely independently. New technology enables work assignments to be dispatched directly from the centre to each worker. External supervision is minimal.

Engineering support clerical workers are also divided into teams, each supporting a particular engineering function. One such team works in its own room and is responsible for posting jobs onto maps for all geographical areas. The work requires equivalent skills and a high degree of interdependence. External supervision is light.

An independent study of the effectiveness of these SMTs found an important relationship between technologies and the appropriateness of SMTs in service functions. Where the technology requires a high level of interdependence, as in the engineering support function, and the need for a high level of employee autonomy, as in the installation and maintenance teams, SMTs were most effective. In the Customer Service area, interdependence and employee autonomy were circumscribed by the design of the work. Teams did not have a distinctive task or set of tasks. Greater interdependence and self-management for teams could have been achieved by redesigning teams around, for instance, the servicing of a particular set of customers.

[43]

or section of the process. This may be a full-time or part-time assignment; it may involve relocation near the shop floor or not. But the idea is that the service team becomes an expert in the particular needs of that section of production. If relocated to the shop floor, more than one service function might share an office, which increases interdisciplinary problem-solving. If not, a cross-functional task team may be formed to improve process and product improvement related to that section of the process or product.

Self-managing service teams have the same characteristics as operational teams. In terms of the work design of the service jobs, personnel will be grouped around a particular set of customers or a particular group of products. In manufacturing, this might mean an interdisciplinary group being formed from specialists responsible for providing a service to the shop floor. It is unusual to find this in manufacturing unless it is an exceptionally large or dispersed site. Usually business teams or dedicated service teams would be used. However, it is increasingly possible to find self-managed service teams in relation to customer service, supplier relations and other service functions that relate to those outside the company.

In the examples above, some distinctive issues arise with service teams. In both cases, defining a complete process in some support or service areas proved complex. The tasks defined show considerable diversity – a completed client or internal customer brief, a whole planning sequence, materials acquisition for a product range or process, etc. Time-scales for these tasks may be very protracted and skill requirements diverse and specialised, making it less likely that one individual can follow through the whole sequence completely. In practice, whole tasks are defined in two main ways. In support teams, they are defined in terms of an integrated set of needs for an internal customer, such as a production team. In other kinds of service teams, they are defined in terms of an external customer, such as a group of clients.

Service teams may also have widely different spatial configurations. Manufacturing support teams might be grouped around production or assembly teams to facilitate access and exchange of information. Information technology can also enable teams whose members are widely dispersed to maintain constant electronic communication. Teams servicing external clients, such as maintenance, repair and distribution personnel, are often widely scattered, meeting up at certain times only.

The extent of, and limits to, multi-skilling are a major issue for service teams. There are likely to be a number of highly specialist skills that are essential to the task of the team. However, multi-skilling throughout the team to this level takes too long and is probably not cost-effective. Effective teamwork does not necessarily require everyone to be interchangeable. Maintaining specialist skills may also be essential to keeping up quality standards. As with operational teams containing specialist skills, payment systems have to be able to reconcile individual skill differences with team-based working.

Service teams face similar problems as operational teams about defining the extent and limits of individual and group autonomy and responsibility. They have to organise tasks, probably involving some degree of rotation, manage cross-training requirements and clarify leadership roles. Intra-organisational boundaries and coordination with other teams also have to be managed.

Cross-functional Task Teams

Contemporary organisations may contain a wide variety of teams based on cross-functional or cross-organisational links and fulfilling a wide range of purposes. Cross-functional task teams, which may be of varying duration, play important roles in both conventional, functionally structured organisations and in matrix type structures where they form the main organisational building block.

In functionally based organisations, cross-functional task teams are an important way of breaking down tendencies to inherent insularity or rigidity. In practice, informal cross-functional links constitute a significant part of organisational life. Informally, most organisations consist of a web of linkages which develop partly to fill organisational needs, particularly those involving interface management. Instituting formal cross-functional task teams can be a way of capitalising on existing, effective intra-organisation linkages, particularly as a way of increasing coordination and lateral communication flows within the organisation. In this context, cross-functional task teams are not a substitute for existing organisational structures, but operate in parallel or as a complement to them.

An Example of Cross-functional Task Teams

Britax Vega Ltd introduced cross-departmental task teams in the context of a major TQM initiative. Their aim was to bring together TQM initiatives with business planning. Their business planning process identified a set of key processes and associated annual objectives for each one. These ranged broadly, covering business planning, supply chain management and human resources issues. Senior managers set up project teams, consisting of managers and other technical and administrative staff, to work jointly on these annual objectives, reporting directly to a policy group of directors.

Cross-functional task teams are likely to play an increasingly important role in organisations moving away from a strongly functional structure to one based more on product or project. These structures are associated with the flattening of hierarchies and blurring of functional boundaries. Self-directed operational teams create a need for clearer lateral links among the support staff. Cross-functional task teams (sometimes called multi-disciplinary teams) are critical to any organisation concerned with technological innovation and new product development, both of which require a high degree of creativity and close coordination throughout all stages of a project.

Temporary task teams are frequently cross-functional task teams, bringing together personnel for a specific, usually time-bound task. However, quality circles and shop floor improvement teams may be limited to operatives. They may also link up different organisations, as in the case of supplier development teams which bring together personnel from different functions from both customers and suppliers.

Team boundaries, in the case of cross-functional task teams, are very different from those described for operational and service teams. In the latter, the team provides the employee's main or entire work focus and is the source of his or her work identity. Cross-functional task teams are usually part-time.

Generally, the visible manifestation of the team is the team meeting. Teams are intended to facilitate the more effective working of primary roles and organisational structures. There are contexts, however, where employees may temporarily spend their whole time 'on secondment' to, for example, a new product development team.

Similarly, leadership of teams does not fall to a specially recruited team leader but is likely to be assigned to a senior person in the team. These differences mean there are differences in managing 'part-time' teams in the wider organisational setting. It is appropriate to ask what is needed from the organisation to set up and support cross-functional task teams in order that they perform effectively.

Probably the most important requirement for effective cross-functional teamwork is the clarification of the task and team authority, together with a set of clear goals and, if relevant, a time frame within which the task or aim is to be carried out. Associated with this is the need to ensure a match between team membership and the task to be carried out. Team members should be chosen because they have an identifiable contribution to make, not simply because it was felt to be a good idea to include someone from every department or section.

Teams also need a clear reporting structure and a sense of their own authority – i.e. how far their powers go before they have to get permission or report progress. Although they tend to be part-time or temporary, training in how to operate as a team, for both members and leaders, may be essential to effective teamworking practices. To be effective, cross-functional task teams must also be given adequate resources, decision-making and follow-through powers. These requirements are unlikely to be met unless the team is fully supported by senior management, both in principle and in practice. Teams of this kind commonly fail because they lack the authority to act on their analysis or recommendations or because the team label disguises authoritarianism or dominance by particular interests. In such circumstances, cynicism quickly develops.

Cross-functional task teams raise particular issues in relation to leadership, authority and representation. Teams may be comprised of a complex configuration of equals and subordinates. Members will have to balance and reconcile possibly

[47]

competing loyalties (especially where there are strong functional divisions) and dispersed loci of authority. For example, the team leader of a new product development team drawn from different functional divisions, may have temporarily greater authority over a team member than the person's functional head. These issues can only be partly addressed through teamwork training. They also require a wider awareness of how the organisation functions, together with mechanisms to manage cross-cutting authority structures. It is important not to treat cross-functional task teams as a substitute for other ways of managing lateral links, such as delegation to key sets of individuals, which might be more appropriate in a given situation.

Summary

Three types of teams operate within manufacturing companies: operational teams, service teams and cross-functional task teams. In order to determine the structure and boundaries of a team, aspects of job design, self-direction and leadership must be considered. The potential for self-direction within a team is defined by the way in which structures and boundaries are set up. Inadequate levels of competence and performance within a team can be traced to problems with the defining structure. Further, teams require both an initial and an ongoing investment in training and development if they are to achieve the strategic benefits of cost reduction, quality enhancement, and innovation improvement.

Further Reading

Buchanan, D. and McCalman, J. 1989. *High Performance Work Systems*. London/New York: Routledge.

Carrington, L. 1991. Working as a team member. *Personnel Today* 22, January.

Ford, C. 1994. Teamwork: key issues and developments. *Occasional Paper No. 54*. London: Advisory, Conciliation and Arbitration Service.

Hirschhorn, L. 1991. *Managing in the New Team Environment*. Reading, Massachusetts: Addison-Wesley.

Incomes Data Services Ltd. 1992. Teamworking. *IDS Study No. 516*. London: IDS.

4

Shifting 'Figure' and 'Ground': Difficulties of Planning and Sequencing Comprehensive Changes

Executives and senior managers sometimes think that it is possible to introduce, develop and reinforce teamworking without too much disruption. Such an idea rests on the assumption that teamwork involves altering a single aspect of organisation. For example, managers commonly express the belief that teamwork is just a matter of changing attitudes, just concerned with working practices on the shop floor, or just about getting the production process right.

But every one of the 20 plus companies participating in the 'teamwork in manufacturing' (TIM) project stands as proof that teamwork requires comprehensive change – that is, changes in multiple aspects of organisation. For example, attitudes, working practices and production processes are all involved, along with a great deal more. Based on the experience of the TIM companies, organisational leaders can anticipate changes in five broad areas of organisation as a normal part of developing teams:

1. Business and organisational strategy
2. Work design and related training
3. Quality, manufacturing and engineering systems
4. Business planning and accounting systems
5. Industrial relations and personnel practices.

Company after company demonstrates that teamwork-related changes come about through multiple initiatives – both simultaneous and sequential, at the same time and one following another (Holti, Neumann, Standing and Stein, 1993). Companies undertake these multiple change initiatives over several years. Each company starts from one of the five places, works at its own pace and in a sequence that reflects the characteristics of its business and the people in it. At any one time, a dominant change initiative will be being given attention and resources, and there will be several others progressing at a slower pace and with less visibility.

Sometimes these multiple change initiatives will be understood by the organisational leaders as connected to an overall strategic direction. More commonly, however, developments take place in a seemingly unconnected way, even though it becomes apparent later that a particular change helps or hinders another. Regardless of how it is understood, teamwork will achieve the business benefits over time only if changes are made to all five aspects of organisation listed above and described below.

The experience of the TIM companies suggests that each aspect of organisation, as an area of change initiative, must be developed in such a way that it makes a positive contribution towards the effectiveness of teamwork: otherwise it may work against teamwork actively or passively. An example of an active force against teamwork would be an industrial relations agreement that blocks particular working practices consistent with teamwork. An example of a passive force against teamwork would be a factory layout that separates sections of the production process, thus preventing a group of operators from taking full responsibility for a section of process or product.

The broad areas for change that need to be managed in

[51]

order to bring about successful teamwork are shown in Figure 4.1. The figure is a circle of five circles, each containing a name for the aspect of organisation to be targeted for change. The figure is intended to illustrate several important points about managing a change towards teamwork.

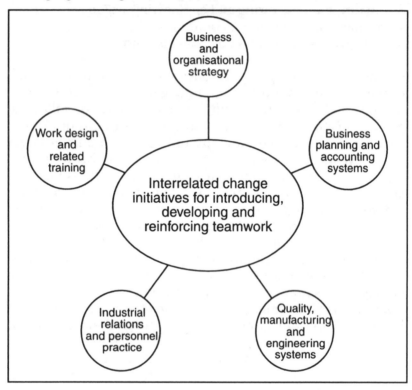

Figure 4.1. Aspects of organisation requiring change initiatives for successful teamwork.
Copyright: The Tavistock Institute, 1993

First, all five aspects of organisation – or areas for change initiative – need to be subjected to developmental activities as a part of managing a comprehensive change to introduce, develop and reinforce teamwork. Few executives and senior managers start with the awareness that this will be the case. Instead, they introduce change initiatives in one of the circles and find themselves being compelled to start up a corresponding change in another circle. For example, a total quality management programme (theoretically located in the the circle labelled 'quality, manufacturing and engineering systems') results in an awareness that locating quality inspectors at the end of the production line discourages operators from paying attention to quality (located in the circle labelled 'work design and related training'). To take another example, a strategic planning process located in the circle labelled 'business and organisational strategy' leads to a determination to improve the quality of raw materials and reliability of product delivery, which are located in the circle labelled 'business planning and accounting systems'.

The second point illustrated by the figure therefore is that organisational and technical change initiatives across these five areas tend to be highly interrelated and interdependent. To be interrelated means that changes in one aspect of organisation connect to, and need to be consistent or complementary with, another. It is difficult to undertake an initiative in any one area without causing or considering a need for change in several other areas. Hence the need to consider the whole picture.

The third point suggested by the figure illustrates a very important element of comprehensive changes. The five areas for change initiative tend to fall within the boundaries of traditional functional departments, or to be of particular concern to certain occupational specialists. These various 'change agents' play a significant role in shaping change initiatives. Alongside each of the five broad areas for initiative within a programme of comprehensive change, one or more 'change professions' or body of organisational expertise have emerged. People with these different types of expertise typically advocate the need for the corresponding types of change initiatives. In practice, there is a good deal of overlap between the areas of concern of different types of 'change professional'. Even so, each tends to start from their own particular conception of what needs changing and which initiatives and recipes should be used.

Change Initiatives Related to Teamwork

The introduction, development and reinforcement of teamwork requires change initiatives in all five aspects of organisation. This means that, at any one time, those who are directing the change will have projects underway within some areas, and projects in other areas awaiting attention. Descriptions of each of the five areas follow, along with a list of methods commonly used within companies for achieving changes and the 'change agents' typically involved. Five separate chapters come next providing more detailed information on each aspect of organisation and its related methods.

Business and organisational strategy refers to activities initiated by executives and senior managers to improve or maintain competitive advantage. These activities always address the enterprise's relations with the external environment, especially issues of products and markets. In order to achieve strategic directions externally, internal organisational strategy must also be specified. For the purposes of this book, introducing some type of teamwork is considered strategic.

Change agents for business and organisational strategy always include executives and, often, senior managers. A corporate adviser or an external consultant may be brought in to work with executives and senior managers. Depending on the method, middle managers and employee representatives may be included.

Initiatives for changing business and organisational strategy imply significant redirection or even reformulation of the company as a whole. Many companies have had success with four basic methods for achieving this:

- Options for the *strategic planning* method include: the top management approach; open systems planning and socio-technical systems analysis; and search conferences.
- Options for the *organisational restructuring* method include: business units or product-based departments; centralised processing functions; and increasing integration across existing functions through cross-functional meetings or redrawing departmental boundaries.
- The method using *flatter hierarchy and redundancies* also includes redefining roles for middle managers.
- Options for *improving customer-supplier relationships* include decreasing the number of suppliers and identifying preferred customers and suppliers.

[54]

Work design and related training developments mean shaping the daily jobs of employees in such a way that individuals increase their self-sufficiency and, at the same time, increase their responsibility and cooperation with a group of others working on a common task. Some versions of team-working also involve increasing the group's accountability to and influence within the larger department or organisation.

Usually, change agents for work design and related training are the senior managers implicated along with professionals from the personnel and training functions. Typically, an external or internal consultant, with a relevant background in organisational development or industrial engineering, provides the work design input. Depending on the method being used, employees who have been working in the jobs, their line managers and technical support specialists will be included in the design process.

Five broad methods have been used with success by many companies changing their work design and related training:

- Options for a *structured design process* include socio-technical systems and job enrichment and enlargement.
- Options for *new line management roles* include: redefining the supervisor position; assigning a team leader from within the group; and encouraging the team to supervise itself without a line manager.
- Options for *relating support functions to operational teams* include: placing support personnel on the teams; integrating the support skills and tasks into the team job description; and integrating the supervisory tasks into the team.
- Options for *building effective teams* include: training needs assessment; training in multiple skills; and consultation about the socio-psychological development of the team.
- Options for *new management roles and styles* include: skills and attitude development; job enlargement or enrichment; and devolution of decision-making from senior managers.

Quality, manufacturing and engineering systems make up the technical core of any production process. Manufacturing systems constitute the techniques, equipment and movement through time and space, by which an order and raw materials are transformed into finished product. Quality systems relate to every point of the manufacturing system by improving performance according to technical and customer specification. Engineering systems underpin both manufacturing and quality systems, being concerned with development and set-up for new products. In teamwork-related changes, developments in these areas tend to do some combination of the following: intensify operator involvement in improving quality; link sales order processing, manufacturing scheduling, stock control and purchasing; locate all operations associated with one product close to one another; mandate cross-functional cooperation in process improvements and new product introductions; and minimise movement of material, work-in-progress and inventory.

Change agents for quality, manufacturing and engineering systems include all the senior technical specialists in the functions implicated: quality engineers and managers, manufacturing engineers and managers, design engineers, materials management and logistics managers, and information systems specialists. Using project management approaches, they may or may not employ external consultants. If not, then someone within the organisation tends to be assigned the task of becoming an expert in the method being used.

Many companies have been successful in changing quality, manufacturing and engineering systems using three basic methods:

- Options for *quality management* include achieving British, European or international standards (e.g. BS-EN-ISO 9000) and total quality management.
- Options for *logistics systems* include: investing in integrated computerised manufacturing control systems, like manufacturing resources planning (MRPII); using a just-in-time (JIT) materials ordering and production planning system; and laying out the factory floor into cellular units.
- Options for *simultaneous engineering* include 'within company' cooperation between designers and manufacturing engineers and 'between company' cooperation with design engineers from supplier and customer organisations.

Business planning and accounting systems provide the means by which executives and senior managers monitor, control and develop the overall performance of the company. Developments compatible with teamwork-related changes involve sharing plans, information and feedback across traditional functional divisions and hierarchical levels. Also, all activities associated with a particular product or stage of the business process are brought together – at least on paper – for the purposes of better planning, monitoring and control. The aim is to provide product or customer-focused manufacturing units with a picture of costs and revenues directly associated with their own activities, as a basis for making improvements. There is usually a related goal of increasing efficiency and decreasing non-essential activities as a way of cutting overhead costs.

Change agents for changing business planning and accounting systems almost always include information technology specialists, as computers can improve both availability and access to financial and planning information. Finance managers, accountants and business planners tend to control the type of system and information available. Especially for systems related to monitoring significant suppliers or customers, purchasing managers might be involved along with the relevant senior manager in charge of a particular product's performance. Depending on the method being used, external consultants might be brought in by business planners or financial managers.

Companies are experimenting with three methods for changing business planning and accounting systems:

- Options for planning based on *process measurement* include critical success factors, key business processes and non-financial measures.
- Options for *team-friendly accounting practices*, those that provide for feedback and control to teams, include activity-based accounting and delegated budgetary control.
- Options for *purchasing initiatives* focus on supplier monitoring and supplier development.

Industrial relations and personnel practices define how a company attracts, retains, develops and motivates the people by whom the work of the organisation gets done. Even the most highly automated manufacturing facility requires people to operate it and to complete all the tasks necessary to produce and deliver finished goods. Human resources management policies and procedures include planning, recruiting, selecting, training, appraising, developing, compensating, communicating, consulting, and negotiating. Through the overt and covert messages embedded in these activities, employees are made aware of and reinforced for behaviours consistent with the needed roles. As a teamwork-based organisation requires different behaviours from one planned along Tayloristic principles, then the industrial relations and personnel policies need to reflect that difference. For example, instead of being rewarded individually for working to narrow job descriptions, operators may be rewarded as a team for working to a broad, group-based job description.

Change agents for changing industrial relations and personnel practice always include senior managers in charge of industrial relations and representatives of the workforce. Frequently, technical specialists within the personnel function provide valuable service in, for example, gathering data on grading or developing precise procedures for training. Internal or external consultants in organisational development, industrial relations and reward systems may be brought in to help.

Six broad methods have been used with satisfaction by many companies for changing industrial relations and personnel practices:

- Options for an *industrial relations framework* include: enabling agreements; 'new deal' agreements; and single status.
- Options for *recruitment and selection* include using psychometric or other forms of testing and hiring from within.
- Options for *pay and grading* of individuals and groups include: job evaluation; pay for skills; and pay for performance.
- Options for *appraisal* are numerous: peer and self-appraisal; upward appraisal; management appraisal; and participative appraisal.
- Options for *communications and consultation* include: team briefing and information sharing; attitude surveys; handover meetings; and employee involvement forums.
- Options for *recognition* and reward outside the payment systems include suggestion schemes, awards and publicity.

As nearly all significant aspects of organisation are implicated in reinforcing and developing teamwork, leaders face *the challenge of managing comprehensive developments and change: this means planning and sequencing multiple, simultaneous and sequential change initiatives.* The list of five aspects of organisation, combined with the variety of methods and tools being used by companies to make changes, indicates the complexity of what is possible. Even if only one option is being pursued under each of the five areas, five change projects could be underway at any one time. Sometimes there are more than one: for example, it would not be unusual for a company making changes related to teamwork to have the following going on at the same time:

- Executives and senior managers are convening information meetings to discuss business performance and strategy, along with the internal cultural and structural changes necessary to improve quality and productivity. (A method for changing business and organisational strategy.)
- An imaginary line is drawn around selected groups of operators and a set of machines; the operators take care of that section of the production process with fewer staff, rotating and covering each other for breaks. (A method for changing work design and related training.)
- A computerised MRPII system is being installed and will be up and running towards the end of the year. (A method for changing quality, manufacturing and engineering systems.)
- The finance department is planning a new management accounting framework to give accurate cost information to teams. (A method for changing business planning and accounting systems.)
- Senior managers hold informal conversations with the representatives from both blue collar and white collar unions on the need for a new way of working in order to meet strategic needs. (A method for changing industrial relations and personnel practices.)

Unfortunately, most popular approaches to change management have embedded in them an assumption of one, albeit major, change project being undertaken at any one time. It might be possible, in this example, to contain the five change initiatives within the boundaries of the particular functional departments and change agents responsible for them. But before long, developments and expansions in each area will begin to impinge on the others or be blocked because of what is happening elsewhere. Complaints that 'too much is being changed at once' will begin to be whispered behind closed doors.

Too Much Change, Too Fast

Once leaders and managers decide that significant structural, relational and cultural changes will be necessary for implementing new strategies and tactics, employees can expect to sustain several years of disruption before some degree of internal stability returns. In the 1970s and 1980s, experienced researchers and professional change practitioners estimated that a 2 to 5-year disruption was typical. Such estimates were based on a few published reports of long-term comprehensive change. In the face of a 1990s boom in highly publicised strategic changes, many management gurus now warn against expectations of ever returning to a condition of stability.

This contrast between disruption and stability has been an important assumption underlying one of the most influential concepts in organisational development. Kurt Lewin (1951) reported observing a period of 'unfreezing' of old attitudes and behaviours, followed by a period of 'refreezing' into new ones. This early, simple explanation of how people in organisations change provides both a description of sequence (first 'unfreezing', followed by 'refreezing') and some indication of pace (time is necessary for people to adjust).

This concept provides a useful, but insufficient description of what goes on during comprehensive change. People in organisations can readily identify when the comprehensive change began, track what change initiatives took place in which order, and state which next steps are on the horizon. In addition to an expressed longing for consolidation and rest, those people responsible for changes inside organisations indicate that the complexity they are experiencing far exceeds any simple notion they hold about sequence and pace.

One crucial difference in thinking about comprehensive

change is that the period of 'unfreezing' lasts much longer than that apparent during the small alterations to work practices being observed by Lewin. In his cases, process improvements and precise attitudes were being slightly changed (e.g. a different way to fold newly manufactured pyjamas; encouraging homemakers to cook organ meats, or offal for their families). In the case of comprehensive changes, the very fabric of the workplace is under reconsideration, resulting in stronger and more varied sources of resistance to letting go of the old ways.

A second crucial difference is that 'refreezing' into new attitudes and behaviours cannot be controlled in a predictable direction. Lewin's work involved altering one type of attitude or behaviour in a context wherein as much as possible stayed the same. A recognisable steady state remained throughout the precise change being undertaken, thus providing a place of sameness for those subjected to change.

In comprehensive change, much that actually constitutes the earlier state is in flux. Job duties, grading structures, payment and even the people with whom one works may change along with technologies, ownership structures, and the behaviour of authority figures. Therefore, employees are reacting to many changes at once: acceptance or adjustment to one change can coexist with rejection or resistance to another. Reactions to the overall period of disruption, and lack of a steady state upon which to rely, can be more important to the overall change effort than any one particular new attitude and behaviour.

The third difference between single changes and comprehensive changes is that *both simultaneous and sequential cycles of 'unfreezing' and 'refreezing' are being experienced by employees as multiple aspects of organisation are being changed.* People in roles typically implicated in implementing change – senior and middle managers, technical specialists, and employee representatives – tend to experience comprehensive change as 'too many things changing all at once'. A complaint frequently heard is 'We don't get to finish with one thing before another comes along'. Given the sheer volume and variety of changes being undertaken in many organisations, this complaint has some validity. It is not unusual to find half a dozen major change projects, each demanding significant resources, being undertaken at once under the rubric of comprehensive change.

[61]

Indeed, depending on how one defines a change project, as many as 24 non-routine developments often can be identified in a large or medium-sized enterprise.

A certain glib philosophy has gained popularity amongst executives and managers as a defence against the complaint of too much change: 'We've all got to become competent at managing continuous change', 'There is no time to get attached to anything, we've got to keep moving', 'The wave of the future is to change, change, change – if you can't take it, go and join the dinosaurs'.

This philosophy barely disguises the adrenalin of fear and the excitement of challenge facing organisational leaders as they 'fight for survival'. The obvious and remarkable correlation of this 'rapid fire, step change' philosophy with major redundancies, as a method of change, creates a paradoxical atmosphere. Organisational members both have to cope with and have to manage new developments that often result in greater individual stress.

A Contradiction in Terms

Three seemingly contradictory tactics are being woven together into approaches to comprehensive change. First, multiple simultaneous developments are initiated, requiring extraordinary workloads on top of routine business demands. At the same time, the numbers of people available to undertake the work are being cut. Methods being used to make such cuts come under different labels: 'removing layers of hierarchy', 'business process re-engineering', 'cross-functional cooperation', and 'activity based management'.

Second, a variety of actions are being taken which result in individuals experiencing their employing organisations as undependable; while, at the same time, initiatives which use ideas of 'employee empowerment', 'teamwork' and 'a shared future' are launched. The initiatives require a degree of commitment, loyalty, and cooperation from employees – or 'psychological presence' (Kahn, 1992) – which the 'violated psychological contract' has taken away. The removal of job security, predictable career paths, and clearly delimited job descriptions – changes considered necessary by organisational leaders for

[62]

competitive advantage – decreases psychological presence at the very time when the organisation needs it the most.

Lastly, many executives and senior managers build their strategic redirection around a 'mission' or 'vision' statement, with corresponding objectives or values. They would like this statement to serve as a unifying force, a template against which decisions can be taken and multiple change projects can be judged for consistency. However, developing a business strategy tends to become, itself, one of many approaches to change – that is, just another change project. While organisational leaders are emphasising the urgent need for strategic coordination and consistent direction, many other actors on the organisational scene are emphasising the equally pressing need for their particular change (e.g. making progress on technological innovations, responding to health, safety and environment legislation, completing requirements for international standard certification).

These three tactics comprise contradictions in the terms of comprehensive change – *situations in which the content of the change appears to be in opposition to the process or methodology of change.* Change a lot, but with less resources. Become more psychologically present to the company, but don't expect commitment from the company in return. Pull together in the same direction, but emphasise the needs of one's specialism.

In the face of such seemingly contradictory terms, senior and middle managers find it difficult to complete one initiative before another one comes along. They report feeling that they are being asked to be more productive while everything is changing around them. Indeed, the tensions between maintaining routine operations and implementing strategic changes constitute one of the most challenging dilemmas of many comprehensive change programmes. Decisions about how to deploy time, money and people necessary to bring about the identified changes – while deploying time, money and people necessary for maintaining continuity – become the decisions of comprehensive change.

Shifting 'Figure' and 'Ground'

Despite the feelings of being overwhelmed and the reality of a significantly increased workload, the evidence in fact indicates that not everything changes at once during comprehensive programmes. Yes, contradictory methodologies are being used by executives and senior managers to bring about drastic, seemingly unprecedented changes. Yes, multiple, simultaneous cycles of 'unfreezing' and 'refreezing' make it practically impossible to control and predict employees' reactions. But, in comparing many organisations, it is possible to glimpse a pattern of managing sequencing and pace that runs through the experience of being overwhelmed. There appears to be an organic, not always conscious, approach for informally testing compatibility amongst change initiatives, along with an intuitive sense of timing and judgement about 'how much our organisation can handle at any one time' (Neumann, 1994).

Clues for this organic approach can be gathered from a 'cooker' metaphor commonly used by companies within the TIM project: 'We've put that on the back-burner for now' and 'It is boiling over, so we have to deal with it'. In combining the metaphor of a ' change cooker' with the idea of multiple, simultaneous and sequential change initiatives, four possibilities for action become apparent. As Figure 4.2 illustrates, it is possible to imagine the main decision-takers in a position of putting some changes 'on the back-burner', being forced to attend to some changes that are 'boiling over', choosing to invest in getting some changes 'cooking', and keeping an eye out for other change initiatives which are 'simmering' but not requiring special attention.

The 'change cooker' is being viewed, then, from the front by those people in a position to decide which change initiatives will be taken in what order. In other words, the main decision-takers control those aspects of organisation which can be changed legitimately. Two concepts from perceptual psychology – 'figure' and 'ground' – refer to the interplay between those targets or processes for change which have the attention – are 'figural' – for the main decision-takers and therefore receive sanction and resources, and those aspects which are temporarily 'on the back-burner', or are not receiving attention and are, therefore, in the background or 'ground' (Wheeler, 1991).

In the TIM project, researchers tested the idea that multiple, simultaneous and sequential change initiatives were a basic

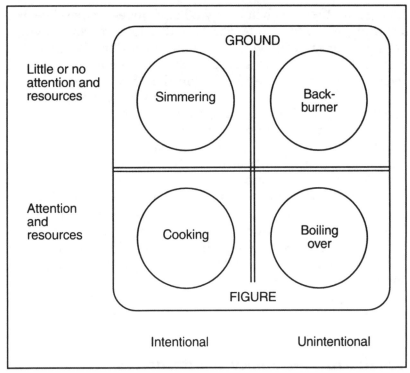

Figure 4.2. The 'cooker' metaphor for shifting figure and ground in comprehensive change.
Copyright: The Tavistock Institute, 1994

characteristic of developing and reinforcing 'teamwork'. What emerges, from the way managers describe their experience of comprehensive change, is a picture of some progress being made towards changing some aspects of organisation until that progress is halted for some reason. Other aspects of organisation are then taken up and as much progress made as possible before something more pressing attracts the attention of the main decision-takers. Usually more than one aspect of organisation is 'figural' – that is, under up-front consideration at any one time – while other aspects are held in the back of the mind.

In other words, *those change initiatives that executives and senior managers legitimate as 'figural' tend to shift into and out of the background at different times in a long-term change effort.* Shifts seem to depend on a variety of dynamics. Successful progress in one change initiative may draw attention to the need to

[65]

change another area before any other changes are possible. For example, increased job flexibility and cellular machine layouts may not progress beyond a certain level due to limitations inherent in the payment system. So a change in the payment system, receiving no attention 'on the back-burner', may be moved to the 'cooking' burner while further developments in job flexibility and cellular design might be set to 'simmer'.

Equally, attempts to make progress in one initiative may be blocked by a lack of progress in another change initiative. For example, repeated difficulties with computerised equipment may leave operators more dependent on technical specialists than they, and the new job design, might suggest. Process improvements to the equipment may have been a 'simmering' issue for the organisation for a long time until the operators threaten to stop cooperating with 'teamwork' unless the equipment is fixed. Such a stance could move technical improvements off a 'simmering' burner and onto the 'boiling over' burner regardless of the main decision-takers' perceptions of what is most important.

Rivalry for Legitimacy and Resources

Increased understanding about how change initiatives shift from 'figure' to 'ground' and back again might help executives and senior managers deal more effectively with comprehensive changes. Tavistock Institute researchers have begun to conceptualise such a shift in terms of the dynamics by which the main decision-takers, or the 'dominant coalition' (Kotter, 1978), perceive a change initiative or decision area as crucial for making progress in a comprehensive change. At any one time, both the number and areas for multiple simultaneous change initiatives depend on decisions taken by the dominant coalition. Such decisions are based on perceptions of what should be 'figural' and what can be considered background or 'ground'.

'Ground' refers to aspects of organisational change which may be explicitly acknowledged by organisational participants, but which are not authorised by the dominant coalition to be progressed. Typically, those aspects of organising perceived by the dominant coalition as not having a strong impact on competitive advantage are more likely to manifest themselves as 'ground'. Over time, various aspects of 'ground' may become central preoccupations and the subject of important change initiatives, at which point they take centre stage as 'figure'.

Based on data accumulated from the TIM research, it appears that this process of some aspects of organisation and technology moving from 'ground' to 'figure' (and back again) results from pressures exerted on the dominant coalition. Pressures come through the web of social and political relations in which the dominant coalition sits, both individually (e.g. as a functional manager or a member of a professional association) and as a group (e.g. senior managers in relation to middle managers)[1]. By both formal and informal mechanisms

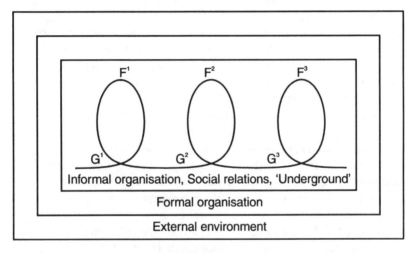

Figure 4.3. Context for figure and ground in comprehensive change.
Copyright: The Tavistock Institute, 1994

(e.g. meetings, conferences, newsletters, chats, working papers, industrial action) members of the dominant coalition, and others who have a stake in the changes, influence the selection of those change initiatives which will receive sanction and

[1]We wish to acknowledge the contribution of Andrew Friedman of the Department of Economics and Accounting, University of Bristol, in the application of the 'figure', 'ground' and 'underground' concepts to organisational change.

[67]

resources. These same mechanisms can be traced as influential in the transfer of knowledge from the organisation's environment, through the individual's professional identity and functional role, and into debates about what to change and how to change it.

These relations tend to involve both psychological and political dynamics and, thus, constitute an 'underground' to the more overt processes of influence being enacted by the dominant coalition. For example, envy of a legitimated change initiative in a rival's department might motivate an exaggeration of the importance of a change initiative in one's own. To take another example, a perceived conflict of interest over a change initiative might motivate employees who are not involved directly to protest on behalf of the targeted employees, out of fear that they will be next. Difficulties in taking decisions about which aspect of organisation and technology should be considered legitimate for attention and resources usually can be traced to unresolved issues being enacted through covert dynamics.

The concept of underground, therefore, refers to processes and issues which have important influences on the dynamics of 'figure' and 'ground' over time, but which are not acknowledged or not immediately visible. Political issues include: which individuals or groups gain or lose influence over what are perceived as core aspects of organising; which groups gain or lose access to financial or other rewards; and which groups or individuals gain or lose security of employment. Psychological and cultural issues include: what norms, ideologies or interpretative frameworks triumph or are displaced; which social defences against anxieties raised by change processes will be sanctioned positively or negatively; and which individuals and groups will be made the scapegoats in service of the changes.

Towards a Planning and Sequencing Methodology

Empirical data from the TIM research show that a process of selection and decision-taking does occur whereby the dominant coalition negotiates over which aspects of organisation will be targeted for change. However, this appears to be one of the challenges of managing change that managers find most difficult. The TIM project has studied this emerging picture of what happens during comprehensive, strategic changes and combined it with the needs for a planning and sequencing methodology expressed by executives and senior managers. Such a methodology needs to take into consideration the interconnections between change initiatives and the multiple stakeholders.

Strategic planning methods are notoriously unitary: there is one mission, one focus, one direction around which everyone, and every change project, is to gather. But clearly these data suggest that multiple change initiatives are going on, albeit in the context of one overriding rhetoric. How to develop a pluralistic method of planning and sequencing comprehensive changes appears to be the challenge.

From the perspective of these main decision-takers, a planning and sequencing methodology needs to assist them in:

- Deciding which aspect of organisation to change in what order
- Dealing thoughtfully with the complicated relationships between interrelated aspects of organisation
- Facilitating cross-functional cooperation between those middle managers and technical specialists charged with the task of implementing changes
- Managing the tensions and competing pressures and conflicts of interest inevitable in comprehensive change.

Chapter 11 of this book offers a planning and sequencing methodology that might address some of these concerns. The intervening chapters map the terrain of possible change initiatives in more detail, as preparation for a fuller discussion of what is involved in planning and sequencing a journey through them. The five areas and their associated methods are considered in the next chapter.

Further Reading

Holti, R.W., Neumann, J.E., Standing, H. and Stein, M. 1993. *Reinforcing and developing 'teamwork' in manufacturing: approaches to the management of change.* London: The Tavistock Institute of Human Relations, Document Number 2T688.

Kahn, W. A. 1992. To be fully there: psychological presence at work. *Human Relations,* Vol. 45, No. 4, pp 321-349.

Kotter, J. 1978. *Organizational dynamics: diagnosis and intervention.* Reading, Massachusetts: Addison Wesley Publishing Company.

Lewin, K. 1951. *Field theory in social science.* New York: Harper and Row.

Neumann, J. E. 1994. Shifting 'figure' and 'ground': sequence and pace during comprehensive organisational changes. *Review 1993/94.* London: The Tavistock Institute, pp. 38-44.

Wheeler, G. 1991. *Gestalt reconsidered: a new approach to contact and resistance.* New York: Gardner Press, Inc.

5

Changing Business and Organisational Strategy

Business and organisational strategy relate to teamwork in the sense that the decision to introduce or develop teamwork in manufacturing is almost always a strategic one. The term 'business strategy' refers to a plan of action instigated by executives and senior managers in order to maintain or improve competitive advantage. During most of the relatively brief period for which the term has been a standard part of the management vocabulary – from the 1930s onwards – business strategies have focused primarily on the enterprise's relationship with the environment outside. Aspects of the business somewhat external to the organisation were involved, such as: product markets, geographical markets, financial structure and the type of competitive advantage managers were striving to achieve in their chosen markets.

More recently, the proven relevance of human and organisational factors to successful implementation of business strategy demonstrates the need for an internal strategy to complement the external one. Thus, aspects of the business internal to the

[71]

organisation have become implicated, such as: overall organisational structure, the use of technology, job design, human resources management policies and management style. These internal strategic concerns need to complement, match and generally support the external strategy of markets and products.

The idea of competitive advantage (Porter, 1985) is that a company orients its strategy around achieving superiority along one of three dimensions: cost, quality or innovation. Practically, most companies operate a strategy that blends more than one, emphasising different elements of their competitive advantage to different aspects of their market. A strategy can be explicit and public within the enterprise, or emergent and of the 'what do we seem to be doing that is working' kind. For the purposes of this book, strategic initiatives which have some sort of comprehensive impact on the life of the internal organisation tend to connect to teamwork.

All three types of teams – operational, service and cross-functional – have proved effective in helping many companies progress towards strategic objectives. By increasing job flexibility and job capability, operational teamwork allows employees to take greater responsibility for improving quality and to work with a smaller number of more highly skilled and productive workers. Service teams improve the speed and relevance of process and product improvements on the shop floor, as well as increase the product knowledge and customised responsiveness of service departments dealing directly with customers. By bringing together people with the full range of necessary specialisations, cross-functional teams can solve a problem or develop an innovation more efficiently and effectively than with the same problem or innovation moving from function to function in a linear fashion.

Increasingly, manufacturing companies attempt to develop some aspect of all three types of teamwork in order to maintain or improve competitive advantage on all three strategic dimensions of cost, quality and innovation. In fact, many managers feel their organisation is attempting to do everything all at once for all reasons. However, when compared with other companies both within their own market and in other industries, it is possible to recognise the particular strategic emphasis of a company. A company will tend to develop one type of teamwork first, over and above the others.

This tendency can be tied to a variety of factors: the managerial philosophies and occupational identities of the executives; the stage of development of the industry of which the company is a part; and the major dimension in which the company is attempting to establish competitive advantage.

Methods for Redirecting the Company

This chapter describes initiatives concerning business and organisational strategy where there are not only clear implications for one or more forms of teamwork but also an important element of discontinuity with the past. It concerns methods and tools for achieving significant redirection of a company in terms of some combination of its external business strategy and internal organisational strategy.

Even when talking about strategic redirection, it is important to recognise that, since organisations are historical entities, no business strategy starts with a clean slate. In arriving at a particular status quo, many previous developments will have paved a way favourable to the new direction desired. Equally, other developments may have resulted in conditions seemingly antithetical to the business strategy now considered necessary by executives and senior managers. In other words, an organisation will have more or less changes to make in order to introduce, develop and reinforce teamwork. The degree of change required depends on how favourable existing conditions are for encouraging the particular type of teamwork deemed suitable for particular strategic purposes.

It is not unusual for members of an organisation, recently informed of a strategic decision to introduce some type of teamwork, to notice a historical connection between the new organisational strategy and various change initiatives of the past. For example, thinking back over a 10-year period, a manager might hear similar messages in: the total quality management programme; the computerised production planning system; an overall mission initiative; and the current strategic intention to develop multi-disciplinary operational teams and cross-functional project management groups for process and product innovation. Given that strategy development is rarely a totally conscious, controlled process initiated by the top managers and implemented in a linear, logical way, such historical connections are inevitable.

This matters because managers and employees sometimes resent the assumptions that strategy only comes from above: they would like credit for their less visible contributions. Indeed, organisational (internal) strategy does not always follow business (external) strategy in a neat sequence – the two can evolve together. In the daily running of the company, many different adjustments are made continuously over time in relation to the company's environment, under the auspices of the different functions or subsections. A business strategy evolves from the accumulated effects of these decentralised adjustments as much, if not more, than it does from a direction set by top management. Most methods for changing business strategy and overall organisational structure focus on increasing consistency between the wishes of top management and the daily behaviours of people carrying out their jobs.

Obviously, not all methods for changing business strategy lead to teamwork. But there are methods which have more to do with teamwork than others. Four major methods for changing business and organisational strategy can be compatible with introducing, developing and reinforcing teamwork:

- Strategic planning methods, associated closely in people's minds with business strategy itself, sometimes use management of change processes that suggest a consultative managerial style consistent with teamwork.
- When senior managers restructure the organisation this usually both communicates significant redirection and makes certain types of teamwork more or less possible.
- When senior managers respond to changed market conditions by flattening hierarchies and making redundancies, this literally removes people from the organisation, creating vacuums into which a type of teamwork can develop.
- Strategic change may emphasise improvements to relationships with customers and suppliers; a type of cooperation, frequently termed 'teamwork', and essential for logistical systems responsive to high-performing shop floor teams.

Strategic Planning

Frequently, strategic planning constitutes the primary method a company uses to change business strategy. Those individuals with the authority to take strategic decisions think about the business pressures facing them and consider how they might respond in a way that benefits the company as they see it from their perspective. All strategic planning methods involve those with authority talking together, in some configuration, about the situation in such a way that leads to decisions being taken.

Types of strategic planning decisions oriented towards the environment external to the company include:

* Entering or leaving geographical markets
* Withdrawing a product or initiating a new development
* Restructuring the financial base.

Types of strategic planning decisions focused more on internal strategy include:

* Restructuring the organisation
* Announcing a different approach to daily operations
* Altering the managerial style
* Commissioning an organisation-wide training programme
* Designing the jobs differently
* Investing in technological innovations.

Usually, some combination of internal and external strategy is considered, although the emphasis tends to be on the former.

After four decades of accumulated research and experience with strategic planning throughout the business world, two practical difficulties persist. The first is that moving quickly from a strategic plan to implementation continues to be difficult in most cases and impossible in many. Both active and passive resistance to strategic changes, especially those affecting livelihoods and requiring major adjustments, slow down implementation. This first difficulty feeds the second: by the time some aspects of strategy are in place, business conditions have changed to the extent that a different emphasis is required.

Strategic planning methods differ in terms of who is

involved in the decision-making discussions and the degree of formal method used to structure the discussions. Formal methods tend to involve gathering more information prior to decision, and using someone in the role of facilitator from outside the planning group. The most common form of strategic planning is that of executives, with or without the involvement of selected senior managers, taking decisions as a part of their normal meetings.

In terms of methods, this *top management approach* relies to a great extent on well established norms for business meetings, chaired by the authorised executive. These serve sufficiently for the proposals, debates and discussions which lead to decisions. Generally, these discussions are structured at a fundamental level by techniques of market analysis, financial analysis of performance, predictions of return on investment and so on.

Increasingly, managers turn to techniques developed at business schools or by management consultants. For example, the SWOT analysis method has been widely disseminated. SWOT is just one example of a tool for analysing the competitive position of a strategic business unit. This simple method asks that four questions, about 'strengths, weaknesses, opportunities and threats', be addressed with serious thought and backed up with research. Based on the answers, actions can be inferred. Internal reports may or may not be supplemented by business consultant reports or other sources of competitive information. There are plenty of business analysis tools for looking at product and financial strategy – far fewer for looking at internal or organisational strategy.

An advantage of this top management method for strategic planning is that it is familiar and consistent with the expectations many people hold of the top management. SWOT or some other business analysis technique can be used by a group of executives and senior managers, with or without an external or internal consultant functioning as a facilitator.

The main disadvantage of the top management approach is that managers and employee representatives most crucial to implementation are left out. Those aspects of strategy which cannot be directed tend to fail. For example, subtle, widespread attitudes and behaviours (commonly termed 'cultural change') typically resist change, and industrial relations strategies can take years to implement.

Further, there is nothing inherent in a technique like the SWOT analysis that will result in a decision to introduce and develop teamwork. Created exclusively with business frameworks, strategic planning techniques tend to ignore human and organisational issues in implementing plans. The top management approach assumes that there is one right way to interpret the business environment, and that the one right way can be directed from the top. These assumptions have been

Using the top management approach for changing business and organisational strategy

The executives and senior managers use existing or special meetings to think through the business pressures facing them and how to respond. Senior managers then work with middle managers to implement these strategic decisions.

Advantages	Problems/Concerns
This approach is familiar to everyone in the organisation and consistent with expectations of top management.	The top management group may be stuck in their ways and have difficulty being innovative.
A rapid response is possible to unexpected difficulties.	Rapid decisions may take extraordinarily long to implement; some will never be implemented.
Unpopular decisions – like redundancies and withdrawal of support for projects – can be taken with a minimum of overt resistance.	There is nothing inherent in this approach that encourages attention to human and organisational factors.
The competence of top management can be tested.	Dependency is increased on top management as those below delay taking independent initiative.

challenged seriously by organisational specialists and business leaders alike.

Social scientists developed *open systems planning* and *socio-technical systems analysis* as methods which would compensate for the drawbacks of the top management approach to strategic planning. Open systems planning incorporates some of the business planning techniques into a method which can be used to encourage managerial and employee involvement in thinking strategically. Typically, top management retain a steering role while representatives of middle management, technical specialists and employee groups take up leadership roles on multiple groups looking at planning and implementation in specific areas.

Open systems planning is combined with socio-technical systems analysis (STS) as a tool for 'scanning the environment', the first step in the most popular version of STS. From open systems planning, significant aspects of the business environment, as they affect the primary task of the organisation, are identified. An assessment is made of the degree of current and potential influence likely to be exerted successfully by those inside the organisation. Possible and desirable futures are discussed and implications for business and organisational strategy proposed.

At this point, socio-technical systems analysis, well regarded as a method for work design, is often used to think through organisational design. The overall flow of work from input through transformation to outputs is identified from a technical perspective. Boundaries are drawn around sensible sections of the business process, initially in terms of technical outputs and then in terms of social or organisational considerations. Decisions are made about centralisation, decentralisation, clusters of task interdependencies and other design criteria relevant to the location and authority for departments, functions and other subsections of the organisation. Using STS during a strategic planning process tends to be focused on the organisational needs emerging from business strategy. Once a decision to restructure has been taken, a more extensive socio-technical systems analysis process may be undertaken.

This method, therefore, increases involvement and links classic questions about the changing environment of the business with questions about organisational structure. By

[78]

Using open systems planning and socio-technical systems analysis for changing business and organisational strategy

Monitored by top management, representatives of groups of managers and employees from all functions and levels of the organisation think about business pressures and determine the organisational and technical changes necessary to respond.

Advantages	Problems/Concerns
Business strategy and human and organisational issues in implementing strategy are addressed simultaneously.	Those human and organisational implications of business strategy which have a negative impact on job security and status are readily transparent – a matter of concern to some top managers who believe in tightly controlling information.
Attitudinal and behaviour change begins to happen immediately as many people are involved in the planning.	Resistance tends to be more direct and apparent earlier rather than later, which some top managers find disturbing.
Because so many people are involved in thinking about strategy, there is less need to 'sell' employees the rationale for certain actions.	Those who have a stake in various decisions will lobby and negotiate for decisions which they consider to be correct from their perspective; therefore conflict will be high.
Implementation can happen almost simultaneously with planning; rapid understanding can be achieved and subtle, unpredictable aspects of implementation undertaken informally.	The parallel infrastructure necessary for using this method is time-consuming; people begin to complain about the encroachment into their other work and off-duty time.

bringing these two concerns together, one of the main difficulties with implementation begins to be addressed. Redesigning organisational structure and jobs in light of the business strategy incorporates changes in daily behaviours into the strategic plan.

Open systems planning and socio-technical systems analysis both eliminate the linear process whereby the top management plan strategy and pass it down the chain of command to be implemented. Instead, only enough planning is completed to point people in a broadly common direction – this is called 'minimum critical specification'. Implementation and planning can proceed in an integrated fashion.

One of the main disadvantages of the open systems and socio-technical analysis approach to strategic planning, however, is the pace at which decisions get taken. Usually, this method sets up a cumbersome infrastructure of meetings running parallel to the chain of command. Because top management rarely authorise the meetings to take actual decisions, lengthy negotiations and power plays add to the time necessary for final decisions. Equally, the representatives on the various planning groups may experience numerous difficulties in communicating with their constituencies and achieving support.

In practice, the only strategic decisions that top management delegate to such a participatory process tend to be those of organisational structure and job design. The chain of command retains the market and product-related decisions. Unfortunately, this tends to decrease the link between business strategy and organisational issues.

A modification of the open systems planning and socio-technical systems method has evolved. The goals of its creators have been to minimise the amount of time necessary for involving a group larger than top management, and to minimise the split between looking at external business strategy and internal organisational strategy. Organisational change practitioners created the notion of a *search conference* in order to combine strategic planning with increased involvement and decreased implementation time. The search conference can combine many different strategic planning techniques already mentioned, but what makes it unique is the attempt to do away with representative groups and to work with as many people from the existing structure as can fit in a room.

Deciding who to involve is a very important aspect of this method. Usually, external consultants work with internal change agents to organise a search conference. They invite key decision-makers in the hierarchy, managers and technical specialists with project management responsibilities from across all sections of the company, and some representatives (both elected and not) from throughout the workforce. Search conferences last 1-3 days, and can take place once or repeatedly over several months with the same or different groups of participants. The organisers pose questions which the participants answer through conversations and working sessions structured in pairs, small groups and the large group. The questions begin with the future of society as a whole, implications for the future of the company, and then move through progressively more detailed planning relevant to the company (Weisbord, 1992):

- What milestones in society, ourselves and this company over the past number of years have brought us and the company to where we are today?
- What external forces are shaping our lives and our company right now?
- What are we proud about and sorry about in our relationship to the company?
- What is our ideal scenario for the future?
- What actions can we plan to take immediately that will move us forward into the future?

Often, following a search conference, planning and implementation groups will continue to work on particular topics. The search conference's main advantage lies in quickly bringing a large number of significant actors in an organisation to a common conclusion. Indeed, if top management commits to this method and insists that those responsible for planning and implementing strategic change are in the room, the potential is great for both completing a plan and working through issues of resistance to implementation.

The disadvantages of all strategic planning methods – the need to communicate and convince those people not involved in the planning and the need to take action after the planning –

A Case of Changing Business and Organisational Strategy with Strategic Planning

Chemco Ltd, the only non-US site of a multinational corporation, used to employ less than 100 people. Most of those employees had been recruited together 20 years previously when the factory was first built. The executives at headquarters decided to invest in the expansion of Chemco by adding a second factory on the same site that made a different product and that used supervisorless shop floor teams.

The Management Team felt overwhelmed by the implications of this expansion. During the two years of construction, start-up and commissioning, they did their best to limit the effect of the second factory on the existing employees. Once the new factory, and its 100 new ambitious operators, was up and running, it became apparent that keeping the two plants separate was not going to be possible. The Management Team decided to engage in some strategic planning to take control of both the old and new plants. They went off-site for three days, with an external consultant, to develop a vision statement which combined the overall corporate business strategy (achieving competitive advantage through quality and value) with a description of the direction they intended for the organisation (emphasising operational teams and cross-functional teams).

Once they had a draft of a vision statement, they each shared it with the direct reports in their department. The majority of middle managers and technical specialists criticised the statement; some even refused to cooperate. The Management Team was very confused about why the negativity was so strong. They began a series of working sessions within each department to help their middle managers and technical specialists to come to terms with the vision statement and to understand their role in the new direction. After about nine months, the Management Team felt confident enough to print the statement in the company newspaper, to post it around the site, and to host information meetings for all employees. The statement became the guidelines – the minimum critical specifications – for several working groups planning and implementing changes in several aspects of organisation.

are not completely eliminated in the search conference. But the theory is that if enough of the significant actors are present together the likelihood of implementation increases and resistance decreases. Search conferences further make a contribution to resolving the problem of delayed implementation in the light of rapidly changing strategic priorities.

Another disadvantage of search conferences, in particular, is that they have been applied only recently to strategic planning inside manufacturing. Their effectiveness, unlike other methods, has yet to be researched and validated across a large number of organisations.

Organisational Restructuring

Changing the structure of an organisation has become a commonplace method used as part of achieving strategic redirection. Executives often consider it crucial for implementing business strategy to reassign significant roles, to redraw departmental boundaries, and to redirect the activities of some sections of the organisation. Indeed, some strategic decisions imply the creation or dissolution of structures.

A new product or new market might require an additional project management or sales structure, led by a specialist selected for his or her likely success in achieving strategic objectives. Some decisions – withdrawing from a market, not expanding the development of a product, benefiting from economies of scale by combining operations into one site – often involve closing down a department or relocating people. Restructuring an organisation so that it supports a strategic decision to introduce, reinforce and develop teamwork tends to imply three general options:

- Structuring into business units or some other product-based form
- Centralising processing functions based on information technology
- Increasing integration across functions.

While all three options require reassignment of personnel, redrawing of structural boundaries and redirecting of emphasis, many companies attempt to improve relationships across functions without changing structural boundaries. The benefit for teamwork of such changes to organisational structures lies in the potential forms of teamwork possible as a result of each option.

Structuring an organisation into *business units* or *product departments* stands in contrast to the more familiar functional departments or process-based units. Senior managers rearrange the operational sections of the manufacturing enterprise. Instead of there being separate manufacturing, quality, and maintenance departments, managers and technical specialists are brought together around a free-standing unit of the business, like a particular product. They work full time on that business unit team, overseeing operational personnel who produce only for that particular business or product – for example, one major customer or one class of products or only those products requiring a unique treatment. Sometimes logistics, sales and customer service will be brought into the same unit or department.

This logic for structure can be used just for the shop floor, line managers, and the technical personnel from the relevant service functions or it can be used to restructure at the level of the organisation as a whole. For example, instead of there being one executive in charge of all operations for the entire enterprise, there may be several executives in charge of particular businesses or products. Duplicating technical and administrative services can be cost-effective in a large enough enterprise. Multinational corporations are experimenting with this logic on an even larger scale with the idea of particular factories being simultaneously a part of a regional structure *and* a part of a global product-based business.

Restructuring into businesses usually carries financial implications. To be held accountable as a profit centre, for example, and to be capable of selecting the best suppliers strengthens the power and autonomy of the business unit. In fact, being able to measure economic performance, and take corrective action, motivates top managers' enthusiasm for this structure.

The advantage of the business unit structure for teamwork is twofold. First, bringing together managers and technical specialists around a common product or free-standing unit of the business creates a team where single jobs stacked up in a hierarchy existed before. The multidisciplinary orientation

Using business units for changing business and organisational strategy

Managers and technical personnel are taken from functional departments and reassigned onto teams focused on the manufacture of particular products or a section of the business.

Advantages	Problems/Concerns
The technical services necessary for product and process development are under the same boss, which decreases conflicting priorities.	The number of technical specialists transferred into the business unit tends to be lower than those available under the functional structure, thus availability is not necessarily increased.
Managers, technicians and operators can identify with, and develop expert knowledge in, the one product or customer around which the business unit is oriented.	Managers and technical specialists tend to be called away from the business unit to work on special projects or difficulties in other business units for which they retain expertise from the previous functional structure.
Through improved quality and speed of technical service provided to operations, quality and productivity can improve.	Operational employees remain dependent on the business unit team to respond; a transfer of relevant skills does not take place automatically in this structure.
Operational employees can be made less dependent on line management by having direct access to technical specialists.	Operational employees sometimes feel shy about requesting services directly from those in a higher status; and specialists sometimes resent those in a lower status making demands on their time.

promises more rapid solutions to the process and product development problems that tend to be delayed indefinitely in a functional structure. Second, with all the technical services necessary for operational teams to solve their problems located within the authority of the business unit team, the likelihood of improved quality and speed of service increases. Theoretically, operators do not need to speak to their line manager who then goes to the line manager in another department to try to get something done; they can request service directly.

Unfortunately, the actual implementation of business units rarely lives up to its theoretical promises. Almost always, when business units are set up, top management take the opportunity when announcing a new structure also to announce redundancies. Thus, a significantly smaller number of employees are brought into the business unit, when compared to the number of people previously performing the same tasks from the centralised service. As pressures to cut costs tend to characterise the motivations for introducing this structure, the more difficult or expensive process and product development problems often persist.

Further, remnants of the functional structure may live on long after the majority of functions have been decentralised into business units. Technical specialists, who retain expertise gained from years of working throughout the operation, can be called away to work in other sections of the factory despite the logical business unit structure. Medium-sized manufacturing facilities find duplication of administrative and technical services too expensive or too cumbersome. Often, a compromise structure operates: part business unit, part strong centralised function. The corresponding ambivalence weakens the business unit structure.

The move towards business units or product-based departments is not the only method for strategic redirection consistent with teamworking. Strong elements of centralisation of organisational structure are also present in many cases. Particularly with advances in information technology, in the form of powerful software and distributed networks, it becomes possible and sensible to *centralise processing services* – like personnel records, production planning and tracking information. The specialised nature of other functions – such as product development – also means that it is often sensible for them to remain centralised.

These centralised services now look different, however, from traditional large centralised functions. Automation means that these processes require fewer personnel. Having a computerised information system on a network covering all relevant sections of the factory means that data collection and input can be decentralised while only the processing of data needs to be centralised. For companies running their plants as cost centres, the centralisation might not even be on-site: modems and centralised main frames can be maintained elsewhere, with the information being downloaded onto personal computers on-site as needed.

For this form of restructuring to work a major investment in computerisation is necessary. Production planning and tracking systems work best when the computerised information system includes terminals at points of production and related operations throughout the factory. Employees then need training in operating this new technology, for which they often expect additional reward. New product development teams often need to be supported by computerised design and engineering equipment: matching this technology at the point of introduction onto the shop floor is expensive. Small and medium-sized enterprises can only invest in computers for new products, not for manufacturing as well. The potential for centralising the processing of personnel records falls down in the implementation: few personnel are trained properly and developed to gather and input the data on a regular basis.

The third common option for using organisational restructuring to change business and organisational strategy in a way consistent with teamwork is to *increase integration and improve communication across functions*. To some extent, business units and centralised processing functions both represent an attempt to improve communication across departments. With business units, people are taken from functions and reassigned to business or product-based units. With centralised processing functions, the network of computerised information technology compensates for the difficulty of sending and receiving information between various sections of the enterprise.

Even so, as long as functions exist within the overall organisational structure, business units and centralised processing

[87]

will not be sufficient to take full advantage of possibilities for increasing communication and integration across functions. There are two basic ways for achieving this objective:

• Establish relevant meetings at which information and ideas can be exchanged and tasks addressed jointly
• Redraw boundaries in such a way that there are few 'hand-overs' between different functions or departments.

The former tends to be described by such terms as project management, improvement groups and problem-solving task forces. The latter tends to be called organisational design or by the currently favoured label 'business process re-engineering'. Both approaches are based on the idea of interdependencies between tasks.

For four decades, organisational researchers have been advising manufacturers to pay attention to the overall flow of work from the input of raw materials to the shipment of finished products. Of special interest must be the degree to which one process of transformation relates to another; the degree to which a part of the organisation's work is dependent on another part for successful completion. A classic way of thinking about this is in terms of three typical types of interdependencies – pooled, sequential and mutual (Thompson, 1963):

• Pooled interdependence means that processes or units of work are relatively independent of each other. Together they contribute to overall organisation goals, but each process or unit can complete their work with little input from other sections of the organisation. If they receive an input from another section or hand one over themselves, the hand-over is relatively whole. For example, a particular product can be manufactured entirely in a business unit before being sent to the warehouse for shipment.
• Sequential interdependence means that the processes or units of work interact in a sequence: in order for the work in one to be completed, the work before it must be done. A simple example would be sequential sections of an assembly line.
• Mutual interdependence means that processes or units of

work must interact with each other continuously in order to complete their work. An example would be a customer service team, where no one person knows everything about the team's multiple products and multiple customers.

The basic principle in strategic redirection through increasing intensity of relating across functions is to facilitate sequential interdependence and mutual interdependence, through clustering activities together in the same department or group, or developing better working links between departments or groups. For example, hand-overs are no longer necessary when all the processes and units of work are brought together into one department, under one boss or coordinating team who are authorised to take decisions about that process or unit of work. A business unit team is an example of how this kind of clustering for manufacturing operations can be achieved.

The same concept can be used to improve the relationship between service functions. For example, order processing, production planning and monitoring, shipping and invoicing have historically tended to be organised in separate departments or groups, linked sequentially. Paperwork on a particular order would be handed over from group to group, often moving between two or more departments. With information technology and the appropriate integrated software, the work can be clustered within one department. Alternatively, a more integrated way of working can be established across the groups involved, even if they remain in separate departments. Each order has one record, to which the various transactions can be added as needed throughout the factory.

Clustering sequential or mutually dependent tasks into one department means redrawing departmental boundaries, reassigning personnel and redirecting the emphases of the new department. As such, this way of improving communication and integration between functions is also a form of restructuring. Less drastic changes may also be highly appropriate. A procedure might be moved from one department to another, for example, or a more integrated way of operating established so that similar record processing procedures cease to be repeated in two different departments.

Even so, employees often do not welcome being grouped with others whom they have regarded historically with suspi-

Using increased integration across functions for changing business and organisational strategy

Sequential flows of work are clustered together into one department as much as possible and those people involved with mutually interdependent work are brought together to work simultaneously on a joint task.

Advantages	Problems/Concerns
Problems which result from mistakes earlier in a sequential flow can be spotted and resolved before they cause difficulty down line.	Employees may have gained years of experience in a particular sequential stage of the process and do not always welcome learning new skills or working with people from other processes.
Processes can be designed in such a way that the work itself is less boring, requiring more complete knowledge and skills than previously.	Employees experience the change as more work without an increase in pay; changing the jobs challenges the existing grading system, held on to by managers and workers alike.
By working together simultaneously on joint tasks, project groups can avoid designing or planning impractical or over-expensive solutions.	One occupational specialism tends to dominate in project groups which then undermines the benefits of interdisciplinary, cross-functional work.
Competition and dysfunctional behaviour between units or departments can no longer block completion of the work.	Individual performance appraisal remains the most popular reward system. This decreases the benefits to the company promised by pooled jobs or mutual work groups.

cion. The likelihood is great of employees feeling they are being asked to undertake extra work without additional pay. Frequently, existing grading systems do not translate easily into the new arrangements and more bad feelings result. It is also a rare departmental manager who willingly transfers sections of his or her operation into another manager's territory.

Perhaps because of the disadvantages of redrawing boundaries, holding a meeting of managers and specialists ranks as the most common approach to dealing with the difficulties inherent in sequential and mutual interdependencies across departmental boundaries. Managers frequently have coordination with other departments as a part of their job description. Bringing together the appropriate managers and technical specialists into an ad hoc problem-solving meeting is a well established and familiar approach. Problems of sequence (e.g. variations created in one section of the manufacturing process which prevent another from meeting production quotas) and reciprocity (e.g. delays in setting up a prototype on the shop floor slowing down the introduction of a new product) can be addressed. However, each manager is held accountable for his or her individual performance and continues to see the world primarily from the perspective of his or her departmental position; there may be very little to require cooperation.

One way to maximise cooperation is to set up project management teams by taking personnel from different departments. Each person then contributes full-time to the overall task from their particular specialism. A manager, assigned to oversee the entire project, carries a degree of authority that outweighs the authority of the original departments. Such a multidisciplinary team has the advantage, by working simultaneously on a joint task, of avoiding designing or planning impractical or too expensive solutions. However, one discipline (often that of the manager) does tend to dominate and this can cause resentment and lack of cooperation.

A Case of Changing Business and Organisational Strategy with Business Units

Tucker Fasteners plc manufactures and distributes rivets throughout the European, Middle East and African markets on behalf of its US parent. Because of delays in agreeing a new industrial relations framework with the trade union, there was some delay in introducing teamwork through job design and cross-training. Some newly automated equipment made it possible to design a number of new manufacturing cells in which production and quality targets could be met readily by small numbers of operators. The company hoped to move to cells entirely once the industrial relations framework problems were sorted out.

In the meantime, it was decided to implement part of the plan by moving to business unit teams. The products were clustered into six types; a Business Unit Manager was assigned along with a Process Improvement Engineer, a Quality Technician, and a former supervisor turned trainer/coach. To as great an extent as possible, all operators working on a particular product were treated as if they were a part of the Business Unit Team even though, in some cases, they were not located together on the shop floor. They trained together in total quality management practices, including team skills, and met together for Business Unit Team briefings.

After a year, the senior managers decided to go from six to five business units. Capital investment funds for bringing together some of the dispersed Business Units were approved at about the same time. The Business Unit Managers began to meet together on a twice-monthly basis with the Operations Manager to coordinate joint problem-solving and to learn from each other's experience.

Flattening Hierarchies and Making Redundancies

Referring to *redundancies* as a method for changing business and organisational strategy may strike some people as a bit ironic. Indeed, many executives and senior managers consider redundancies as a decision of last resort; more a reaction that they feel forced into than a choice they have taken positively. Some of those employees made redundant as a part of a business strategy seriously question the competence of a top management who cannot develop the business and retain employment at the same time.

But the facts speak for themselves. The overwhelming majority of companies involved in the 'teamwork in manufacturing' project announced significant redundancies at least once, several more than twice, during a 5-10 year period of comprehensive change. Those redundancies made it possible, even mandatory, to introduce, develop and reinforce teamwork.

Sometimes, the redundancies were tied to automation or some other form of new technology. The more automated section of the manufacturing process ran with fewer people. In such an instance, a smaller number of employees made teamwork a viable option, but not a requirement.

Most of the time, top management order redundancies as a response to declining market shares, or as an important part of cost-cutting programmes to retain market share. Introducing changes in working practices like multi-skilling, job rotation and cellular manufacturing – all elements of many companies' teamworking efforts – makes it possible to work with fewer operators. But the biggest facilitator of cutting numbers in the overall labour force lies in the theoretical promises and practical realities of operating with fewer levels of hierarchy.

Flattening hierarchy refers both to operating with fewer levels of authority (i.e. those who can direct the behaviour of others) and with fewer grading differences amongst employees. The latter, theoretically, removes differentiation between workers who are making similar contributions to the business and encourages cooperation within and across the boundaries of operational teams. In reality, lower status employees like a flatter grading structure because they tend to be elevated in skill training, status, opportunity for develop-

[93]

Using flattened hierarchies for changing business and organisational strategy

Senior managers define differently the jobs of their direct-report and line managers, remove middle layers of authority and delegate problem-solving and decision-making to the point where the need for the decision originally arises; usually, a flatter grading structure is also implemented.

Advantages	Problems/Concerns
Problem-solving and decision-making must be delegated to the lowest level possible because middle managers are no longer present to address them.	Many decisions tend to be 'delegated upwards' as employees lack information, training, confidence or willingness to take risky decisions, resulting in an overloaded top management.
A better flow of communication and cooperation can emerge between line and top management because there is no one to filter that communication; implementation of changes and improvements can be easier.	Managers report over-working in order to do the 3-4 jobs that have been collapsed into the one; piled on top of the routine job, cross-functional and management of change meetings can overwhelm the best of managers.
Through making redundancies, a process can be implemented to retain those employees and managers considered to be making a contribution to the company.	The emotional and financial wounds left by several cycles of redundancies (usually felt to be unfair) may not heal in time to capture back the goodwill of the employees. Company loyalty and identification may be lost from the majority of workers and managers.

The simplified hierarchy and grading systems can free up creativity and release accumulated resentment.	Employees and managers of higher status will resent and resist changes to their privileges; compromises will be struck which leave symbolic inequities and differentials in place regardless of a management philosophy to the contrary.

ment and sometimes even pay. Higher status operational employees resent the loss of difference and tend to resist mightily: craftsmen, staff with company cars and the highest-grade operators (many of whom sweated through the steep grading structure to get to where they are) frequently obstruct progress. To the extent that a flatter grading structure facilitates multi-skilling and job rotation, fewer employees are needed to cover the same number of jobs.

With fewer levels of authority, the principle operates differently. Instead of employees being changed in order to develop new forms of work, the organisation is changed and the people made to fit in or made redundant. Top management decide to remove positions, by eliminating whole layers of middle management. Often, those who are making the changes think through only the line and senior management posts. Once the entire middle (between two and three layers usually) has been removed, the remaining managers must find a way to make the flatter structure work. Typically, senior managers announce the introduction of business units or business process re-engineering at the same time as they announce redundancies and flatter hierarchies.

Defining new roles for managers who remain challenges the managers themselves, their bosses and those within the training and development function. A period of emotional shock gives way to lassitude. Managers report that they await direction from top management about how to proceed. Meanwhile, they maintain those aspects of the job that strike them as most central. At the same time, top management tend to look for signs of greater initiative and innovation in process and product development. Theoretically, line managers and service managers become crucial actors in the management of

[95]

change, especially as far as the encouragement, education and development of the operational personnel are concerned. In a slightly more recent trend, senior managers expect remaining

A Case of Changing Business Strategy by Flattening Hierarchies and Making Redundancies

In the years leading up to 1992, **Leyland DAF** at Preston had been able to make significant progress on introducing and developing operational teamwork in the manufacture of trucks. In cooperation with its trade unions, the senior managers had established business units and a team structure around most of the assembly plant and had achieved some cross-training. However, several difficulties defied solution. For example, service to the operational teams was not as effective as it might have been due to poor cross-functional relationships; the same issue blocked the introduction and development of teamwork within the service departments.

In 1992, shares were suspended in the Dutch multinational that owned Leyland, and the UK sites went into receivership. In a matter of months, the UK company had been split into several companies, two management buyouts arranged and approximately 2,500 employees made redundant.

In preparing the Preston truck operation for a buyout, senior managers capitalised on and further developed their new team-based working practices which helped considerably in justifying the company's continued viability with its new backers. The strategic organisational and cultural changes, started in 1990, had already resulted in a flattening of hierarchies, with new roles for departmental managers. Within the service departments, project management teams and teams devoted to particular sections of the shop floor were being used. For example, business unit management teams including manufacturing engineers were formed within the assembly area and quality technicians were also integrated on to the assembly line teams. Within the new company, **Leyland Trucks Manufacturing Ltd**, a complicated infrastructure of planning and review meetings emerged fairly quickly to begin to increase integration across service departments.

and line managers to be involved in actively developing the business and managing relationships with customers.

Managers who are being expected to behave according to new roles require some sort of transitional phase. Available training packages emphasise 'coaching and facilitating skills', and it is not uncommon to find all the remaining managers being put through 2-3 days of some sort of training programme. Management developers tell stories of how they must adapt their courses to allow these 'shell-shocked' managers the opportunity to deal with their feelings – a blend of fear, inadequacy, guilt and anger. Grief needs to be worked through in order to prepare for taking up a new role.

Many managers claim that they need straightforward training in new business and technical skills. The not uncommon experience of being expected to use a personal computer without any training is a good metaphor for how managers feel about being expected to fit into new roles. Training in new managerial skills covers only a proportion of the new challenges. In addition to new business and technical skills, managers need help adjusting to the psychodynamics of a flatter structure. For example, being more visible to the executives and being held accountable directly for measurable results can be terrifying.

Improving Customer and Supplier Relationships

Redirecting change in business and organisational strategy by improving customer and supplier relationships has become an important method for many manufacturers. Selection and development of preferred suppliers and customers gains popularity as the benefits achieved by some companies become public. Interestingly, the strategic decision to work in special relationships with preferred customers and suppliers can be understood as redefining the boundaries of the organisation at points of input and output.

A strategy popular during better financial times was to buy one's corporate customers, so that a certain market for one's product would be guaranteed, or to buy one's suppliers, so that the source of raw material would be certain. The trouble with this strategy was that, once the recession hit, the additional costs of the expanded company were difficult to sustain. Improving the supplier-customer relationship is a less drastic way to try to achieve some degree of control over sources of raw material and predictable sales figures.

Inadequate knowledge about customers' anticipated needs for product can make planning and organising for work a matter of experience and guesswork. As a customer's needs change – for example, smaller batch sizes or dramatically different specifications – a manufacturer can lose business if the necessary adjustments and developments are not made. Further, as both manufacturer and customer strive to achieve competitive advantage through cost reduction or quality enhancement, both parties have much to lose or gain by failed negotiations on cost or persistent difficulties with process and product improvement.

Persistent difficulties with quality and productivity can often be traced to defects in raw materials. Wastage rates can soar and machines stand idle while technicians attempt to compensate for poor-quality inputs. Equally, matching both production process and capability to customers' needs can make or break a company. When a customer develops a new product, the capability of suppliers to invest in corresponding developments in process to manufacture relevant components may determine whether the customer is retained or lost.

In the light of the importance of both suppliers and customers to a manufacturing company, improving relationships is strategic. Two options, sometimes used together and other times used separately, are emerging in relation to teamwork. The first option is to decrease the number of suppliers; the second is to identify preferred suppliers and customers with whom special deals on price and disclosure are agreed. Some sort of collaborative activity such as improving quality or reducing cost is agreed.

- *Decreasing the number of suppliers* has the effect of decreasing the volume of administration and transaction costs. The size of market share increases for the suppliers retained. They respond by agreeing to improve service, to ensure quality standards and to cooperate with technical specialists in improving process. Sometimes, a just-in-time delivery schedule forms part of the agreement to accept a larger proportion of a customer's business.

- *Identifying preferred suppliers and customers* does not mean automatically that there are fewer suppliers and customers. Preferred suppliers and customers agree to disclose actual costs in some areas to each other in order to identify cost savings for both parties. This sort of disclosure implies that each party can help each other out, or even require certain improvements, for the benefit of the whole. It would be typical in such a situation for technical specialists and sales representatives in both companies to spend time inside each others' sites, solving problems and planning jointly. The basic principle underlying this type of 'partnership' arrangement is a long-term mutual commitment to the continued viability of both parties.

The advantages and disadvantages of both of these options are roughly the same. Theoretically, both parties benefit from improved quality, cooperation on price and process improvements, and pace of new product introduction. By breaking down the barriers to sharing information and to helping solve mutual problems, both parties join together against competitors. Thus, their competitive advantage improves.

In practice, the customer tends to be the stronger partner. With the inherent threat of awarding their business to another supplier, the customer can exert influence which can verge towards direct control. Supplier executives and senior managers may feel a danger of losing control over their own company's strategic decisions because of vulnerability to potential loss of business. When one customer constitutes a significant proportion of business, then growing the business is the only way to strengthen the supplier's hand. Even that action does not remove the threat entirely.

Improving customer and supplier relationships can be crucial for introducing and developing teamwork internal to a company's operations. If poor raw materials cause frequent breakdowns and poor-quality finished goods, then operators learn that productivity and quality are out of their control. Instead of taking responsibility for solving problems, they will blame the suppliers and their dependence on technical specialists will remain strong.

[99]

At a relatively early stage of team development, team members can take responsibility for monitoring and ordering raw materials and for moving their completed work onto the next step in sending the product to the customer. However, the more the internal and external supply chain is controlled by

Using improved customer and supplier relationships for changing business and organisational strategy

Executives set up a system for identifying and selecting a limited number of preferred customers and suppliers; these are supported by agreements and collaboration on product and process improvements, aimed at improving quality and reducing costs.

Advantages	Problems/Concerns
This arrangement motivates a supplier to ensure quality and make process improvements more closely in line with the company's specifications.	The company is more vulnerable to difficulties within the supplier; if for whatever reason the supplier cannot deliver, other suppliers may have been alienated or unprepared to meet specifications.
A customer can be preferential to one's product because of the price advantages and match with specific needs.	If the customer does not continue to buy the agreed amount of product, other markets or distribution channels may not be open soon enough to prevent financial crisis.
It is possible to achieve disclosure of actual costs underlying prices and to open up engineering and technical channels of mutual influence.	Both suppliers and customers have other companies that they deal with; suppliers especially can be overwhelmed with competing demands which threaten to take their business in conflicting directions.

By negotiating mutually beneficial cooperative relationships, customers and suppliers can both achieve a greater proportion of the market, guarantee quality product and block competitors' access to suppliers and distributors.	A preferred customer can have influence bordering on direct control over one's business through the power of proportion of the company's business that customer represents.

another department or level of hierarchy, the less autonomous the team will be. A just-in-time or kanban system can be readily controlled by operational teams. Cooperation from the supplier is necessary. Later on in the life of a team, they can be involved directly with customers in problem-solving and plan-

A Case of Changing Business Strategy with Improved Customer and Supplier Relationships

Cleaning Filters Incorporated is a medium-sized manufacturer of large, customised filtration systems that clean fluids used in the manufacture of automobiles. Over the past three years, three of their customers have introduced preferred supplier programmes and Cleaning Filters has been selected by all three.

While these relationships guaranteed steady flow of work, it also forced a growth to their business they were not prepared to handle. They had to bring many new people onto projects with little socialisation to the practices of the company. More senior engineers, including the founder-managers, increasingly were summoned to one or more of their customers for 1-2 day long meetings. It was as if they were being treated as employees, involved in more and more aspects of planning and maintenance of the filtration systems. In desperation, the senior managers worked longer and longer hours and promoted others into important department management roles. Unfortunately, the others were not experienced managers and personnel difficulties began to escalate. The senior managers had handled such difficulties with sensitivity and skill previously, but they were not in the office of their own company enough.

ning sessions and increasing mutual understanding about process and product improvements.

Initiative Areas Interconnected with Business and Organisational Strategy

Executives, senior managers and other change agents involved in changing business and organisational strategy, in a direction complementary with teamwork, may find it useful to keep in mind other interconnected change initiatives. It would not be an exaggeration to say that all of the other four aspects of organisation are interconnected with business and organisational strategy. However, at a minimum, operational teamwork

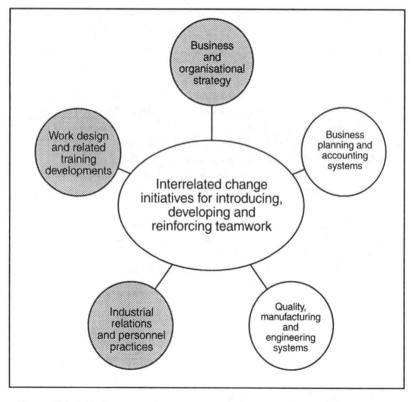

Figure 5.1. Initiative areas interconnected with business and organisational strategy.

[102]

A Case of Stalled Teamwork Due to Business and Organisational Strategy

Acco-Rexel Limited (Llangeinor) has been manufacturing stapling machines for 20 years on behalf of its multinational parent, known for its office supplies. For most of its history, Acco-Rexel was structured along functional lines, although its operations were split into staple production and stapling machines production. The Operations Director of the stapling machines department was keen to introduce and develop teamwork. He experimented with two different versions of teamwork: quality improvement teams located in each of the six sections of manufacturing and one of assembly; and grouping employees around a set of machines in one section, cross-training them on multiple machines and promoting one of the operators into the role of team leader. Both experiments resulted in limited success, but not the degree of quality and productivity improvement the Operations Director had expected.

Little progress was made on developing teamworking further for a couple of years. Then, an emerging business and organisational strategy for Europe identified the strategic potential of self-regulating teams. This particular site was a cost centre: keeping costs low was of primary importance. Two elements of the business strategy - maintaining low costs and increasing flexibility - were judged to be related positively to teamwork. By flattening hierarchies, automating certain aspects of production and cross-training their operators, managers hoped to improve quality and productivity without having to employ more people. Plans were started for developing a more effective form of teamwork.

cannot be implemented without changes to job design and related training developments and without changes to industrial relations and personnel practices.

Questions for Understanding Business and Organisational Strategy

• What strategic decisions have been taken in the last couple of years related to the company's relationship to its external environment? For example, product markets, geographical markets, financial structure and competitive advantage.

- What types of teams have been introduced in this company: operational, service and/or cross-functional? Which strategic rationale do managers offer for teamwork: cost reduction, quality enhancement or innovation?

- To what extent has strategic planning been used in this company? When was the last planning process? Who was involved and how formal was the planning process? Which aspects of the plan have been implemented, which are being implemented now and which ones seem to have been dropped?

- Have there been any major restructuring efforts recently in this company? To what extent, if at all, has the company moved away from a functional to a product-based or business unit structure? Are there indications of significant investment in information technology that has or might suggest centralised processing functions? To what extent, if at all, are cross-functional problem-solving or project groups used; have departmental boundaries been redrawn recently?

- When, if ever, were the last redundancies in this company? How many people were made redundant, from what levels of hierarchy and which sections? How many levels of hierarchy does the company have? How does this compare to historical numbers of levels?

- What recent changes to their roles, if any, have been experienced by line and middle managers and by technical specialists? Has the company, in the last few years, commissioned training and development programmes offered throughout the organisation? Is there reference to a different managerial style on any public statements of 'mission', 'vision' or strategy?

- What is the nature of the supplier and customer relationships in this company? How many suppliers and how many customers are there, with what proportion of the business? Have there been any supplier development or customer development programmes in the last few years? What sort of materials handling system is in operation on the shop floor? How much control do the operators have over incoming and outgoing product?

[104]

Further Reading

Dopson, S. and Stewart, R. 1990. What is happening to middle management? *British Journal of Management*, Vol. 1, 3-16.

Johnson, G. and Scholes, K. 1993. *Exploring Corporate Strategy*: Text and Cases, 3rd Edition. New York: Prentice Hall.

Laming, R. 1993. *Beyond Partnership. Strategies for Innovation and Lean Supply*. New York: Prentice Hall International.

Mintzberg, H. 1991. The effective organization: forces and forms. *Sloan Management Review*, Winter, 54-67.

Morris, D. and Bandon, J. 1993. *Re-engineering Your Business*. New York: McGraw Hill Inc.

Pasmore, W. A. 1988, *Designing Effective Organisations: The Sociotechnical Systems Perspective*. New York: John Wiley & Sons.

Porter, M.E. 1985. *Competitive Advantage: Creating and Sustaining Superior Performance*. New York: The Press Press.

Schonberger, R. J. 1986. *World Class Manufacturing*. New York: Free Press.

Thompson, J. D. 1967. *Organisations in Action*. New York: McGraw Hill Inc.

Weisbord, W. R. 1992. *Discovering Common Ground*. San Francisco: Berrett-Koehler Publishers.

6

Changing Work Design and Related Training

The redesign of jobs is an intrinsic aspect of setting up team-work. It is not possible to develop proper teams without at least some degree of restructuring of existing jobs. Much of the interest in group-based job design originated with concerns about individual, employee motivation and resulting losses in productivity as a consequence of 'traditional' mass production. For several decades work design has been a very important way in which the problems of poor motivation and low commitment among the workforce have been addressed.

Unlike changes to quality, manufacturing and engineering systems – the other major area of change initiative that significantly affects job design – initiatives for changing work design and related training developments specifically take into consideration the social and psychological needs of employees. Nearly five decades of research about and practice with work design underpins a few basic principles which are thought (and in many cases have actually been demonstrated) to do this.

- Give employees maximum variety in their work
- Improve employees' control over work processes (including discretion in how to complete tasks)
- Devolve decision-making and problem-solving
- Develop a more participatory work culture
- Make available feedback on performance.

Approaches to work design, which are closely linked to effecting motivational changes in the workforce, thus also have a clear link with the main principles behind group-based work. An explicit goal of work design is to find a way to address the needs of the technology and the needs of the human beings who must operate that technology. More technologically oriented managers have become interested in work design and related training developments because change initiatives which ignore the social and psychological needs of employees are rarely used to the optimal extent possible.

Scientific management, now generally seen as traditional work design, developed with the mass production of standard items for a relatively undifferentiated consumer market. With this approach to work design, tasks are broken down into a series of simple operations, on the principle that the more simple and repetitive the task, the less the room for error. In manufacturing and assembly operations, people are considered not much more than extensions of their machines with little room for discretion or using their brain in carrying out their work. All jobs are very precisely specified so that they can be standardised and subject to checking by managers. Jobs are grouped into functional specialisms with very clear boundaries between them. All jobs are classified into grades and paid at different rates. Managers and supervisors carry out all coordinating tasks and exercise 'management by control'.

This way of designing work has been associated persistently with poor workforce morale and motivation. Highly repetitive jobs and lack of control cause people to 'switch off', do the minimum they can get away with and feel apathetic or even hostile towards the organisation. The highly specialised and detailed division of tasks, with its associated pay grades and status distinctions, creates rigid and unnecessary demarcations which prevent or discourage employees from cooperating across functional lines or enhancing their skills.

[107]

Such behaviour on the part of workers, whatever its cause, is increasingly at odds with managerial needs for the operation of new manufacturing technologies and a suitable response to fiercely competitive markets. Fighting compeititive advantage out on the terrain of quality and meeting different customer needs requires more 'switched on' employees, who feel motivated by meeting performance targets and challenging learning situations. Traditional shop floor jobs discourage innovation, improvement and problem-solving, and reinforce narrow lines of knowledge. The new technologies require better motivated employees who can take more individual and collective responsibility, involving themselves more fully with the goals of the organisation. This is the context in which teamwork is largely being introduced, and there has thus been a coming together of market imperatives with concerns about how to improve employee motivation and commitment.

Many organisations that have achieved some degree of proper teamwork have done so by changing work design. But work design is not enough on its own. Team members, their managers and technical service staff must be prepared for teamwork with effective training and development. Companies have successfully used five basic methods for changing work design and related training developments. Mostly, change agents select an option from under each method to tackle work system design issues as they emerge.

- Following a structured work design framework
- Clarifying team leader roles
- Relating support functions to teams
- Developing team competence and effectiveness
- Evolving new management roles and styles.

Structured Work Design Framework

Frameworks for structured work design have been developed by social scientists. A framework includes a theoretical rationale, some principles for applying the theory and a method for studying, planning and implementing new job designs. Two of the most influential work design frameworks have been used to challenge scientific management. Both job enrichment or enlargement and socio-technical systems make direct links between motivation and work design. Both are highly relevant to the design of work systems based on teams.

Job enrichment or *enlargement* usually means expanding individual jobs laterally or horizontally or both. This entails widening the range of operating tasks by adding in other like tasks, and/or adding in coordinating tasks. This enables employees to develop their skills and experience. It introduces much greater variety into their work and potentially offers greater individual autonomy and responsibility. Such changes are generally linked to greater job satisfaction which in turn produces a higher level of motivation.

Enriching or enlarging jobs can be an aim in its own right. It can also be a first step in introducing or developing teamwork. The kinds of motivational changes (i.e. enhanced skills, greater variety and improved job satisfaction) involved are necessary for teamwork to succeed. Applying the concepts of job enlargement to a group of jobs – by expanding the jobs to be included in the group laterally or horizontally or both – is an integral part of self-directed teams. Although improving motivation was not their primary aim, several of the TIM companies have effectively used this approach to work design as the route to developing teams through greater job flexibility.

A Case of Changing Work Design and Related Training With Job Enrichment and Enlargement

Paperworks Ltd began their change process by breaking down demarcations and rigid job descriptions and forming flexible teams where operators carried out the range of tasks associated with a particular process. They also began to involve and train employees in business planning and quality-enhancement problem-solving techniques. They thus expanded jobs both sideways and upwards, increasing employees' sense of involvement in the organisation as a whole.

A number of the TIM companies began by enlarging jobs through a process of mainly sideways multi-skilling. This required them simultaneously to renegotiate their industrial relations policies, which had evolved in the context of 'traditional' job evaluation and design. Beginning the process in this way had the advantage of not having major implications for physical layout. One company found that simply moving machinery closer together made it easier to introduce multi-skilling.

A number of boundary issues have to be addressed in designing more flexible jobs. How much flexibility is a key question. Flexibility may mean complete interchangeability across a range of closely associated tasks, enabling rotation of jobs among a spatially or technically defined group of people. Minimal flexibility can mean what one company described as 'deputisation' – providing enough cross-skilling to enable employees to cover a range of jobs in the event of absences and other contingencies. In the case of expanding jobs to include coordinating tasks, this will have implications for the design of supervisory jobs.

Jobs are defined across time as well as space. Where shift work operates, the same task continues over a time boundary but with different personnel. Challenges of work design include such questions as: how to effect coordination and handover between shift personnel; and how to provide a sense of completeness to jobs without sacrificing coordination or setting up inter-shift competition.

Teams particularly can build up very strong relationships, developing their own rules and boundaries and excluding others, thus vitiating flexibility. One company found that their production teams, though well motivated, had settled into a competitive dynamic with teams on the next shift and this was interfering with coordination. They set up cross-shift improvement teams to look at quality control and found that the problem resolved itself.

The other major framework for structured work design is *socio-technical systems analysis*, which originated with the work of The Tavistock Institute in early postwar manufacturing and mining industries. There are several variants of socio-technical systems analysis actively in use: the 12-step method developed for Shell UK by Michael Foster and colleagues at The Tavistock Institute; the work restructuring method developed by Schumacher in the UK; and another one developed by Lou Davis in the US. All of these 'STS' methods have been adopted with some success by leading international corporations and more local companies as well. The principal features are,

Using job enrichment and enlargement for changing work design and related training developments

By expanding jobs laterally and/or horizontally, the range of operating tasks is widened by adding in other similar tasks or widening the variety of tasks carried out by an individual.

Advantages	Problems/Concerns
It gives employees greater variety and responsibility in their work and potentially increases interest and motivation.	Employees do not necessarily all welcome change. If they have been comfortably carrying out the same job for a long period of time, they may prefer to continue in the same way.
Job enrichment and enlargement are a useful route to increasing flexibility through multi-skilling.	Trade unions, particularly those representing craft employees, may resist if they believe their members' jobs are threatened.
It is possible to expand jobs to include supervisory and wider coordinating tasks.	Supervisors and 'white collar' staff may not cooperate, feeling that their jobs and style of operation are threatened.
Job enrichment or enlargement can be a first step towards introducing teamwork.	Unless attention is paid to the group-based design of jobs,

however, similar. At the heart of socio-technical systems is the concern to get a better match between the needs of the task and human needs for greater involvement, autonomy and responsibility in the workplace (Neumann, 1989).

A key concept of socio-technical systems is that of 'joint optimisation'. Work systems are a coming together of a technology of production and a set of human interactions. The

[111]

needs of both technical and human, or social, subsystems have to be met jointly to achieve the optimal output. If either is maximised at the expense of the other, productivity declines and employees become demotivated and alienated from their work. In this view, traditional work design is seen as skewed towards optimising the technical over the social subsystem. A value of the socio-technical systems method is that people should complement machines (and vice versa), rather than be subservient to them. Thus, socio-technical systems design focuses on the total work system as its unit of analysis, rather than on distinct tasks or jobs.

The idea of the semi-autonomous work group – or self-regulating teams – is central to much socio-technical systems thinking. Empirical work in the 1950s demonstrated an important fit between productivity and a high degree of control by employees over the conditions around the performance of a task. Further, the task itself must be meaningful in the sense of constituting a whole stage or process of production. Self-regulating teams feature in many socio-technical systems-based work designs as a way of achieving this. Team boundaries are drawn at natural breaks (or 'transformations') in a total production process: the set of tasks involved is grouped together and performed by the group as a whole. As with work design focused on job enrichment, self-regulating teams imply flexible working and multi-skilling. However, they go much further in developing a high degree of self-direction, enabling people to develop maximum levels of autonomy and responsibility within the work group and in the group's relationship to the rest of the organisation.

Socio-technical approaches also imply much wider organisational changes. They are associated with flat organisations, participative management styles and minimal direct management – the antithesis of scientific management. The resurgence of interest in socio-technical systems theory derives partly from the potential of self-regulating teams for furthering organisational development and innovation. Though the idea was developed in a very different era, they also mesh well with the need for greater technological knowledge and higher levels of responsibility among employees.

Jobs designed according to socio-technical principles will, not surprisingly, bear little resemblance to conventional job classifications. A job such as welding, for instance, will cease to be a work identity ('I am a welder') and become a skill which will be an aspect of the job of all team members working on a process which requires welding.

A Case of Work Design and Related Training Developments Using Socio-technical Systems Analysis

UK Metals Ltd used a form of socio-technical systems work redesign to develop their integrated manufacturing teams. They wanted to put in place teams conceived of as groups of self-managing people who would be fully responsible for the product and its quality in their area.

They employed a method called key task analysis. This is a mapping process designed to identify, chart and analyse all activities involved in the processing of material to and from the customer. On the basis of this analysis, all production lines and departments were divided up into segments, with new jobs formed by grouping together the tasks necessary to run a complete process. Existing demarcations and grading structures were disregarded for the purpose of the analysis and the new jobs were regraded. The new work teams cut across former operator-craft divisions, with some craft tasks going into process teams.

Socio-technical systems methodologies can imply quite comprehensive changes to job design, especially if self-regulating teams are a desired outcome. However, as the cases quoted here demonstrate, this structured framework is flexible enough to be applied to a range of work design issues without necessarily entailing a complete reorganisation. Most importantly from a job design point of view, this approach strongly encourages equal consideration of both the social and technical subsystems in conjunction with the other.

In its most generic sense, therefore, work design means the grouping of tasks into jobs and jobs into work groups. To carry out work design, it is necessary to look at the relationship between the production process, the equipment, the tasks required to operate the equipment and the tasks needed to

A Case of Changing Work Design and Related Training Developments Using Socio-technical Systems Analysis

New IT Systems Ltd used a socio-technical systems methodology to reorganise a customer service function where the quality of the service product was very variable. They looked at the transformational steps involved in the process of repairing and returning equipment in order to identify waste and redundancy in the process.

One finding was that a serial number check was carried out seven times over. Moving to bar coding produced substantial savings. At the same time they looked at the social subsystem, carrying out an inventory of activities and identifying strengths and weaknesses among staff. This resulted in changes to the management structure of the function, reducing the numbers of managers and devolving responsibility downwards. They did not, however, reorganise the function into self-managing teams. A previous experience in trying to do this had failed to deliver the service improvements needed. It was felt that the attempt had been too hasty, lacking the necessary organisational development to support such a major change.

coordinate all of these. This mapping process is the same whether manufacturing or service activities are being considered.

However, how radical a restructuring is required will depend on the kind of teamworking aimed for. Developing semi-autonomous work groups, for instance, will require comprehensive redesign. It is important to note also that redesigning jobs for teamworking has important industrial relations and human resources implications. It is also often connected to initiatives in manufacturing engineering, and may have implications for physical layouts as well.

Both job enrichment/enlargement and socio-technical systems analysis can be undertaken by senior managers and technical specialists working on their own or with the assistance of an external or internal consultant. As both frameworks require some specialist knowledge about motivation and about the psychological principles underpinning work design, it is unlikely that this method would be attempted without some professional assistance. Both options require direct observation and evaluation of existing jobs. Job enrichment/enlargement concerns itself only with motivation and satisfaction of employees; socio-technical analysis addresses both social and technical needs. The latter method almost always involves a planning group with representatives from different functions, different job grades and different levels of hierarchy. The former typically is undertaken by managers and then communicated to the workforce.

Clarifying Team Leader Roles

The issue of what happens to line management in teamwork typically exercises the minds of top management in the early days of deciding to introduce teams. Management of teams constitutes a key aspect of the structure and boundaries of operational teams and cannot be considered without reference to decisions about the degree of self-direction. Effective leadership is equally an important feature of cross-functional task teams. In none of these cases does leadership necessarily have to reside in one person – it can be designed in as an aspect of several people's jobs, with associated implications for their training and development.

Three main options for leadership roles in permanent teams have been used effectively by companies: teams with the supervisor as leader; teams with a leader and no supervisor; and teams with no team leader or supervisor.

Deciding to have *teams with the supervisor as the leader* enables teamwork to be introduced without a complete transformation of first line management. The supervisors remain technically outside the operational team, retaining their role of mediating agent between management and shop floor. However, the content of their role is likely to be significantly changed. In this kind of arrangement, team members probably have broadly equal skills, enabling them to take responsibility for direct operational tasks and to be flexible in covering for each other.

The supervisor/team leader generally takes responsibility for coordinating and administrative tasks. These include

[115]

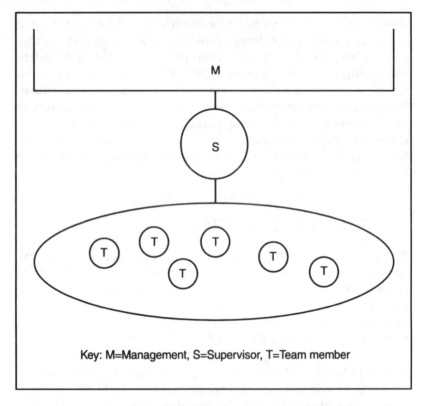

Key: M=Management, S=Supervisor, T=Team member

Figure 6.1. Teams with supervisor as leader.

personnel administration, setting and monitoring targets, and leading problem-solving and improvement activities. At least in the beginning, they are likely to take a lead in training and assessing training needs but with the aim of developing cross-training within the team over time. Pay differentials are likely to be retained in some form between supervisors and team members.

The responsibility of management is for developing overall business strategy and ensuring it is communicated to the teams. Management also continues to take responsibility for the recruitment and management of supervisors and for the central support functions required by the teams.

There are some advantages to creating team leaders from existing supervisory or line management roles. The incumbents are close to the shop floor, tend to be suitably technically skilled and have a detailed knowledge of work practices and personnel. They are already in a key position to push through changes because of their position in the chain of communication, facing both inwards and outwards.

Changing supervisors into team leaders can also be a source of problems and concerns. Supervisors and line managers are often the employees who feel most threatened by the introduction of teamworking at shop floor level. They may reasonably fear the loss of their job. They may also fear loss of status and

Using supervisors as team leaders for changing work design and related training

Existing supervisory staff are redeployed as operations team leaders with appropriate training to support the change in content and style of their job.

Advantages	Problems/Concerns
Having supervisors in team leader roles enables production areas to operate with greater continuity, retaining first line management and existing relationships between supervisors and operators.	Supervisors may be too caught in their traditional ways of operating to be able to respond to the changes needed in their role.
The supervisor is generally technically well qualified for the role and is familiar with work practices and the people in the team.	Team leaders need 'people' skills which are not always possessed by supervisors in a traditional manufacturing enterprise.
They are in a key position to act as change agents because they relate both to the shop floor and the management.	Supervisors may fear loss of status and the forms of control they are accustomed to, leading to inappropriate ways of relating to their teams and resentment from team members.

the control which was inherent in a hierarchically organised structure. Those who have spent many years working their way up to their present position may justifiably resent having to accept suggestions from people with less skills and knowledge. Most of all, they will be expected to exercise management and leadership skills significantly different in some ways from the ones they have previously used. Instead of issuing instructions, ensuring compliance with procedural rules and resolving problems on behalf of subordinates, they will need to facilitate or enable others to organise task performance, take responsibility and resolve problems themselves.

Having *teams with a leader and no supervisor* forces the creation of a new position of team leader and challenges the continued existence of a first line management role. Generally recruited from operatives, but possibly also from first line management, this leader is positioned within the team and is

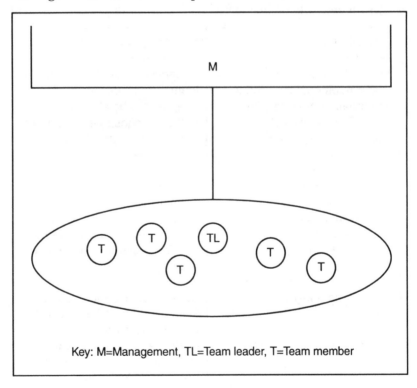

Key: M=Management, TL=Team leader, T=Team member

Figure 6.2. Teams with a leader and no supervisor.

likely to be a working team leader or at least able to cover for gaps or absences. Team members take responsibility for direct operational tasks. They should be in a position to cross-train each other on all basic tasks and may also take a share in administrative and coordination tasks.

The team leader carries out operational tasks as well as taking responsibility for leading problem-solving and improvement activities, liaising with managers and with other team leaders and carrying out some administrative tasks. If the position retains characteristics similar to a supervisor – e.g. managerial control – then, probably, the team leader may be paid more than team members. If the position is more like a chargehand or 'super operator', then the pay may be the same or slightly more.

Management continues to be responsible for overall business strategy and its communication to teams, as well as those support functions which have not been absorbed into the teams. However, the role of management is likely to become less directive and more concerned with managing the boundaries between teams and the wider organisation.

The advantages of recruiting the team leader from among operatives accrue from the fact that they have intimate local knowledge of technical and organisational processes and the personalities and concerns of potential team members. As they are already part of the group from which teams are being recruited, they are likely to be able to establish trust quickly and easily.

A common problem of this approach is a lack of confidence stemming from having historically been in a subordinate position, and from old assumptions carried over from a traditional work design. Difficulties may be experienced in establishing appropriate authority within the team (especially ones containing support staff of conventionally higher status) and in relation to managers. New team leaders may also lack some of the technical and social skills needed to move straight into such a role.

With *teams with no leader or supervisor*, leadership is dispersed within the team, with different types of liaison and leadership roles being taken up for different aspects of the task. All members take equal formal responsibility for all tasks within the team. They are able to cross-train each other and

[119]

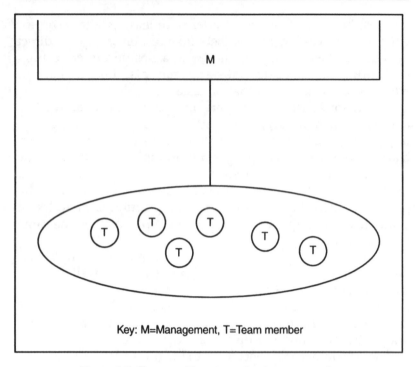

Figure 6.3. Teams with no team leader or supervisor.

carry out their own quality and improvement activities. The team may manage their own personnel matters, including selection and induction of new members and minor disciplinary issues. Staff from support functions may assist in this process or be attached to teams on a temporary or permanent basis. They have a facilitative rather than a hierarchical relationship to the teams. Payment systems need to reflect both the increase in individual skill levels and group-based productivity. Management is again responsible for overall business strategy and its communication to teams, but plays a more facilitative than directive role which is aimed at providing the conditions to enable teams to function in an optimal way.

Teams without a formal leader tend to be associated with a high degree of self-direction where team members already have multiple interchangeable technical and self/group management skills. Such teams are not necessarily leaderless. They may rotate leadership roles among themselves, or have

[120]

an agreed division of labour, of varying flexibility, in relation to tasks which involve leadership. The advantages of self-regulating teams lie in the degree of personal responsibility and commitment which comes with having a high level of social and technical skill and the self-direction to use it. High levels of competence and performance can be achieved, along with a more satisfied workforce.

'More satisfied' does not mean that all employees maintain total satisfaction with this way of working. To some, a job is still a job. The disadvantages of self-regulating teams can result in intense frustrations. If team members cannot manage collective processes of decision-making or intergroup conflict sufficiently, then task performance can suffer. If tied to reward, falling performance due to group dynamics can cause frustrated anger as easily as it can motivate improvement. It can also happen that too many 'leaders' emerge and the group is unable to contain the struggle for dominance. When an employee leaves for whatever reasons, a new recruit cannot immediately step in and take up that person's vacancy in the sense of multi-skills and the leadership roles he or she had been holding. This can throw a group off its stride for a bit, which may affect comfort levels more than actual production performance. These disadvantages point to the importance, for this kind of arrangement, of on-going training on how to manage group processes.

A Case of Changing Work Design and Related Training By Introducing Teams Without Leaders or Supervisors

Chemco, the UK site of a US multinational corporation, built a second factory onto the same site as a 20-year-old facility. While the building was being constructed, an executive from the US initiated a work design project at Chemco's new factory. They decided that the new operators should work in self-regulating teams without supervisors. When this decision was communicated within the existing factory, the supervisors were very angry. Many middle and senior managers, who themselves had worked as supervisors during their careers, shared a general belief that operators could not manage themselves. But the US executive persisted.

New operators were selected for both their potential chemical knowledge and their ratings on a test of interpersonal skills. They were given extensive technical training and, after a period of close daily contact with technical specialists, were involved in the commissioning and start-up of the new building. Because of their special training and intended supervisorless groups, senior managers negotiated an entry grade for the new operators with the trade union that was equivalent to the highest grade in the existing factory. The existing operators were very angry about this and expressed it in open hostility towards the new operators.

Once the new factory was up and running, the US executive took great pride in telling anyone who would listen that it had been the easiest and most rapid start-up period that the company had ever had with a new plant. The new operators did operate the plant in self-regulating teams, initially by staying in the job for which they were trained originally and then by cross-training in all the positions in two big sections of plant. Team meetings and special team skills training helped them carry out their work together. Eventually, the operators in the older factory insisted on being allowed to go through their own work design. Once their jobs were redesigned into self-regulating teams, a new payment system was introduced for rewarding team competence and performance.

The above three options for clarifying the team leader role are not the only ones being used within the TIM companies. Although these options treat supervisors and team leaders as alternatives (and teamwork usually implies considerable changes to the supervisory role, if not its abolition), some companies have successfully combined the two. One company made their chief engineers into team leaders, giving them purchasing responsibilities and accountability for a budget. Supervisors do the day-to-day supervision of team operations and report to the team leader, who is in turn responsible to the shift manager. The solution adopted has to make sense in the context where it is to operate. Clarity of roles and lines of accountability that satisfy workers *and* productivity requirements are more important than following a prescription.

[122]

Relating Support Functions to Teams

Teamwork can mean substantial changes in the way support functions of various kinds relate to operational teams. Quality and maintenance are the two services most frequently addressed through work design because of their daily importance to meeting targets. But training and development, personnel, manufacturing engineering, and product development may ultimately figure in the success of operational teams.

Companies have used three options for relating support functions to teams. First, support functions such as engineering and maintenance can be dispersed and put into production teams. Second, supervisory tasks can be integrated into shop floor jobs. Third, central support functions, such as personnel services, can be redesigned around teams.

Integrating support functions into operational teams can be done by simply making a specialist a full-time member of the team, by training in basic and intermediate specialists skills while a separate function provides advanced input, and by combining the two. Multi-skilling operators to undertake maintenance, repair and basic engineering tasks can improve both productivity and motivation among operators. It can improve quality by, for instance, giving operators responsibility for controlling variances. Decisions on the extent and degree of multi-skilling also involve a range of industrial relations and human resource issues, such as flexibility agreements, payment and grading systems and recruitment and selection.

Two critical issues here are how far to go and how to manage resistance from those whose jobs are restructured through integration. In practice, multi-skilling does not always mean complete interchangeability. Indeed, as one manager commented: 'We don't expect everyone to become completely multi-skilled but we do push people so there is a steady upward growth in the skill level.' An alternative, particularly where specialist skills are needed and it is not viable to train everyone, is to attach specialists to a team or teams. The feasibility of this will depend partly on whether there is sufficient work to sustain the specialist.

[123]

Using integrated support personnel for changing work design and related training	
The jobs of support personnel are redesigned around operations teams by placing them in the teams so that their work is integrated with the requirements of the team.	
Advantages	**Problems/Concerns**
This provides immediate service and specialist resources to the teams as and when they need it, saving them having to go and seek the appropriate person when the need occurs.	Unless there is sufficient work for the specialist, it may not achieve the efficiency gains that were intended.
It can be a way of breaking down craft and status distinctions, producing a more fruitful way of working across the workforce.	Because it challenges cherished status distinctions, it may be resisted or even sabotaged by higher status employees particularly, unless carefully handled.
Support staff can find this way of working rewarding and stimulating as it brings them much closer to the manufacturing process.	Support staff can feel very isolated from their functional colleagues and mechanisms will be needed to enable them to maintain those relationships.

Groundwork is needed to prepare the way for this kind of integration through multi-skilling. Not all companies are in a position to recruit new staff and thus rethink the process from the selection stage. Involving particularly those employees whose skill identities are at risk in the design and preparation of the process is likely to pay off both in goodwill and efficiency.

Integrating supervisory tasks into the job descriptions of operational teams can be a way of enlarging or enriching jobs or part of a wider move towards self-directed work teams.

Moving to self-directed work teams has major implications for first line management. One of the aims of self-direction is to devolve responsibility for what are traditionally supervisory tasks down to the shop floor. This may entail the removal of the supervisory level altogether, or redefining the role of supervisor away from checking and control to that of boundary management and team support. In either event, resistance from supervisors may be anticipated as their domain of responsibility appears to shrink. Less expectedly, problems may arise in the teams themselves. One company found that when they removed the supervisors, some work groups simply abdicated responsibility upwards to the next line of management, while some groups began behaving in an elitist way towards other groups. This points to a situation in which the change process was insufficiently thought through and prepared for, at both shop floor and management level.

Supervisors carry out a range of tasks which could potentially be devolved to production team members, such as: scheduling of work, appraisal of team members and disciplinary procedures. These tasks require different combinations of technical and social skills which, in turn, mean specific training, development and support needs. Some, for example appraisal and discipline, which need a high level of development of 'people' skills, are probably tasks for a more advanced, mature team.

This points to the need to think about the devolution of supervisory tasks as a process over time which is related to the degree of development of self-directed teams. Chapter 10 on continuously developing teams goes into this in more detail. While there are examples of teams successfully handling intra-team discipline, in other teamworking contexts a deliberate decision may be taken to exclude it. There are no prescriptive answers as to exactly which tasks should be devolved. What 'feels right' in one context may be inappropriate in another.

Redesigning central functions for improved support of teamworking usually means some combination of service teams dedicated to particular operational teams and some redesigning of the service function itself to disengage routine from nonroutine work. Routine, daily work involves relating to operational

[125]

teams in some way. Nonroutine work tends to link to longer-term projects and capital investment.

With the development of greater degrees of self-direction in production teams, the role of central support functions is likely to change as teams take on further responsibilities which might previously have been carried out centrally. Service departments may move to a role which is focused more on providing the conditions and resources (such as training) to enable teams to carry out tasks effectively. Support functions can be integrated into production management teams: for example, one manager or specialist from each function with daily involvement in the product can be assigned to a perma-nent, full-time business unit. A less drastic step is to convene a cross-functional task team of the same personnel on a daily or weekly basis for purposes of communication and coordination.

The most drastic move to achieve functional and spatial integration is to remove support staff from their central func-tions and place them physically closer to teams, under the direction of the production manager. This can result in improved relationships and services; however, the support staff tend to feel isolated socially from others doing similar work.

A Case of Changing Work Design and Related Training by Redesigning a Central Function

UK Metals Ltd carried out a major reorganisation of its personnel functions to support teamworking in its manufacturing areas on two separate sites. Instead of continuing with separate training and development departments, the whole section was reorganised into two integrated groups which covered both training and devel-opment: one supporting one site and one supporting the other. This was a first step in a more comprehensive reorganisation, with manufacturing engineering to be similarly dispersed.

Introducing and developing teamwork in production areas often tends to prompt the question, not only of how central support functions can support teamwork effectively, but whether teamwork should also be extended into support areas.

[126]

A Case of Changing Work Design and Related Training by Redesigning a Central Function

Leyland Trucks reorganised its assembly area into business units containing teams of multi-skilled operators. They took manufacturing engineers out of their functional department and attached them to the two business units where they are dedicated to particular teams and report directly to business unit managers.

Within a small to medium-sized manufacturing facility there can be arguments in both directions. Small administrative and technical departments, once freed from unnecessary levels of hierarchy, readily adjust to cross-training and working as a professional service team.

However, one company carried out a detailed review of the tasks of their support functions. They concluded that it would not be appropriate to transfer the style of operational teamwork into support functions. The work of the functions was highly structured, distinct and answered specific needs. The senior managers could see no obvious advantage in moving to flexible teams. They opted instead to introduce what they called 'service excellence' – focusing on process improvements within and between functions to increase the effectiveness of the services provided to both internal and external customers. These improvements focused on work flow as a whole, not just problem-solving, and emphasised working together both within and across functions.

The above examples indicate a number of salient concerns. First, decisions are required on what central support functions are needed to support teamwork. Second, support functions and teams need in some way to be brought closer together, whether spatially or in terms of breaking down cultural or psychological boundaries. Third, support functions themselves need to be rethought in terms of how their work is organised in a teamwork environment. This may not necessarily mean introducing teamwork, but it will mean attention to work flows across boundaries and to whether outcomes support the teams.

[127]

Developing Competent and Effective Teams

Developing competent and effective teams is a critical method for changing work design and related training. A good work design on paper will not come to life without sufficient training and development of all the people who can make or break the success of that design. Many an elegant work design has failed because the people involved, to use the words of a personnel director, 'didn't give it a chance'.

The options for developing competent and effective teams focus on development as much as training. Having gained relevant skills is not enough if employees' attitudes and emotions work against their effective use of those skills. The three options most commonly used under this method of developing competent and effective teams are:

- Training needs assessment
- Training for multi-skilled team members
- Providing external consultation on team effectiveness.

The development of teamwork produces training needs in relation to both technical and social skills. The need to enhance technical skills is generally connected to multi-skilling, but teamwork generates its own distinctive needs in terms of the social and interpersonal skills necessary to make teams function effectively. Training can be an expensive and time-consuming activity. It needs to be thought through carefully and to be tied to specific, identifiable needs and purposes. It is just as possible to over-train people (leaving them frustrated at not being able to use their new skills) as to under-train them (leaving them bored and dissatisfied).

Training also needs to be appropriately reinforced through on-going developmental interventions. Regular coaching sessions, self and peer assessments, group review meetings and refreshment courses may be more important than the original training. Research suggests that 'one-off' episodes of training rarely make a sustained difference to employee performance. This is especially the case where training takes place off-site and those 'trained' cannot transfer their experience to real work situations.

Carrying out some form of *training needs assessment* is an

important first step in the process of planning training for teamwork. This can be done internally, if the capacity exists, or by bringing in outside expertise. Whichever it is, it must link with overall objectives behind training.

Cases of Changing Work Design and Related Training Developments With Training Needs Assessment

International Chemicals wanted to develop more skill flexibility in their employees and less rigid, mechanistic job descriptions through teamwork. They carried out their own data gathering on what skills operators would like to learn, then – if it matched a need in the company – sent them on an appropriate course. At the same time, they involved supervisors in the process by getting them to choose which of a range of necessary skills (such as employee counselling) they wanted to develop and providing the training.

Paperworks Ltd, on the other hand, linked their needs assessment to the Investors in People programme which they were already pursuing. They commissioned a needs assessment from a local training college. They then agreed an action plan with the local TEC adviser, in which training for teamwork became part of a more comprehensive training package on human resources and other issues, including health and safety.

Teamwork training needs should also be considered in the light of existing training capacity and strategies. In one company, an extensive training programme is driven by the system of appraisal, with the training team following up on individual appraisals and providing any recommended training through a collective fund. This provides a ready-made framework for slotting in teamwork related needs. Training clearly overlaps, then, with other decision-making arenas.

Training is also not a politics free zone. The issue of *training for multi-skilled teamwork* can similarly impinge upon industrial relations. In one company, union officials 'blew a fuse' when it was specified that all skills were to be in production teams. So they were sent on an introductory course on teamworking to

[129]

reassure them and 'win them over'. Another company found that they had developed a tendency to send the least useful people on training courses because it was easier to release them, pointing to the need to give training a much higher profile and get senior managers to demonstrate their commitment to it.

Political sensitivities, especially concerning those who may be placed in potentially vulnerable positions by moving to teamwork, can be eased by developing their training role. Former supervisors or expert senior operators are often in a good position to provide technical training, while not necessarily being well suited to take up a participative management role. In one company, some engineers carried out some of the technical training while others were moved into capital

Using training for multi-skilled operators for changing work design and related training

Training is an essential component of preparing operators to take up multi-skilled roles in teams where the tasks have been reconfigured for flexibility.

Advantages	Problems/Concerns
Training is generally welcomed by operators as a way of enhancing their skills and increasing job satisfaction.	Training is sometimes delivered in isolation from the place of work; learning does not transfer to the job.
Training needs for multi-skilling can often be partly fulfilled by using existing expertise within the organisation.	Training needs for multi-skilling are complex. Not everyone who has technical expertise is necessarily a good trainer.
Multi-skilling can be highly cost-effective in improving quality and productivity.	Limits to multi-skilling must be considered. It is possible to overskill people, leaving them dissatisfied when they are unable to practise all the skills they have learnt.

[130]

projects work. In some cases, those who are 'surplus' after the selection for new positions in a teamwork structure can usefully be redeployed into training and mentoring roles for the new teams.

Most teamworking organisations will seek to develop their own training capacity and devolve it as far down the organisation as possible. One company reorganised into a cellular structure and, after a period of training, put their module leaders in charge of training. They then sent the next level down, 'cell leaders', on a similar course. They are now able to do most of their own training internally.

Ideally, production teams should be able to develop cross-training for basic tasks, but there can be limits to cross-training which must be recognised. Some products may involve a particularly difficult technology, requiring highly specialised skills which rules out cross-training within the cell. Cross-training can then be encouraged by moving people across the cells to learn new skills.

Most executives and senior managers discover to their suprise that all three types of teams need *external consultation on team effectiveness*. Effective teams usually need building. It is rare for them simply to evolve without some training or mentoring in the social competences associated with successful group work. This is one issue where the changing role of the first line manager has received the most criticism.

In scientific management, the role of the supervisor was to control, to coordinate and to provide some on-the-job instruction. The emphasis was on technical competence of the supervisor and his or her direct reports. Human factors were to be managed in such a way that they did not cause difficulties with the work. With team-based work designs, the role of the team leader or newly defined supervisor still includes technical competence. But the importance of 'coaching' as a management style has started to emerge. The trouble is that the ability to provide consultation on issues of group effectiveness, which are not technical in origin, is not broadly distributed in the population. The theory and practice of group effectiveness is a specialty in its own right. Therefore, the company faces the option of employing external specialists to provide consultation, developing internal consultants or developing their team leaders into group specialists.

[131]

But what is an effective team? Hackman and Oldham suggest two broad criteria for effectiveness. The first is that the productive output of the group meets the requirements of the organisation. It is no good having well-functioning teams in the social sense if their productivity falls below what is needed. Teams must therefore be technically and organisationally effective. The second is that the group must be a successful social unit without counterproductive patterns of behaviour which block effectiveness. These criteria sound relatively simple but can be less easy to achieve in practice.

The technical and organisational effectiveness of a team will depend to a large extent on how well teamwork has been designed – that is, whether the team tasks make technical and organisational sense and whether team members have the necessary technical competence to carry out their tasks. The rest depends on the degree to which the teams do function as

---

A Case of Changing Work Design and Related Training Developments With External Consultation on Team Effectiveness

BottleMake Ltd had self-regulating teams well established amongst their operators. At the time, it was not possible to integrate the quality technicians and the maintenance craftsmen into the team. A few months previously, the quality technicians had been integrated into the team and cross-training with operators had begun. Maintenance craftsmen had agreed to attend team meetings, in their role as members of a dedicated service team, on assignment from a central service function. The team meetings, however, were widely considered a waste of time. Despite extensive training in team meeting and problem-solving skills, the teams failed to tackle the process improvements necessary to manage themselves.

A consultant from the Training Department began attending their meetings to help out: before long, he withdrew because he felt as if he had been turned into the team's supervisor. Only when a manager on secondment from another factory within BottleMake's corporation began to provide group process consultation did the group begin to manage itself better. The consultation worked so well that other teams began to ask for help.

[132]

successful social entities. Most of the practical emphasis on this issue within companies has focused on recruitment and selection of 'good team players'.

There are different theories about what makes a 'good team player'. The best-known ones, such as Belbin's, tend to focus on personality types and suggest that people take on roles in groups which are linked to their personality type. Based on this kind of theory it is commonly suggested that groups need to be balanced and heterogeneous in terms of their membership.

There are a number of difficulties in applying this kind of approach to team building. First, it is a theory rather than an unconditional truth. There is some evidence that many people are more multi-faceted and adaptable in a group situation than this theory implies. Second, the luxury of choice may be absent – organisations have to build with what they already have. Probably at minimum what is needed is a counselling process for those who feel unable to adapt to teamwork and a procedure for managing casualties. Techniques for managing interpersonal processes within groups more effectively (such as how to conduct meetings, resolve conflicts, deal with dominating individuals and encourage passive ones) can be taught.

What has received less attention in the literature on team building is the influence of social characteristics, such as age, ethnic identity and gender, on how groups function. It is not unusual for gender divisions in a workforce to overlay skill and grade distinctions, and hinder the development of a multi-skilled team. Such divisions are often firmly entrenched in the manufacturing industry in particular. Perhaps the most important learning point here is that these divisions have to be first acknowledged and named before progress can be made in confronting their implications for building effective teams. In one company, where a clear distinction existed between the 'unskilled' women operatives and the 'skilled' male employees, it was necessary to redress inequalities in the payment and grading systems, while recognising that this would cause resentment among the men. At the level of developing effective interpersonal relations in teams, enabling people to discuss and become aware of the ways in which stereotyping of subgroups or individuals may block working relationships can be a valuable part of teambuilding activities.

[133]

This issue, and others like it, illustrates the degree of social and psychological complexity that self-regulating teams in particular may be being asked to manage. Once team structures and boundaries are in place, once technical and social skills have been taught, then on-going interventions to facilitate, encourage and reinforce effective team functioning are required. This might take the form of a quarterly review meeting with the team and a consultant; or a combination of on-going skill training, review and assessment may work best. The important point is to avoid a situation where the teams have been put in place, trained and then left for years without any additional development. This, unfortunately, does happen.

Designing New Management Roles and Styles

The extent to which management styles need to change in a teamworking organisation has already been stressed. This need encompasses all levels of management and overlaps with the wider changes which many organisations are currently experiencing. The changes in management style which TIM companies typically describe as needed to support teamwork fall broadly into three categories: changes in roles, changes in attitudes and behaviour, and changes in expectations.

In terms of *changing roles*, at all levels roles become less 'hands on' or involved with day-to-day 'firefighting' and more concerned with delegating and devolving decision-making. Roles become concerned with setting up the conditions which enable team members to operate effectively, including developing people, making resources available and identifying and planning the organisational development needs required to support teams. Managers also tend to find themselves involved more centrally in communicating business plans and decisions down the organisation.

The roles of supervisors and first line managers will undergo similar changes. Supervisors have to learn to work across areas rather than guarding their own 'territories'. One company saw its supervisors as front line change agents. It involved them in the development and communication of a more competitive business strategy and trained them, according to their choice, in particular skills such as employee counselling which were needed to support teamworking.

In terms of *changing attitudes and behaviour*, this essentially means developing a style which is in keeping with the changes in roles – enabling others to carry out their roles and maintaining a 'hands off' approach, facilitating rather than directing task performance, developing interpersonal, coaching and

Using a change in managerial attitudes and behaviour for changing work design and related training

Managers are required to change or modify attitudes and behaviour from more traditional modes in order that they can assist and facilitate appropriate teamworking behaviour both among themselves and those whom they manage.

Advantages	Problems/Concerns
Promoting and encouraging changes at managerial level gives the right message to the whole organisation.	It is important to ensure that managers are not given conflicting messages – 'give staff more room to make mistakes... we will hold you responsible if anything goes wrong'.
Managers can become key change agents in reinforcing and developing teamwork.	Many managers find the rapid changes frightening. They fear for their own jobs as those below them take on more responsibility. They need attention themselves in managing the change process.
More enabling and facilitating management styles tend to draw greater motivation from those being managed.	The managed themselves may not always appreciate the change in style, regarding it cynically as another management 'ploy' and testing out the manager to see if it is 'real'.

counselling skills. Moving managers into change agent roles means requiring them to manage for uncertainty and constant change. These changes can require major personal adjustments for those managers accustomed to a directive management style in a context of long-term stability.

In terms of *changes in expectations,* many of the external symbols of status, such as cars, clothing and separate facilities, are likely to be substantially eroded in a teamworking organisation. Flatter hierarchies, together with the larger context of change and uncertainty can also mean that jobs are more short-lived, there is less expectation of a long-term assured future, and conventional career paths no longer exist.

Changing management style involves both formal and informal processes. At a formal level, various kinds of training and organisational development can be undertaken. At an informal level, individuals themselves are faced with complex demands which relate to both their interpersonal skills and their personal capacity to manage major changes in their working environment.

There can also be a problem of conflicting demands on the managers themselves. One company found that their management training initiative brought out the problem of mixed

A Case of Changing Work Design and Related Training By Changing Managerial Attitudes and Behaviour

International Chemical's experience exemplifies how these processes operate hand in hand. The whole company went through a 'vision and values' process concerned with changing management style. This involved training and development activities on leadership, empowerment, realising people's potential and recognising the value of difference. An 'awayday' was organised for the top 50 managers and this resulted in some leaving because it conflicted with their long-held values about how to manage. Managers generally found it a struggle to change values. One recalled how he had called all his supervisors together, explained the process and said: 'This is how I want to behave but it will be hard. If I don't behave that way, come and tell me.'

messages, in that managers were being told to take responsibility for making improvements, but expected at the same time to follow already instigated quality control procedures strictly.

The experience of the TIM companies suggests that changing management style typically involves at least a three-stage approach.

First, a number of companies carried out surveys among the workforce on perceptions of the role of the manager, canvassing both managers and non-managers and setting up workshops to feed the material back.

Second, this is then used as the basis, either for developing training materials, or for working with external consultants to develop a programme. Decisions then have to be made on what levels of management should be trained together. One company put on an organisation-wide programme for all junior managers and supervisors across the different functions. This led to some resentment that – as the company clearly saw the programme as a major organisational intervention – it had not encompassed all managers. Other companies have set up more specific programmes for particular groups, such as supervisors. One, for instance, set up a two-day course for supervisors in leadership skills, covering team processes and team roles. They then produced their own training document.

Third, the changes have to be developed and reinforced. As with other training initiatives, it is important to revisit and reappraise management development. Further rounds of surveys among the workforce can provide the basis for planning for further training needs.

What training cannot necessarily do is to resolve problems of career structure and mobility within organisations and, hence, the problem of expectations. Several of the TIM companies have begun to confront this issue through developing strategies for lateral movement within the company, particularly for middle managers who are often most affected by the flattening of hierarchies. Teamwork, while contributing to the dilemma of what constitutes a 'career' path, also opens up other kinds of opportunities. People may move sideways to work in other functions, technical and administrative staff can be attached as resource persons to teams, and 'surplus' managers can find new roles in organisational development.

Initiative Areas Interconnected with Work Design and Related Training Developments

Top managers and other change agents involved in changing work design and related training developments towards teamworking may find it useful to keep in mind other interconnected change initiatives. Given the intensive resources required, it is highly unlikely that significant changes to work design would be started without a strategic direction to do so.

Some companies draw an imaginary line around a group of workers on the shop floor and instruct them to help each other out, and then called that teamwork. But proper teamwork requires redesign of jobs. And, for the redesign of jobs to be successful over a long period of time, there must be corre-

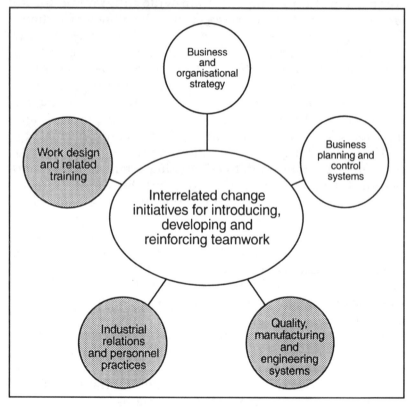

Figure 6.4. Initiative areas interconnected with work design and related training.

sponding changes to industrial relations and personnel practices (so people are being reinforced to behave in roles consistent with teamwork) and to quality, manufacturing and engineering systems (so that operational teams fit in with and are encouraged by production systems).

A Case of Successful Teamwork Due to Work Design and Related Training

International Chemicals used Schumacher 'work restructuring' principles to redesign several production units within the company. They used the concept of a whole transformation in a product or process as the basis for setting up semi-autonomous work teams. Major changes were necessary in order for the company to remain competitive. Multi-skilling, total flexibility and teamwork were to be the essential ingredients. The company set up a central control room to bring people back from dispersed locations into one large room with shared facilities and different groups. Previously, they had separate control rooms on each site, which were no longer economical because of changes in technology; 200 people were moved in all, starting with those closest to the new location. Remote control technology was brought in to enable them to deal with a machine located two miles away. This helped to break down the culture where people only worked on their own machines.

The company looked at teamworking in relation to shifts. Managers found that most of the key skills were located in the 9-5 staff rather than the 24-hour staff, so the shift staff were trained in technical, mechanical and planning skills in order to develop semi-autonomous shift teams. They now experience a lot less breakdowns as these can get fixed on the night shift.

The Schumacher approach meant designing jobs around whole tasks and developing consistency through the organisation. It also involved using a more participatory style of management. It moved the company from a structure which had a technical, operations and customer service department to a process-based structure, beginning from raw materials through chemical processes to warehousing and shipping. Work redesign turned the old technical department into an improvement area which included some customer services. To emphasise preventative maintenance, a new maintenance area was created, combining technicians and equipment specialists.

Many managers think that the most significant element in the company's success was achieving a change to industrial relations and personnel practices. About mid-way through the structured design process, everyone was moved to staff pay and contracts. This change laid the ground for a degree of cross-training and flexibility that would not have been possible under the old agreement.

Questions for Understanding Work Design and Related Training Developments

- To what extent are employees in this company working in group-based jobs and to what extent are their jobs individual and separate?
- How motivated or demotivated do the employees seem to be by the way their jobs are currently designed? What evidence exists for ratings in terms of job dissatisfaction, figures on absenteeism and turnover?
- What types of people would make good team leaders in this organisation? What jobs are they located in now? What sort of selection, training and development will be required to help them take up a new role?
- Thinking about the top management's overall objectives in introducing teamwork, how might support functions be reorganised to meet them?
- What levels and kinds of training are likely to be necessary in order to develop the appropriate social, technical and organisational skills for teamwork?
- What changes will be necessary in the roles and styles of managers to support teamwork?

Further Reading

Birchall, D. 1978. Work system design and the quality of working life. *OMEGA – International Journal of Management Science* 6 (5), pp. 433-442.

Cherns, A. 1987. Principles of socio-technical design revisited. *Human Relations* 40 (3) pp. 153-162.

Fisher, K. 1993. *Leading Self-Directed Work Teams: A Guide to Developing New Team Leadership Skills.* New York: McGraw-Hill.

Hackman, J.R. and Oldham, G.R. 1980. *Work Redesign.* Reading, Massachusetts: Addison Wesley Publishing Company Inc.

Neumann, J.E. 1989. Why people don't participate in organizational change. *Research in Organizational Change and Development,* Volume 3, pp. 181-212.

Pava, C. 1986. Redesigning sociotechnical systems design: concepts and methods for the 1990s. *The Journal of Applied Behavioural Science* 22 (3), pp. 201-221.

7

Changing Quality, Manufacturing and Engineering Systems

Three closely linked sets of techniques lie at the heart of new approaches to the coordination, planning and control of manufacturing activities. The first, quality management, concerns preventative approaches to achieving quality in manufactured goods. It is based on the idea that the key to output quality lies in understanding the capabilities of the processes involved and then seeking to improve them continuously.

Historically, those more capable and dependable processes resulting from the application of quality management techniques have paved the way for the second set of techniques, concerning integrated manufacturing logistics, often referred to under the heading of manufacturing systems engineering. The focus of these is sequencing and scheduling the chain of commercial transactions and physical operations involved in ordering, making and supplying a product so that there is great precision in the matching of supply to demand at all points in the chain, with minimum waste and costly inventory.

Finally, the scope for what can be achieved by the application of these two sets of techniques can be further increased if products are designed to pose fewer quality and logistical problems during the various stages of manufacturing and procurement. Hence the importance of 'design for manufacture'.

The links between these techniques are profound. Equally, they all have fundamental implications for teamworking. The first two require high levels of employee motivation, flexibility and problem-solving in manufacturing operations, and so some form of teamworking in operations may be highly relevant to their successful implementation. The third requires in-depth cross-functional collaboration between product design and manufacturing process engineers, and so, in a similar way, cross-functional teams offer an implementation route. Another way of thinking about this is that these three sets of techniques offer tools which operations, service and cross-functional teams can take up and use to make sure that the work they do is effective for the organisation as a whole.

Quality Management

Ideas of quality assurance and quality systems are in many ways the starting point for most recent developments in manufacturing techniques. The modern manufacturing sector shares an assumption that customers – whether private or public, corporate or individual – will not tolerate goods which do not conform to an accepted specification or certain basic standards of reliability. Furthermore, few would now advocate that simple inspection of finished goods offers a commercially viable route to achieving the required standards in output quality. Instead, the practice of quality assurance has become widespread, where companies set up systems and procedures for making sure that desired product quality is achieved during the course of manufacture, rather than 'inspected out' at the end.

In post-war quality management thinking, quality has become defined as 'fitness for purpose', in the sense of being adequate for the needs of the customer (Juran, 1988). This is seen as having two components:

- *Quality of design*, i.e. the extent to which a product is specified to meet the characteristics desired by its users

[143]

- *Quality of conformance,* i.e. the extent to which processes for manufacturing result in products that conform to the specification.

A company's *quality system* amounts to a set of procedures for making sure that quality objectives are met in terms of setting a desired quality of design and achieving an acceptable level of conformance to it.

According to Dale and Oakland (1991), quality systems may need to cover any or all of the following activities, depending on the nature of a company and its role:

- Marketing and market research
- Design specification engineering and product development
- Procurement of materials and plant
- Production preparation, process planning and development
- Production
- Inspection, testing and examination
- Packaging and storage
- Sales and distribution
- Installation and operation
- Technical assistance and maintenance
- Disposal after use.

Experiences within TIM companies illustrate two broad options for proceeding with the development of quality systems in a teamwork environment. These two options – applying quality systems standards and implementing total quality management – are not at all contradictory, and are often used to complement one another. They do, however, represent different emphases within an overall quality management framework. Respectively, they focus on documenting and enforcing existing quality practices, as opposed to gaining employee participation in improving quality procedures and standards.

The British Standards Institution (BSI) is the body responsible – by royal charter – for laying down and disseminating national standards in a wide range of fields. In 1979, in response to government and industry concerns that lack of standards for quality systems could harm the competitiveness of British Industry, the BSI first launched a general set of industrial quality systems standards, known ever since as BS 5750. Based on *quality systems requirements* developed for NATO and Ministry of Defence procurement, the idea of BS 5750 was that it would provide a basis for companies to achieve a place on an 'approved' list, regardless of whether or not their goods are defence-related. Subsequently, BS 5750 has formed the major basis for the similar International Standards Office ISO 9000 set of standards.

BS 5750 and ISO 9000 require that companies have a quality policy appropriate to its business objectives and a comprehensive set of documented procedures for all aspects of quality control, covering the monitoring of activities, the detection and correction of error, and the initiation of action to prevent recurrence of non-conforming product. These procedures must specify the roles – including responsibility, authority and working relationships – of all those responsible for any aspect of quality, and must be available and well known to those involved.

In practice, gaining accreditation for these quality system standards involves several person-months of work in defining procedures and documenting them. Several TIM companies reported that senior managers had originally decided to 'go for BS 5750' simply as a marketing aid, because they thought it would improve their position to have accreditation, or they felt they would be disadvantaged if they did not have it. For companies which had already given considerable thought to quality systems, gaining BS 5750 became one of a number of fairly routine development initiatives, with two or three staff allocated to it for a significant proportion of their time, drawing on staff from particular areas in drafting procedures relevant to them, and coordinating documentation into the standards required. For others, gaining accreditation to BS 5750 was seen as a way of consolidating changes that had already been made in logistical and quality systems, rather than a change project as such. Benefits were largely in marketing terms.

For some, even when initiated from a marketing perspective, the process of finding out what was needed for accreditation led senior managers to appreciate the importance of quality systems and quality improvement for the first time. Defining procedures for BS 5750 became a springboard for considering a more dynamic approach to quality improvement.

[145]

The potential influence of BS 5750 on the work of operational teams is that it lays down procedures for how work should be carried out. It also suggests that there may be conflicts between a top-down notion of where procedures come from and the ethos of self-regulating teams. People are unlikely to take both to working with a great deal of responsibility for what they do and according to highly defined procedures. Many companies look to solving this dilemma by making BS 5750 accreditation a subsidiary part of a wider programme of quality system improvement, where operational and quality control procedures are defined and improved much closer to work-group level. This more participative approach to quality management amounts to what is commonly called total quality management.

As this book goes into production, accreditation bodies have begun the process of harmonisation of standards. The British Standards Institute, the European Committee for Standardisation and the International Standards Organisation have developed a joint standard at the national, European and international levels known as 'BS-EN-ISO 9000'.

Total quality management refers both to an overall philosophy of striving for constant improvement in quality standards through employee involvement and a set of tools and techniques, mainly statistically-based, which allow employees at all levels to carry out data-based investigations of quality performance and initiate improvements. There are a number of different versions of total quality management propagated by a number of famous American and Japanese 'gurus', but most share a few underlying principles:

1. The idea, originally developed by Shewhart at Bell Laboratories during the 1930s, that, once errors in the operation of product processes have been eliminated, variations in product characteristics are the result of variabilities and imperfections in production processes and raw materials. Product quality in the sense of conformance to standard can be improved only by understanding the nature of this 'common cause' variation, and finding out what lies behind it, so that it can be reduced. Variations due to errors or breakdowns are known as 'special causes'.
2. Since most variations from standard stem from the charac-

teristics of processes or materials, rather than operator errors, it is the responsibility of management to ensure that processes are improved. This can be done by making a public commitment to improving quality through improving processes, making the resources and techniques available to all employees to undertake analyses of variation and implement process improvements, and providing an environment where employees feel motivated to use initiative and make improvements.

3. Operators need to be given the authority to take responsibility for the quality of the goods they manufacture. In particular they need to be responsible for inspecting their own output, with clear means, preferably based on visible inspection according to unambiguous criteria, for determining what is acceptable. Operators should also have the authority to stop production if the process is not adequate to meet this standard. Special causes of variation can in principle be eliminated by these measures.

4. Both design quality and conformance quality should be improved continuously, by applying a set of tools and techniques to significant streams of activities or processes within organisations. Activities should be improved to meet more fully the requirements defined by the customer – internal or external – who receives the output. Commonly used techniques include:

Design quality
- Quality function deployment (QFD), i.e. use of a set of matrices for relating customer requirements to design characteristics
- Taguchi methods of statistical analysis, for making performance less sensitive to variations in design parameters
- Failure mode and effect analysis (FMEA)
- Fault tree analysis.

Conformance quality
- Competitive benchmarking
- Pareto voting on options for tackling problems
- Statistical process control (SPC) and control charts
- Tree or systematic diagrams for analysing causes of variation

[147]

- 'Cost of quality' analysis, where the costs of non-conformance are assessed in terms of returns or maintenance required after products have reached the customer, and level of 'internal' wastage, in the form of scrap or rework.
- Interrelationship diagrams
5. The way to implement this philosophy and apply the techniques is to set up some form of parallel 'quality organisation'. At the top of this might be a director level or corporate TQM steering committee, which sets overall quality policies, defines the broad approaches to be used and then delegates particular process analysis and improvement activities to other groups, usually drawn from all the functions involved in the particular process. This 'quality organisation' is based on the principles that all staff have knowledge and experience relevant to process analysis and quality improvement, and that they are more likely to develop a commitment to quality improvement if asked to participate in it.
6. The establishment of the 'quality organisation' needs to be linked to widespread training in the principles and techniques of preventative quality control.

There are fundamental similarities between the principles of TQM and most rationales for teamworking. Both share the notion of creating a 'culture change', where employees feel motivated and responsible for improving the effectiveness of processes they work with. However, experiences from the TIM companies back up a picture that emerges from other research into the fate of TQM in UK manufacturing. Companies often find that TQM by itself is insufficient to steer their enterprise towards chosen business goals. They need to struggle to find which elements of TQM to combine with which other initiatives for improving employee participation and commitment.

TIM companies encountered a number of problems with implementing TQM. First, senior and middle managers in operations tend to experience attending cross-functional improvement team meetings as an additional demand, which takes them away from 'running the factory'. It may take some time for improvement activity to become recognised as valid, particularly if managers feel their real value is in their ability at 'fire-fighting'. Some TQM managers also cited line

Using Total Quality Management to change quality systems

Managers organise widespread training in TQM philosophy and techniques and encourage process improvement activity based on monitoring of process performance.

Advantages	Problems/Concerns
Focus on the requirements placed by customers on processes helps break down rivalries between different functions or departments involved.	Improvement activity is time-consuming; managers may be reluctant to invest in it, particularly if they feel they know all the answers already or fear others may show them up.
Provides techniques for bringing about long-term improvement in processes, rather than 'fire-fighting' current problems without fully understanding causes.	Both managers and employees may be suspicious of the tools and techniques associated with TQM because they seem unfamiliar and full of unnecessary jargon.
TQM tools and techniques provide a common language for understanding quality and how processes affect it, and for spreading this understanding within the organisation.	The timing of TQM training appears to be crucial. If there is a long gap between training and the chance to use techniques learned in improvement activities, cynicism is very likely.
If not implemented too rigidly, TQM is compatible with many other kinds of change initiatives, including self-regulating teams.	TQM programmes may produce a need to rethink reward systems, particularly if there are existing rewards for suggestions and improvements. These are generally thought to work against the collective ethos required for TQM.

managers' reluctance to invite the ideas of employees for fear of hearing something they hadn't thought of as the real reason quality improvement activity received little support.

The most important condition for the successful take-off of quality improvement appears to be finding a way of integrating it with operational activity, so that there is not in fact a parallel 'quality organisation' vying for attention and resources with the main operating structure. In some cases, TQM tools and techniques have been brought into self-regulating teams, to underpin process improvement within the team area. Thus one manager was able to say: 'We don't have a quality programme anymore ... it's integrated with everything we do, so we don't even talk about it.'

One common solution to the split between TQM and operations is to encourage or require shop floor teams to use various TQM tools for undertaking process improvements. Almost all TIM companies have achieved some level of success in terms of operatives charting processes using statistic process control (SPC). These data are used as a basis for eliminating 'special causes'. Genuine success in tackling 'common causes' is probably much rarer.

A further model of integration can be found in a number of TIM companies. After several programmes of TQM training, managers set up a limited number of *ad hoc* cross-functional improvement groups at any one time, in response to problems perceived by operating departments. This ensures that quality improvement activity is seen as directly relevant to operating realities.

A Case of Changing Quality, Manufacturing and Engineering Systems Using BS 5750/ISO 9000

At **Paper Products plc** in Lancashire, an external consultant guided the management team through a process of documenting quality procedures. This led them to realise that quality was suffering because of a lack of standardisation in how many operations were carried out. Achieving accreditation took three years, but by the end the Managing Director was convinced that the by now comprehensive set of quality procedures should provide a basis for gathering and analysing data on weak spots in the production process where improvements were needed. BS 5750 was a route into a programme for quality improvement.

At the same time, Paper Products' managers encountered a number of difficulties with BS 5750 which are typical of those reported by other companies. The set of manuals for each operation may be seen as 'a paper tiger': shop floor workers may be too intimidated by the volume of procedures and jargon used to incorporate them in their day-to-day work. The quality systems manager therefore undertook an extensive rewriting of procedures to make them more usable.

Manufacturing Logistics and Layouts

One of the distinctive features of more recent developments in teamwork in the manufacturing sector has been the major role played by manufacturing systems personnel in the introduction of team-based forms of organisation. Manufacturing systems engineering approaches, particularly those which have come to be associated with 'world class' manufacturing and 'lean production', often drive teamwork initiatives. There are typically two areas in which manufacturing managers are associated with the introduction and development of teamwork.

First, 'computer aided production management' (CAPM) or 'manufacturing resources planning' (MRPII) systems trans-

[151]

form the planning and scheduling of production, integrating the supply of factors of production, i.e. materials, plant and labour, with customer demand. These may or may not be combined with other techniques for matching supply and demand in flows of materials so as to minimise inventories within distribution, production and supply, falling under the general heading of 'just-in-time' (JIT) materials management.

Second, cell-based manufacturing layouts enable all the operations associated with a product to be located close together, minimising the movement of materials and the amount of work-in-progress. Such layouts are often combined with JIT scheduling. Both systems – which in practice are often closely linked – require a degree of employee flexibility and changes in organisational boundaries that are often associated with teams at both shop floor and cross-functional levels.

Manufacturing resources planning systems – known as MRPII to distinguish them from earlier less integrated materials requirements planning (MRP) systems – have comprehensive goals. They aim to provide computer support for an integrated approach to planning requirements for both materials and manufacturing capacity. In principle MRPII systems allow planners to make firm judgements about immediate needs – for today and this week – and make increasingly less definitive provisions for longer-term time scales – next month and the next three quarters.

While the idea of an integrated computerised database is fundamental to making MRPII systems possible, it is a mistake to conceive of them as simply a computer system. They call for a considerable amount of human activity in terms of collecting data, inputting it and making decisions on the basis of reports produced by the computer. In most implementations, several aspects of MRPII amount to entirely new domains of planning which have never been done explicitly within the organisation.

As a total process, MRPII has a strong human component as well as an information technology one. Various forms of team-working have a great relevance to delivering the potential benefits of this system – improved performance in meeting customer orders, greater certainty in planning production and ordering materials, and reduced inventory levels for both finished goods and materials.

[152]

An MRPII system ideally consists of four different planning subsystems, all working from an integrated common database (Spreadbury, 1994) and interrelated with one another, so that in reality they work simultaneously, each one updating the other. Not all of these planning functions are present in all implementations of MRPII. In most manufacturing organisations, operation of these systems is predominantly the responsibility of a production planning, materials management or logistics function, working in collaboration with others, in particular operations, sales and finance.

- *Business, sales and operations planning (S&OP)*. Production planners use accurate data on demand forecasts, sales performance, manufacturing performance and finished product inventory to produce a monthly sales and manufacturing schedule for each product family. This is used to update targets for sales and production set in the annual business plan, which also sets parameters for capacity and labour needs. The monthly plan will be finalised in a meeting between the planning and operations functions, and provides a technical basis for improving cooperation and integration between these two functions.
- *Master production scheduling (MPS)*. Production planners use the computer system to break down the monthly S&OP into a firm production plan for the coming week, including detailed breakdowns of needs for particular materials. As plant becomes temporarily unavailable or people go sick, and as anticipated orders fail to arrive or are exceeded, planners need to modify the monthly plan. This involves close liaison with operations personnel as to what manufacturing capacity and inventory is actually available. The MPS then provides a basis for daily production schedules for each product family.
- *Materials requirements planning (MRP)*. The computer system provides support for turning the MPS into a detailed specification of materials required, with increasing certainty for shorter time scales. In principle, the MRP subsystem can forecast materials requirements up to two years ahead if fed with appropriate forecasts for sales and accurate bills of materials for all products. The MRP subsystem focuses in particular on calculating minimum safe materials inventory

levels, taking into account supplier lead times and likely variances in demand levels.

- *Capacity requirements planning (CRP)*. This part of this system relates the MPS to a detailed planning of loading of particular products on specific cells, pieces of plant or work centres, based on knowledge of the detailed capacity requirements of each product. The CRP is generally produced in tentative form for some months ahead, so that the MPS can be adjusted if necessary. The goal of the CRP is not necessarily to arrive at perfect utilisation of plant at all times, but to identify when plant is going to be under- or over-utilised, so that labour can be transferred or extra capacity acquired temporarily. The idea of the CRP is highly dependent on the flexibility of operators within a cell, and greatly benefits from the ability of a shop floor team to make adjustments in the amount of time spent on producing different products.

There are two further elements to MRPII, the first essential and the second highly desirable:

- *Production and inventory control.* For the planning systems to work, they need to be fed with accurate data as to what is actually happening on the shop floor and in the warehouse. This can take the form of direct entry of stock movements, or of the progress of a job or batch into networked terminals by supervisors, team leaders or operators, or for some types of plant, automated data capture. A manual system of job cards may suffice, although data then need to be entered by a production or inventory clerk. The use of JIT kanbans – described below – can also function as an effective method of monitoring production. Most of these methods imply a considerable degree of responsibility for keeping accurate records at operator level on the shop floor or in the warehouse. Again, the benefits of MRPII are greatly enhanced if operational teams are able to take on this role in a dependable fashion.
- *Integration with computerised accounting systems.* This can take two forms: sales and operations forecasts can be linked to the management accounting systems that produce cash flow and other financial forecasts; and purchase orders and

[154]

payment of accounts can be linked with the order receipts function within the inventory control subsystem. This kind of integration improves relations between operations and management accounting functions, in particular freeing up accountants and financial controllers to do more detailed forecasting and investigative work rather than manage a duplicate tracking system. However, these benefits depend very concretely on the accuracy of data entered in the warehouse or shop floor. Again, operator teams able to take this responsibility offer enormous benefits.

Within the TIM project, a number of companies have sophisticated MRPII implementations moving in the direction of many of these six features. However, most continue to struggle with accuracy of data, both in terms of tracking what is happening on the shop floor and future demand from customers. This commonly results in a master production schedule that requires considerable informal modification on a weekly or even daily basis, as orders suddenly become urgent and the production plan cannot accommodate them.

Several TIM companies have combined the overall production and inventory planning framework of an MRPII system with some form of *just-in-time (JIT) production*. MRPII has come from Western developments in integrated computerised databases and JIT arose in a relatively low technology but revolutionary Japanese approach to manufacturing, but many TIM companies are finding ways of combining elements of both.

The term JIT is in fact used to mean a number of different, if related, things. There are two meanings:

- An overall philosophy of linking demand, production and supply in a very direct fashion. Usually attributed to the production system developed by Toyota during the 1960s and 1970s, this philosophy builds on the ideals of TQM (Womack *et al.*, 1990). If production processes can be made extremely reliable in terms of the quality they are capable of, through continuous improvement by the people that operate them, it is possible to reduce buffer stocks.

  If, furthermore, forecasting of demand can be improved and production processes made extremely flexible by finding ways of drastically decreasing machine set-up times, then it is possible further to reduce stocks of finished product. The ideal is to have a production process that can respond directly and almost instantaneously to variations in demand for different products on a 'pull' system, in contrast to the 'push' system of works orders that an MRPII system produces.

A third element in the overall philosophy is that the whole supply chain can be organised on these principles – so that distributors and suppliers work on a just-in-time, minimal inventory basis. Suppliers, for example, may be asked to take responsibility for delivering materials only when needed to the input end of an assembler's production processes.

The final element is an emphasis throughout the production process and supply chain on eliminating waste and 'lean' use of resources. In addition to the pervasive principle of minimum inventory, the philosophy emphasises careful balancing of work centre speeds, minimal transport and waiting times for materials within a production process, as well as elimination of scrap due to imperfect manufacturing procedures.

• JIT is also a set of techniques for detailed production scheduling and control. The best known of these is the kanban 'pull' system for coordinating successive stages in the manufacture of a product. Each work centre or cell in the process works to fill a small number of pallets or carts that make up the allowable stock of inputs to the next stage. In turn, each work centre expects the previous one to replace its own 'kanbans' of input parts or materials only as fast as they are used up. The result is a very simple, clearly visible way of matching supply and demand along the length of production process.

Several TIM companies have seen the master production schedule (MPS) element of MRPII as a part of achieving lower inventory within an overall JIT philosophy. They have also used kanban shop floor scheduling as a way of controlling materials flow on the shop floor, once works orders according to the capacity requirements plan (CRP) and MPS have been produced. TIM companies also illustrate that the relevance of

JIT production flows to teamworking is very much bound up with a cellular approach to production layouts which usually accompanies it.

Cellular manufacturing in itself is not new, originating in the group technology approach to manufacturing which was developed during the 1950s. Rather than putting like machines with like, this approach to manufacturing groups together all the machinery, assembly operations, and other resources required to manufacture a particular product, family of products, or significant sub-assembly. In the factory as whole, this may lead to a larger number of smaller machines, compared with conventional function-based shop layouts, where workers operate one functionally dedicated type of machine only, and where assembly is carried out in a separate part of the factory. The resulting product-focused layout is the basis for most cell-based forms of manufacturing, although cells can be based on other groupings, such as processes or materials. Its advantages have been well documented. It can improve workflow and decrease work-in-progress by reducing materials handling. Tooling and set-up times for machines are also decreased, because cell staff become expert in the needs of particular products. Above all, cellular layouts provide a basis for clearly visible JIT production flows. Delivery tends to become more reliable.

Combined with JIT and MRPII systems, cellular manufacturing has become an extremely important means of responding to competitive pressures and managing much higher levels of market uncertainty. However, it also needs much greater attention to human and organisational factors in implementation than is often realised. Cells are organisations of people, not just technology.

It is possible to introduce product-focused cells without developing teamworking in its stronger forms. At minimum, cellular working requires some grouping of operators able to manage all the tasks associated with the manufacture of the product (or process, if cells are not product-based). As cell-based manufacturing tends to involve a wider range of less dedicated machinery, there must be a sufficient level of multi-skilling to ensure flexibility within the cell. In terms of the link with job design, therefore, at minimum, operators' jobs are

[157]

likely to be 'enriched' by giving them more task variety. Changes in materials handling, particularly the introduction of kanbans, together with a more customer-driven, quality-focused approach to manufacturing, mean that more responsibility will be devolved to cell members. This in turn will require corresponding changes in the roles of supervisory and support staff. The need for much greater functional flexibility will have implications for training, and possibly for industrial relations policy as well (see Chapter 9 on industrial relations and personnel practices).

Both JIT and MRPII systems, in conjunction with cell-based working, do, however, predispose towards the introduction of self-directed, multi-skilled production teams. This is because much higher levels of skill, cross-functional cooperation, commitment and employee participation are required in order to maximise their advantages.

From the point of view of operators, JIT requires a new way of working that is contingent on understanding why eliminating rather than building up inventory is a good thing. It also requires a human resource approach which supports the new world view. Conventional payment and reward systems, craft demarcations and supervisory practices do not generally support a system which requires operators to monitor the throughput of materials, stop work on a process when a kanban is full, and move elsewhere to help other operatives clear a bottleneck or carry out preventative maintenance on a machine.

Experiences from other TIM companies suggest that the change in world view may also have to accommodate a less than perfect switch to the new system. One company, having introduced cellular manufacturing based on JIT principles, found that the low inventory message had to be countermanded when there was a fall in the demand for products. In order to have people doing useful work rather than nothing at all they deliberately encouraged the build-up of inventory again.

At the same time, these systems also depend on a much higher level of skill and commitment from operators. This generates a considerable training requirement, both in relation to the information technology component of the systems and the organisational culture which supports them. JIT tends to push accountability for quality down to the cells and requires problem-solving within the cell. Operators' roles become centrally concerned with quality and improvement activities. Increased operator control over the workflow means giving operators greater responsibility and autonomy. Supervisors' and first line managers' roles have to change to reflect this shift in responsibility. Instead of being mainly concerned with policing and control activities, roles need to be redefined to support and facilitate greater operator responsibility. Teamwork-based cellular manufacturing also tends to go along with a reduced managerial and supervisory hierarchy.

In many organisations, changes in manufacturing systems engineering are seen as affecting manufacturing employees only. But the changes clearly have implications for staff in other support functions. Product-focused manufacturing, JIT and MRPII systems all require much greater coordination between the functions. Eliminating buffer stocks makes it essential that purchasing, sales and manufacturing parts of the organisation work closely together. The integration of supply and demand brought about by MRPII entails much closer integration along the whole chain of activities which 'pull' production through the system. In some companies, cellular manufacturing has gone together with the setting up of semi-autonomous business units, with implications for central finance functions. There is an important role for cross-functional teams, both at the level of implementation of new manufacturing engineering systems and to develop and monitor inter-functional coordination.

Cellular manufacturing clearly means major changes in working and organisational practices. Without the support and commitment of the workforce, manufacturing systems engineering changes in themselves will be unlikely to deliver the hoped for gains in efficiency, waste reduction, productivity and customer satisfaction. Moving to self-directed teamwork, with a parallel commitment from management to greater employee participation in decisions which affect them, is one way forward. However, many human and organisational issues are likely to arise along the way.

A number of major concerns are commonly voiced by employees facing these kinds of changes. First, people fear losing their jobs. Much of the force of manufacturing approaches such as JIT and cell-based working lies in their capacity to cut manufacturing costs through removing waste at all levels of the operation and to introduce greater flexibility among employees. For example, kanban systems and low inventory mean greatly reduced materials handling, which affects handlers and stores personnel. Increased automation creates an immediate concern about what happens to spare operator capacity. These fears, unless addressed and managed,

Using cellular layouts and MRPII to change quality, manufacturing and engineering systems

Manufacturing systems engineers group together machining and assembly operations concerned with particular products or sub-assemblies in the same location, and link them with production scheduling systems that minimise inventory and work-in-progress.

Advantages	Problems/Concerns
It improves workflow and decreases the amount of inventory and work-in-progress, resulting in reduced materials handling and waste and more reliable delivery.	For employees, cellular manufacturing and associated logistical changes may raise fears of job losses, leading to resistance and industrial relations problems. This can seriously impede the development of teamwork if it becomes seen as a disguise for making redundancies.
Cell-based working provides the opportunity for job enrichment and multi-skilling for operators, as well as for greater individual and group responsibility for tasks.	It will require corresponding attention to work design and human resources policies which support such changes, including trainings, pay and grading systems and management and supervisory roles and style.

Cellular manufacturing fits well with advanced forms of team-work, i.e. semi-autonomous work groups, benefiting greatly from the increased self-direction and motivation of such teams.	Cell-based manufacturing, MRPII and JIT can all increase the work stress on operation teams because of the tight workflow discipline and coordination involved. This can reduce the degree to which teams can operate with some discretion over work scheduling.

will be at odds with the need for greater employee commitment and may mean that attempts to introduce genuine team-working will be met by hostility. Getting rid of people may, in the end, be necessary, but there are more imaginative responses.

A Case of Changing Quality, Manufacturing and Engineering Systems with Cellular Manufacturing and MRPII

When **Filmco** invested in new machines to create extra capacity, they changed the ratio of people to machines to two per two machines instead of three to two. Instead of making operators redundant, they reconstituted operators' jobs to add in 10 per cent of time for product improvement and management of health and safety issues. They also put an end to the process of continually increasing overtime to the point where operators were working five 12-hour shifts per week, rather than increasing staffing levels. The savings on the overtime bill offset the additional wage bill to hire extra people.

Second, particular groups of employees may fear loss of skills or of income as a result of the changes. The drive for greater flexibility affects craft employees who see their skill status being 'diluted'. Rationalising production flow often reduces the amount of overtime needed. One TIM company introduced a JIT system into their warehousing operations but experienced considerable opposition from the warehouse employees as they stood to lose their regular Saturday overtime. As the chapter on industrial relations and personnel practices spells out in more detail, it is important to anticipate these areas of concern and resistance.

Third, employees often fear that the changes mean more stress and an intensification of their workloads. While managers may talk up the greater autonomy and responsibility of cell-based teamwork, and the opportunities to increase their skills, operators may see simply a demand to do more work, with less natural breaks and less resources. Both sides have a point. As one TIM company testifies, teamwork based on cellular manufacturing generally produced a positive response from the workforce, providing greater task variety and gaining strong commitment to teamwork.

It has become conventional wisdom to argue that the new manufacturing approaches are an improvement over the more traditional assembly line in terms of the quality of employees' working lives. This is, however, to ignore some of the new pressures and constraints that systems such as JIT can impose. This is especially an issue in relation to the introduction of semi-autonomous work teams. If some degree of autonomy is essential to the successful introduction and development of teams, a critical question concerns what kind of autonomy is possible with current manufacturing systems engineering approaches.

One of the features of traditional approaches based on the build-up of inventories is that inventory provides a buffer between one process and the next, thereby helping to manage uncertainties in the workflow. Where semi-autonomous teams operate, buffer inventories provide important task and boundary markers for teams and reinforce an individual team's discretion over how it completes its task.

New manufacturing approaches remove inventory and create much greater interdependence between teams, with an associated loss of discretion over decisions within the team about work scheduling and pace. Tight coordination between teams becomes the prime need. Klein (1991) suggests that where new manufacturing practices result in a loss of individual discretion and autonomy, attempts must be made to develop some form of collective autonomy where the teams are able collectively to exercise some discretion over areas such as task design. Those concerned with making manufacturing

[162]

A Case of Changing Quality, Manufacturing and Engineering Systems with Cellular MRPII and JIT

Tucker Fasteners introduced cellular manufacturing as part of a wider attempt to develop a manufacturing system that would be more responsive to customers. This entailed adding JIT to the existing MRP system in order to develop more responsive planning of production, and make changes in layout to move towards product-based cells. The MRP system took in customer orders and broke them down into work orders but could not tell production personnel what was needed to be produced at any given time. Without a coordinated approach to production planning, work-in-progress would build up to eight weeks. The company aimed to get this down to two.

They began by looking at the products and assigning product families to modules (groupings of cells) and separate products to cells. The modules, known as 'focused manufacturing units', are staffed by a leader, a planner, an engineer and a quality person. These personnel support the groups in each cell, which consists of between two and twelve production workers. Plans are in progress for the site to be re-laid out and machinery reconfigured and repositioned. A kanban system is being introduced, including an electronic kanban operating between buildings on site. A master schedule will feed work to the cells.

Cell workers became responsible for improvement activities and for manual aspects of total productive maintenance on their machinery. They now spend 30 per cent of their time on improvement activities and only 70 per cent in the day-to-day running of the cells. Numbers in the cells are determined mainly by the technology. Cross-training has not always been possible with some highly specialised tasks: where it is not, cross-training takes place across cells. The move to cell-based working required a great deal of training for production workers and staff. It also caused the company to move away from the old production bonus system.

This case underscores the complexity of the issues raised by changing manufacturing and engineering systems. Layout changes, setting up cell-based work groups, introducing systems of production planning and coordination which cut right across organisational boundaries and managing human resource issues can all become part of the production manager's task.

systems decisions need to consider the potential contradiction between aspects of the new approaches and the idea of greater autonomy for individual employees.

Design for Manufacture

Designing products with a view to their cost of manufacture as well as their attractiveness to customers amounts to an essential complement to other aspects of quality management as well as to obtaining the benefits of new manufacturing and logistical systems. The set of methods and techniques for achieving design for manufacture are generally known as 'simultaneous engineering'. This refers to the idea of bringing all stages in the development or improvement of a new product and its manufacturing process closer together through overlapping the stages of product and process design in time. Like the other techniques described in this chapter, it too requires organisational changes involving teamwork to succeed. In the planning of a new product, design, production planning, product and process engineering functions are brought together to save project time and resolve problems as the project progresses. The benefits of simultaneous engineering lie in:

- The potential both for removing design faults and sorting out problems at a much earlier stage, and thus in speeding up the process from design to prototyping to product launch
- 'Designing cost out of the product', through identifying cheaper materials or manufacturing methods and eliminating or modifying features that may cause problematic and unreliable manufacturing process steps.

All this requires a major change in how the personnel involved understand their role, as well as cooperation between groups who do not normally work together and who may even distrust or hold stereotyped views of each other. These issues apply in slightly different ways to two different situations in which simultaneous engineering may be used – within the same company and involving several different companies involved in the same product supply chain.

[164]

Simultaneous engineering within a company usually takes place within a temporary new product design or introduction team, with members usually drawn from a product development department, the manufacturing process function within the operations department or the engineering department, and from the marketing or sales function.

The task of the team is to spot and address design trade-offs, in terms of customer requirements and cost of manufacture, and to ensure that manufacturing processes are designed as quickly as possible so that the product gets to market as quickly as possible. This generally involves using a number of problem-solving techniques imported from the Japanese car industry, particularly 'quality function deployment' (QFD), where relatively qualitative consumer preferences input by marketing – 'a nice smooth ride' for a car – are turned into more precise design targets – maximum noise and vibration levels (Francis, 1994).

There is evidence within TIM companies not only of this kind of new product introduction team, but also of arrangements where shop floor operatives are directly consulted by design engineers when making improvements to products and processes. One company has both product and process engineers located within manufacturing areas. After some initial resistance to recognising the validity of knowledge of experienced shop floor workers, design engineers have come to appreciate the benefits of drawing on their expertise in changing design features to reduce cost and improve quality production reliability.

Inter-organisational simultaneous engineering is probably most developed within the UK in the car and aerospace industries. In the car industry, those companies which undertake design work in the UK involve key suppliers at an early stage. This is particularly important when suppliers possess particular technological competencies that original equipment manufacturers (OEMs) do not. Thus, for example, Rover Group designs interior trims jointly with its moulded plastic components suppliers, drawing on their expertise in plastics – some geometric shapes are more expensive to manufacture than others.

While both original equipment manufacturers within the TIM project and their suppliers express great enthusiasm for

[165]

Using simultaneous engineering to change quality, manufacturing and engineering systems

Product design and manufacturing process engineers collaborate to reduce costs of manufacture and ease the path of introduction of a new product.

Advantages	Problems/Concerns
Simultaneous engineering enables the expertise of several functions within a manufacturing company to be brought together in cross-functional teams, with clear benefits to the process of new product development.	It requires people to work together who may have no history of collaborating outside their particular function or discipline. Without attention to the human and organisational aspects of operating in cross-functional teams, they will be less than optimally effective.
Product development teams can also include shop floor operators and craft workers, who can provide valuable input on the assembly implications or problems of design decisions.	Because of long-entrenched distinctions between 'white collar' and 'blue collar' staff, it can be difficult to overcome suspicion or hostility to working collaboratively.
Simultaneous engineering collaboration between original equipment manufacturing (OEMs) and their suppliers can benefit both partners by providing expertise not available in-house for the OEM, and securing the supplier's relationship with the customer.	For both sides, it can be difficult to draw acceptable boundaries between 'team' type collaboration and their respective commercial interests. OEMs wish to reserve the right to look competitively for other suppliers. Suppliers are reluctant to provide their full expertise if they suspect the customer might still go elsewhere.

A Case of Changing Quality, Manufacturing and Engineering Systems by Using Simultaneous Engineering

When **Leyland Trucks** became an independent company, responsible for their own product development, they had to devise an organisational mechanism to do this, in the context of a company which had been extremely functionally based with each function answerable directly to managers in the former Dutch parent company. They had to overcome several problems in developing effective product development or improvement teams.

First, relations between the assembly area personnel and the design engineers needed to be improved. Class and occupational divisions caused strains. Engineers did not find it easy to accept that assembly operatives could contribute to product improvement or development, feeling that they did not understand engineering constraints. Assembly personnel felt that the engineers were an exclusive group unable to respond to wider priorities or understand the relationship between designing and building. Relationships improved after the functions, which were situated a considerable distance apart, were consolidated within the assembly site and teambuilding work was undertaken both within and across functions.

Second, greater awareness of the purpose of prototyping had to be developed through an educational process. Both engineers and assemblers tended to see it as a 'right first time' instead of an experimental stage. Thus, if anything went wrong, it was seen as a failure, rather than as a useful piece of intelligence to be acted upon.

Third, effective cross-functional teams had to be put in place, involving assembly, engineering and purchasing functions, to see projects through. These teams needed to be flexible in composition, drawing in individuals at different stages of the process as particular needs arose. This meant both giving the teams some continuity of core personnel with sufficient authority to make decisions which would not be countermanded by a particular function, and making available adequate resources – finance, time and personnel – to enable the teams to operate effectively. It meant, in other words, superimposing a matrix style project-based organisation onto a functional one. In this process, training and team building played an important role.

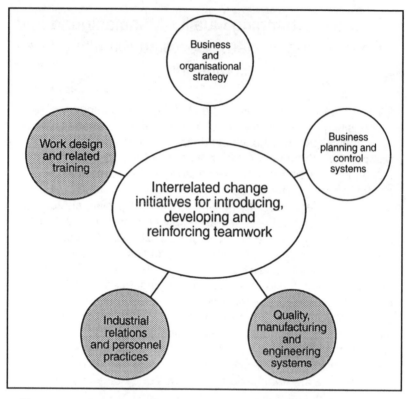

Figure 7.1. *Initiative areas interconnected with quality, manufacturing and engineering.*

the benefits of this kind of simultaneous engineering, both parties experience themselves also managing significant tensions, which concern drawing a boundary between the collaborative aspects and the need to keep the commercial nature of the relationship in mind. Suppliers generally feel that they should be involved even further in design and earlier than OEMs allow them to be. They also resent the fact that some OEMs typically invite two or more key suppliers to take part in initial simultaneous engineering for a component, and then select between the two as to who will actually get the production order. This makes the supplier wary about contributing good ideas, while at the same time feeling they have no option. The result is a certain rationing of the supplier's design expertise.

[168]

A Case of Successful Teamwork Due To Quality, Manufacturing and Engineering Systems

The Leigh site of **BICC Cables** produces metallic telecommunications cables. Faced with increasing competitive pressures, the manufacturing unit adopted a programme of just-in-time manufacturing and teamworking aimed at minimising waste, lowering inventory, eliminating manufacturing bottlenecks and improving responsiveness to customers.

The Personnel Director explains how they did this: 'The unit was reorganised from a process-based operation to a dedicated product layout. Traditional process-based organisation meant that machine layout was inefficient and materials handling excessive because of the long distances between processes. Product-flow was hindered because of the many different processes involved in manufacturing a large product range. The result was that bottlenecks built up around machines and increases in output were difficult to achieve. Cellular layout was introduced, with the product range split into four families and machines laid out so that all processes needed to manufacture a product family were contained in manufacturing cells. Layout changes and product-based manufacturing greatly improved both materials handling and product flow, but changes were needed on the human side.

'The traditional supervisory structure was replaced by a simplified structure with cell leaders responsible directly to the unit manager and with full responsibility for all aspects of the manufacture of their product and for the production workers assigned to their cells. But greater employee involvement was needed to meet the business objectives of the change. The business unit embarked on two major training and development initiatives in JIT and teamworking. Over several months, all the cell leaders and members, together with relevant support staff, voluntarily attended a series of off-site (out of hours) workshops, facilitated by an outside consultant, for teamwork training. On-site training was provided for the implementation of JIT.

'Teamwork training focused on linking the business needs to teamwork, and developing cell leaders' and members' own understanding of how teamwork could facilitate more effective working practices. Beginning from some healthy scepticism, the workshop participants moved to thinking constructively about how teamwork could be more satisfying for individual workers.

'JIT training was undertaken in one cell to begin with, using a firm of outside consultants to start the process off. Training was done through a game which enabled employees to learn the basic principles. This was followed up by further training and information sessions stressing the need to manage bottlenecks and control inventory. A simulation of a kanban system was set up on the factory floor to help people learn by practice. This training was gradually extended to all the cells. In association with the introduction of JIT, a programme of skill enhancement was set up. The new manufacturing environment meant that much greater skill flexibility was required of operators. At the same time, the old pay and conditions were no longer appropriate to the new environment. A single-status package was introduced with an integrated grading structure and skills-based pay. As a consequence of all the changes, the site experienced major improvements in inventory control, customer delivery requirements, scrap levels and quality. On the people side, absenteeism decreased markedly and much greater interest and participation among employees was noted.'

Initiative Areas Interconnected with Quality, Manufacturing and Engineering Systems

Senior managers and other change agents involved in changing quality, manufacturing and engineering systems may find it useful to keep in mind other interconnected change initiatives. These initiatives are at the very heart of new approaches to manufacturing. But issues of work design and related training and industrial relations and personnel practices are likely to be the most central to their successful implementation.

Questions for Understanding Quality, Manufacturing and Engineering Systems

- What policies and procedures does this company have in place for improving (a) the design quality and (b) the conformance quality of what it manufactures?
- If the organisation has a TQM or quality improvement initiative underway, how effective is it in terms of its goals? What appears to be helping people get involved, and what is hindering them?
- What production planning and control systems are currently in use? Is a great deal of time spent in adjusting short-term plans to deal with orders that suddenly become urgent? Are suppliers and distributors involved in planning and scheduling? What is the longest time-scale available in the company's current forecasting systems? What would be the benefits of extending it?
- What is the rationale behind the company's current production layout? Could production planning and control be improved by changing it? What would be the costs of changing it now, or at some point in the future?
- How accurate is the information available on the state of production plans and inventories?
- How is new product introduction or improvement currently handled? Who is involved, and what do they do? What areas of expertise could be brought to bear in a process of simultaneous engineering which currently are not? What could be done to bring wider perspectives to bear?

Further Reading

Bessant, J. 1991. *Managing Advanced Manufacturing Technology*. Oxford: NCC Blackwell Ltd.

Kidd, P. 1994. *Agile Manufacturing*. Wokingham: Addison-Wesley Publishing Company.

[171]

Klein, J.A. 1991. A Re-examination of Autonomy in the Light of New Manufacturing Practices. *Human Relations* 44 (1), pp.21-38.

Storey, J. (ed.) 1994. *New Wave Manufacturing Strategies.* London: Paul Chapman Publishing Ltd.

8

Changing Company Planning and Accounting Control Systems

Various forms of teamworking can play a role in manufacturing operations, in a service or support function, or in cross-
functional liaison or improvement activities, and this is often
linked to developments in quality, logistical and engineering
systems. Team arrangements allow individuals to become
aware of a wider picture of the requirements placed on them
and improve their understanding of feedback as to how well
they are doing. Consequently, people working in teams can
simultaneously contribute more to organisational purposes
and performance and experience more influence over their
work.

Another way of thinking about this is that teamwork by its
very nature implies a cooperative approach to the planning,
execution and monitoring of work. It offers individuals expo-
sure to a wider horizon of information and therefore the possibility of taking part in more comprehensive planning and
monitoring to take account of future conditions or possible
contingencies. Planning can be both short-term in focus,

concerned with adjusting current systems to external contingencies, but also longer term, in terms of identifying how systems can be improved and developed to meet future needs. Similarly, the quality, logistical and engineering systems changes described in the previous chapter can be thought of as ways of increasing the sophistication with which manufacturing activities can be planned and controlled in the light of demands placed upon them.

In practically all cases of teamwork within TIM companies, teams are set up in the context of modified systems for overall monitoring and development of activities at the level of the company as a whole. On a larger scale, these systems reflect the basic teamwork principles of sharing of information and feedback and planning across traditional functional divisions, to provide a better basis for adapting to contingencies. Company level systems for monitoring and developing manufacturing set a framework within which the gains of teamwork can be realised. In practice, there is no clear pattern as to whether lower-level teamwork or modified higher-level systems of planning and monitoring emerge first. As with most aspects of teamwork-related change described in this book, there is evidence of interdependence between the two levels of change, so that progress at one level needs to be matched by corresponding progress at the other. It is, however, possible to identify a number of broad headings where companies may find it relevant to make changes in setting up systems for planning and control.

The setting up of focused business units within a company, or cellular production layouts within a factory illustrates one fundamental type of change in systems for overall planning and monitoring. It allows activities associated with the different stages of manufacturing – and sometimes designing and marketing – of a particular product or product family to be planned, monitored and controlled in relation to one another. The whole point of setting up focused business units is to encourage them to perform as businesses, with a high degree of control over both their revenues and costs.

In this chapter, three further kinds of methods are described which companies may use, often in combination, for changing overall systems for monitoring company performance and planning development in ways that reinforce teamwork.

First, the identification of measures that can be applied to key business processes plays a fundamental role in monitoring and developing world class manufacturing at company level. Closely associated with the idea of product-focused business units is a way of thinking about activities within them in terms of sequences of transformations of inputs into outputs, commonly referred to as 'business processes'. The idea here is to identify a set of key business processes within a company – including for example 'manufacturing operations', 'materials management', 'sales and distribution', 'new product development', etc., and then identify a limited number of key measures that indicate how far these processes are contributing to key success factors relevant to its business strategy.

Second, companies use both financial and non-financial measures for monitoring current process standards and setting future targets. Recent years have seen the emergence and spread of new approaches to both kinds of measures, as a basis for overall monitoring and control. Methods have emerged within the TIM project for company-level monitoring of non-financial measures. These can be used both for short-term planning and control, as well as for planning longer-term development and improvement activities. Also, new approaches to management accounting, utilising activity-based techniques, are complementing devolved financial control and decision-making in various kinds of teams and business units. The purpose of activity-based techniques is to offer greater precision in planning and tracking costs of all resources consumed with a business process.

Third, new approaches to manufacturing logistics and simultaneous engineering demand and enable more collaborative ways of working with key suppliers. These involve cross-functional and even cross-organisational teams, as well as having important implications for what operational teams can achieve. This opens up the possibility of extending the boundaries of planning, monitoring, development and improvement work to include key suppliers. The final section of this chapter examines various methods for supplier development currently available to those in purchasing departments charged with this responsibility.

Monitoring and Developing Overall Business Processes

Applying non-financial performance measures to activities perhaps lies at the heart of the new state-of-the-art company-level planning and control systems. The idea of defining, tracking and acting on non-financial performance measures stems in turn from two basic concepts: critical success factors and key business processes. Together these provide a framework for translating the demands of the external market into things that can be measured, tracked and controlled within the company.

Critical success factors are a way of expressing overall business and organisational strategy. They are simply the areas where the company needs to succeed in order to make real its chosen route to competitive advantage. As such, they may emphasise each of the basic strategic options of cost, quality or innovation to a greater or lesser extent, as well as chosen key aspects of internal or organisational strategy. Typical critical success factors chosen by TIM companies are:

- Improving market share in established markets
- Entering new markets
- Improving customer satisfaction and reducing complaints
- Improving profitability, in terms of added value per employee, return on investment, and actual turnover in proportion to a break-even level
- Increasing employee motivation, skills and participation in process improvements
- Applying state-of-the-art technology in products and processes.

This list indicates the kind of overall measurements executives and senior managers use to monitor company performance with respect to critical success factors. Some are financial, some non-financial. Whichever they are, these measures are usually only meaningful to calculate on an annual basis, or at most quarterly. The concept of business processes and the systems of measurement that can be used in conjunction with them provides a mechanism for tracking performance on a more continuous basis, so that problems in performance at the level of critical success factors can be anticipated and prevented. The most basic aim behind this approach to planning and controlling is to prevent surprises at year end.

The term *business process* is one which many managers have recently found useful to describe sequences of activity within a company which transform inputs – materials, labour, information – into a significant output. The whole activity system of a manufacturing company can be thought of in terms of a set of business processes necessary for the company to produce and sell products in the present and have the capacity to continue to do so for the foreseeable future. Companies using this framework usually identify a small number of key business processes, which they recognise as the main building blocks of what the company needs to do. Each may then be regarded as made up of a number of subprocesses. Typical examples are:

- Overall business planning and control
- Product design and development
- Manufacturing operations
- Process development
- People development
- Supply chain management
- Marketing and sales
- Customer service.

Central to business process analysis is the idea that there are process owners and process customers, with the process owner responsible for meeting the requirements of the customer in a viable way, although also having to take account of other stakeholders. This kind of thinking can be used to achieve greater integration across functions or departments, and even to design departmental boundaries. This chapter focuses on the systems of monitoring, planning and development that go along with increasing integration across functions (which is another way of describing business process thinking), described in more strategic terms in Chapter 5 on business and organisational strategy.

Once critical success factors have led to identification of key

[177]

Time-related metrics	Quality-related metrics	Innovation metrics
Responsiveness to service requests	Number of defects identified per employee	Number of exploratory activities
Manufacturing cycle efficiency	Number of field repairs	Number of patents applied for
Change-over times	Amount of scrap	Ratio of unsuccessful to successful product introductions
New product introduction time	Customer returns	Parts count trend
Distance travelled by parts within plant	Number and frequency of customer complaints	Fraction of workforce with degrees and advanced degrees
On-time delivery performance	Turnover of employees	Fraction of people participating in suggestion schemes, continuous improvement
Ratio of direct to indirect labour	Fraction of people trained in SPC, TQM	Fraction of people trained in team working
Throughput times	Fraction of sales to repeat customers	Number of suggestions per employee Material types usage trend

Figure 8.1. Some key time, quality and innovation metrics.
(Reproduced from Agile Manufacturing, Forging New Frontiers, by Paul T. Kidd).

business processes, it is then possible to attach more detailed measures to each one, for the purpose of monitoring, detecting and correcting problems and guiding long-term improvement. These measures tend to be at a more detailed and operational level than the critical success factors themselves, but still refer to the overall performance of the business process. As Figure 8.1 shows, Kidd (1994) has summarised relevant measures that may be applied to business processes by grouping them according to whether they focus on concern for time, quality or innovative aspects of performance. Companies generally select from this range according to the overall business strategy and the aspects of performance that need to be emphasised in a particular key business process.

Using non-financial measures on key business processes to change company planning and accounting systems

Company level critical success factors are used to identify key business processes, which are then monitored using a small number of performance measures. These are used both for short-term monitoring and control and for identifying longer-term improvements.

Advantages	Problems/Concerns
It translates external requirements into things that can be tracked and controlled within the company.	It can be seen as bureaucratic and an additional burden – there is an appropriate level of measurement.
It allows improvement to be measured over time, gives people a sense of having feedback.	It can lead to ossification and stifling of initiative if groups do not have some influence in selecting the measures to be used.

These non-financial measures of performance provide a basis for guiding the work of operations, service and cross-functional teams. They allow middle managers and team leaders to derive lower-level systems of measurement which allow team members to receive feedback on what they are achieving, while at the same time knowing how their contribution to a larger picture of company performance is being assessed.

One big issue in operationalising non-financial performance measures at lower levels is how far one moves into measuring process parameters. The basic philosophy here stems from TQM, that the output performance of a process stems from the activities carried out within it. Accordingly, measuring and controlling how activities are carried out within the process should provide a way of assuring that output performance will be to the desired standard.

One pole of the argument is that 'if it isn't measured it doesn't happen', meaning that no one will give attention to it. Accordingly, it is vital to measure and monitor as many things as possible. The opposite view is that a culture of measures and targets can lead to a new kind of bureaucracy, even of scientific management, which saps initiative and understanding of what leads to good performance. In one TIM company customer service department, managers have decided to abandon

Case of Changing Company Planning and Accounting Systems By Using Non-financial Measures

Figure 8.2 shows how **Britax Vega** has related a set of key business processes to what its directors see as the critical success factors. The figure, based on documentation produced in an annual round of business planning in which all managers within the company were consulted, shows the largely non-financial measures that were attached to each key business process. However, it also shows the focus for improvement work identified for each business process. Directors appointed managers from different functions to work as a project team on the defined development topic for each business process. This illustrates how this kind of system for planning and monitoring can be used for identifying longer-term development issues and defining the tasks and objectives of cross-functional improvement teams.

[180]

BRITAX VEGA IMPROVEMENT PROCESS
CORRELATION MATRIX

KEY BUSINESS PROCESS	KEY ANNUAL TASKS AND OBJECTIVES (1994)	PROCESS TARGETS — WHAT THE PROCESS NEEDS TO ACHIEVE	Employee satisfaction (Absenteeism, Employee turnover, No. suggestions, Opinion survey)	Customer satisfaction (Reject levels, Assessment scores, Internal assessment)	Profitability (Breakeven/sales ratio, R.O.A.M., sales/employee)	Market share (By product group as a whole)
People management	Implement appraisal scheme for managers. Determine company-wide reward/recognition schemes	Pride in the company, a motivated workforce fully competent to do the job and improve it	●	◐	●	◐
Manufacturing conversion	Define the method to achieve O.E.E. of 85% and implement. In each unit to promote easier working practices and secure company targets	Stock turns of 100 p.a. Internal rejects of 100 p.p.m. Overall equip. effectiveness 85%. Labour cost of sales 8.9%	◐	●	●	◐
New product introduction	Improve the effectiveness of the new product introduction process to secure company targets. Select two projects to demonstrate effectiveness	ppm internal & external rejects. Costs at or below target. Every department meeting timing requirements weekly	●	●	●	◐
Business planning		A clear strategy understood by all, enabling company targets to be met	◐	◐	●	●
Product and process development		Satisfying the customer needs by the provision of creative proven designs/processes when required	◐	●	◐	●
Supply chain management	Establish use of improvement techniques with key suppliers. Introduce line side deliveries	Daily deliveries to line. 20 p.p.m. rejects by 1997. Paperless system. Suppliers capable of making continuous improvement	◐	●	●	◐
Customer service		A pro-active understanding of the current and future needs of the customer and implement agreed actions	◐	●	◐	●

Figure 8.2. One company's improvement plans.

[181]

detailed process measures. Employees now monitor and discuss key customer-related output measures, and meet monthly to discuss the causes of problems and possible areas for improvement. As the department manager puts it: 'We now only measure what the customer sees.'

Devolving Authority for Financial Performance and Decision-Making

Many conceptions of teamwork and related ideas of business units and cellular manufacturing imply greater financial decision-making at the level of the business unit, cell or team. If business units or teams are to take greater control over their destiny, they need to have the financial data and decision-making authority to make this possible. Two basic methods tend to contribute to the kinds of changes required in financial control and management accounting systems needed to achieve this.

The first concerns introducing a *system of devolved budgets* and a corresponding hierarchy of authorisation levels for decisions to spend money, which gives business units and teams a degree of autonomy in how they spend money, in particular on process improvements. In this kind of arrangement, for example, a team leader may be authorised to make decisions to purchase equipment up to a budget of £500 per year, while a business unit manager has a minor equipment budget of £5,000 per year.

The second set of methods perhaps implies more fundamental change from current typical arrangements. *Activity-based techniques for management accounting* focus on providing more appropriate financial measures of performance, which can reveal what is happening in terms of the costs being consumed within a business process.

'Activity-based costing' (ABC) and 'Activity-based management' (ABM) have emerged in recent years in response to shortcomings of traditional approaches to management accounting for this kind of purpose. Closely linked to the costing conventions required by financial accounting for the valuation of stock, traditional cost accounting calculates costs of products based on labour and material costs consumed, and an allocation of factory overheads – in practice, in proportion to the amount of machine time or labour time involved in making the product. This system works fine when the main cost component is labour costs. While this was appropriate in the nineteenth century, modern manufacturing plants typically produce cost breakdowns of 5-15 per cent direct labour, 30 per cent direct materials and 55 per cent overheads in the sense of buildings, equipment and indirect labour costs, meaning service and managerial roles (Kidd, 1994).

This kind of profile means that controlling costs for a product or product family within a business unit needs to focus above all on identifying which overhead costs are directly relevant, so that they can be controlled. ABC aims to achieve exactly this, and so provides a management accounting framework for understanding the financial performance of product-based business units. By implication ABC and associated forms of ABM can provide operations, service and cross-functional teams with a more direct appreciation of the cost implications of their work.

Fundamental to both ABC and ABM is the idea of *activity analysis*. Traditional cost accounting deals primarily with cost objects in the form of outputs, i.e. products or services, perhaps grouped according to type of product or type of customer. ABC and ABM in effect focus on the costs of sequences of activities that make up business processes involved in making products or delivering services. Once this kind of activity analysis has been carried out, costs are attributed to the activities involved on the basis of the resources consumed in these activities.

As the authors (Friedman and Lyne, 1994) of a recent review of experiences with activity-based accounting and management techniques point out, activity analysis carried out on a comprehensive basis within a company allows a great deal of flexibility in how activity streams are combined into business processes for the purpose of calculating their costs. Depending on how activities and the costs calculated for them are combined, managers can look not only at traditional cost objects – end-products or services – but also at the costs of a wide range of smaller-scale activity streams.

[183]

The second fundamental feature of this set of tools lies in abandoning the distinction between direct costs (i.e. labour and materials consumed) and indirect costs (i.e. overheads) attributed to a product or service. The aim is to identify all the activity streams involving any sort of variability in the amount of resources required from one product to the next. Activity-based analysis for a product would typically include the design, marketing and purchasing activities as well as the 'direct' manufacturing operations, unless there are good grounds for assuming that design, marketing and purchasing activities and the resources they consume are spread very evenly across different products.

To summarise ABC as applied to product costing, direct labour costs are first attributed to manufacturing activities exactly as in traditional cost accounting. The main focus of ABC is then to find a way of reflecting how much cost stems from other sources of variability which have traditionally been seen as 'overheads' – such as purchasing or warehousing. In the language of ABC, *cost drivers* need to be identified to indicate how much of particular company-level *cost pool* – for example, the total costs of purchasing resources or warehousing resources – should be attributed to a product. To identify cost drivers, cost analysts need to develop an understanding of the streams of activities involved, and what makes them consume more or less resources.

Figure 8.3 shows the relation between cost pools, cost drivers and product costs, drawn from the CAM-I ABC model (Raffish and Turner, 1991; also reproduced in Kidd, 1994). It illustrates the case of purchasing activities. The vertical 'cost view' of the diagram shows that the number of purchase orders required for producing a certain volume of product X is the most obvious factor shaping product X's consumption of the purchasing resources making up the total company purchasing cost pool. However, the horizontal 'process view' concerns the actual flow of information and activities involved in making purchasing orders. Consideration of this view leads to identification of a more fundamental cost driver – the nature of requirements for materials associated with the product. This shapes the frequency of purchase orders and so the amount of purchasing resource consumed.

In terms of its relation to various kinds of teamwork, prob-

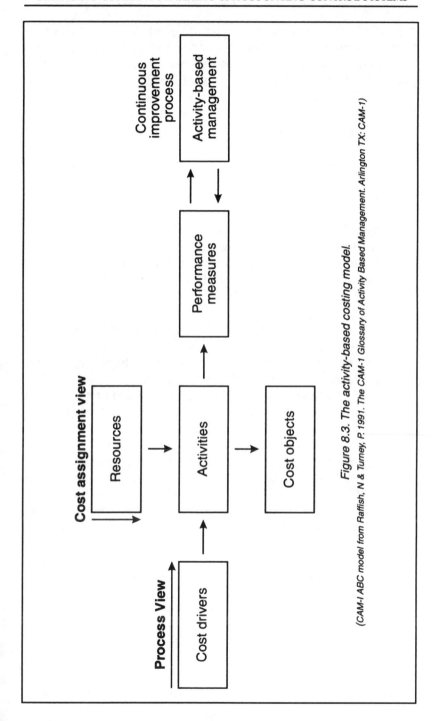

Figure 8.3. The activity-based costing model.

(CAM-I ABC model from Raffish, N & Turney, P. 1991. The CAM-1 Glossary of Activity Based Management. Arlington TX: CAM-1)

ably the most significant current usage of ABC is its application to manufacturing products or support processes as a basis
for executives and managers to make decisions as to whether a
product or support process is viable. ABC can be used to
support decisions as to what operations, support or cross-functional teams are actually charged with undertaking.

Activity analysis and the identification of cost drivers can
also serve a number of other purposes in the general domain
of planning and control systems relevant to teamwork. In
addition to applying ABC to products or processes, usually to
test out their viability, Friedmann and Lyne (1994) identify:

- *Activity-based resource management.* Activity analysis and
  allocation of costs can be used to identify the 'true cost' of
  operations for a business unit or even an operational team
  within a business unit, including all the support function
  resources that are actually consumed. This allows a business unit or operations team to make decisions about which
  resources or specialisms it makes sense for it to have within
  its boundary, and also provides a basis for systems of
  internal charging, typically between operational teams and
  support teams. In one TIM company, the application of ABC
  analysis to business units has allowed teams to work out
  when it makes financial sense for them to 'rent' an operator
  or an engineer from another business unit, and also to fix
  rates at which their own staff can be rented out.
- *Activity-based cost management* or *activity-based management.*
  Figure 8.3 also suggests that once a cost driver has been
  identified, a number of non-financial measures of performance can be derived for activities, which can then serve as
  a means of monitoring the costs accruing to this product or
  activity. This is the principle behind activity-based cost
  management, which can provide a framework within which
  teams or business units are expected to monitor their
  performance. A closely related technique, activity-based
  management, usually takes the form of simply identifying
  activity flows and then categorising activities according to
  whether or not they add value to the product, and whether
  or not they are essential. These judgements can then be
  used as a basis for redesigning flows of activities on the
  basis of minimising non-valued activities. This kind of tech-

nique is most commonly used when support functions are being redesigned, and so may have a fundamental impact on the design of service teams.

Using activity-based techniques for changing company planning and control systems

Activity flows associated with a product, service, customer, or business process are analysed. Cost drivers are identified for the purpose of understanding how the costs of resources consumed in activities should be allocated to different activities. The resulting activity analyses and costs are used for decision-making about reducing costs, usually through the redesign of activities or the abandonment of particular products or processes.

Advantages	Problems/Concerns
ABC tackles the issue of which products are profitable and which are not, instead of spreading 'overhead' equally over all products, regardless of how much resources they consume. They provide information on costs which operations managers tend to see as more real and relevant to their needs in controlling costs.	Activity-based techniques require cooperation from accountants in the finance department who manage the data required to build up activity-based costs. Accountants may resist the idea of an alternative or additional costing system, particularly if the impetus to adopt ABC comes from outside the finance department.
ABC/ABM provide a basis for focusing long-term and short-term improvement activity. They provide a management accounting basis that supports many teamwork-related initiatives, e.g. total quality management, focused business units.	Activity-based cost management and ABM are likely to be resisted by people in service roles, if the purpose of the exercise is explained as 'reducing overheads'. Explicit statements about avoiding redundancies are usually needed to counter this.

Relations between management accountancy staff and operational managers can greatly improve. Finance staff develop a much greater understanding of operational and support activities and where costs stem from. Non-financial managers appreciate accounting information that relates directly to actual processes and operating viability.	A comprehensive approach to ABC or activity-based cost management can involve entirely replacing existing costing systems. The new ABC systems are then unlikely to provide information required for financial accounting purposes. This may lead to a need for two parallel systems (much less of a problem if ABC is used only in a few areas).
ABC/ABM can provide a common framework and language throughout a company which supports greater awareness of costs.	Expertise with ABC models is unlikely to be present within a firm at the outset and needs to be bought in. If bought in the form of the consultancy, there is a danger that outside accountants will apply the model, produce reports and leave, without passing on an understanding of the model to internal staff.

Activity-based techniques are relatively new. While companies within the TIM project and elsewhere in the UK are using them, often with assistance of large accountancy-based consultancy firms, most are gradually extending the degree and range of use, from an initial small scale. Data are available as to some of the impacts, from within the TIM project itself and from Friedmann and Lyne's study at Bristol University. The table above summarises what is currently known.

A Case of Changing Overall Planning and Accounting Systems with Activity-based Costing

Components Ltd, a medium-sized company with two factories in central England, is owned by a multinational holding company. It supplies specialised large batch engineered components, mainly to large UK and European vehicle manufacturers, and jealously guards traditions of autonomy in its business and technology strategy stemming from its previous history as an independent company.

Over the last five years or so, senior managers have made a decision to concentrate on five basic component groups, and also to concentrate on a number of large preferred customers. They have on the whole been successful in winning a 'preferred supplier' status with these customers. All this has involved a number of quality improvement and process improvement projects, involving cross-functional teams of staff employees.

The directors became worried as to whether or not projects were cost-effective in terms of their benefits weighed against the cost of carrying them out. In response, the Finance Director instigated an activity analysis of the work flows involved in a number of projects, identified cost drivers and used them to produce costings for the staff time involved in each projects. These costings were used by the group of directors to make decisions to maintain or abandon the cross-functional team projects.

Supplier Development Initiatives

Techniques like MRPII, JIT and simultaneous engineering require various forms of teamworking within a manufacturing company and more collaborative relations with suppliers for the full benefits to be realised. Particularly in the case of design for manufacture, this leads to the setting up of inter-organisational teamworking arrangements.

The establishment of collaboration with key suppliers on issues of logistics and product design also opens up the possibilities of still greater collaboration in terms of planning and control of the supply chain as a whole. Final assemblers of manufactured goods, or original equipment manufacturers (OEMs), have in recent years been seeking ways to influence the development of suppliers through joint planning, monitoring and development of their business processes. Two options are currently in use for supplier development:

- Techniques for making short-term improvements in quality and reducing cost in supplier companies
- Programmes for comprehensive assessment of supplier performance and processes as a basis for identifying long-term improvement opportunities.

The main form of short-term joint planning, in addition to simultaneous engineering and just-in-time ordering, concerns 'open book' investigations of costs of manufacture of existing components by suppliers, on the basis that cost savings will be shared between the supplier and assembler. In terms of longer-term joint planning, OEMs in several sectors are now competing with one another to offer extensive advice to their chosen elite suppliers on new manufacturing, quality management and logistical techniques. This may include running benchmarking schemes by which suppliers receive feedback concerning how far they have come in adopting modern customer-focused manufacturing concepts. The Rover Group case, at the end of this chapter, illustrates this kind of scheme.

However, there appear to be a number of difficult issues that assemblers and suppliers are currently negotiating for ideas of joint planning and supplier development to move forward.

First, there are issues where suppliers enter into some form of *'open book' activity* with assemblers, revealing information about costs as a basis for finding ways of reducing them. Even though this occurs on the formal understanding that gains are to be shared, there is a tendency for suppliers to feel that the assembler should be taking a similar risk, in the form of divulging new information itself – for example, about its cost and business targets for the year. Schooled in an adversarial climate to look out for imbalances of power and information, supplier staff are sensitive to the fact that assemblers could take advantage of the much greater information they now have about many aspects of their suppliers' activities, in particular where their costs come from. A characteristic supplier stance is to seek to gain more information from the assembler about their performance expectations of suppliers. At the same time, suppliers are typically preoccupied with defining a boundary about what it is legitimate for the assembler to know about them as part of the 'partnership' and what is the suppliers' 'own business'.

Further, suppliers become anxious that the assembler will 'leak' information about particular manufacturing advances or other trade secrets which the supplier has shared with it to the other key suppliers used by the assembler for the particular component group concerned. The supplier becomes anxious about premature loss of hard-won sources of technological advantage over its close competitors.

Using supplier development initiatives for changing company planning and control systems	
Staff from original equipment manufacturers (OEMs) become involved with suppliers in measuring performance of business processes and planning improvement activities.	
Advantages	**Problems/Concerns**
It provides a mechanism for new manufacturing methods and teamworking principles to be passed on from larger to smaller companies.	It is important that staff from OEMs do not assume that they have nothing to learn from suppliers, who may be more advanced in particular aspects of manufacturing or organising.
It allows OEMs to build up a picture of how suppliers progress over time.	Suppliers may become overwhelmed with the demands of assessment and improvement activities instigated by different OEMs, and do not have time to steer their own course.

More generally, there appears to be a subterranean ambiguity in the atmosphere of the *joint planning and 'partnership' relationships* currently emerging between suppliers and assemblers. The form of these arrangements is that OEM staff work alongside supplier staff on some form of assessment and development of supplier processes. The processes concerned are usually manufacturing, engineering and quality systems, but sometimes include general management, financial management and human resources management. Even operational and service teams are the subject of assessment and development.

On the positive side, suppliers are experiencing assemblers as now offering almost a bewildering variety of forms of help. These have allowed them to move much more quickly in adopting modern manufacturing concepts, usually according to a Japanese-inspired 'lean manufacturing' model of low inventory, product-focused cells, flexible teams of operators undertaking their own quality control, and minimal numbers of support staff. At the same time, there is a tension between experiencing assemblers as offering help and experiencing them as carrying out new forms of surveillance. While suppliers at one level welcome visits from assembler company staff to introduce new techniques or carry out a 'benchmarking' survey, they may also feel that the assembler is gradually building up knowledge of all aspects of their operation, and moulding them more and more in a definite image.

Yet another source of tension concerns the experience of suppliers of having to respond to a wide variety of different joint planning initiatives, launched by the handful of different major OEMs with whom they trade. While many of these initiatives are intended to give the supplier techniques and abilities that will enable it to behave more independently, suppliers may find that the need to respond to the letter of a number of different improvement initiatives or techniques prevents them from giving attention to what they themselves see as priorities for improving the service they offer.

A Case of Changing Company Planning and Control Systems Through Supplier Development

Rover Group has developed its own supplier business specification standard, known as RG2000, which it applies to suppliers to help them develop their overall capability and performance. In an activity which Rover Purchasing stresses is entirely separate from decision-making as to which suppliers should receive orders, teams of Rover technical and commercial staff have visited all major component suppliers to administer an in-depth assessment questionnaire, in a data gathering process that lasts several days. Rover staff interview senior members of all the main functions, using a structured questionnaire and multiple sets of rankings to assess the current state of the supplier's main business processes, relative to the total quality improvement practices which Rover itself has adopted. The main headings for this audit are: quality systems; project management for new products; total quality improvement; and business improvement. The last heading involves assessing the supplier's processes for corporate management, operational accounting, product development, operations management, and human resources management.

Once the audit has taken place, Rover Purchasing staff prepare a detailed feedback presentation, including ratings for each section of the audit and overall. Rover staff stress that the purpose of the feedback is not to deliver a judgement, but to provide a basis for discussing an improvement plan with the supplier. The supplier undertakes to make certain improvements in its processes, and to improve its overall score by a certain percentage in the coming twelve months.

Both Rover Purchasing and their suppliers attach considerable value to the RG2000 process as a form of mutual development. Suppliers in particular value the comprehensive nature of the assessment and range of measures, which means that all aspects of their processes are considered. A number of suppliers who pride themselves on their own development activities have found the RG2000 process useful in identifying blind spots.

There are, however, tensions and issues with the audit process, which at the time of writing Rover Purchasing is considering. In spite of Rover's intentions, suppliers may find the audit inquisitorial, and seek to cover up evidence that it would be useful to discuss. Some suppliers also feel that the framework for the audit is too rigid, and doesn't take account of the improvement issues and techniques that are relevant to their particular production process and technology. On the Rover side, there is a concern to find more effective ways of influencing the less tangible aspects of supplier development, such as the development of a genuine culture of involvement in quality improvement.

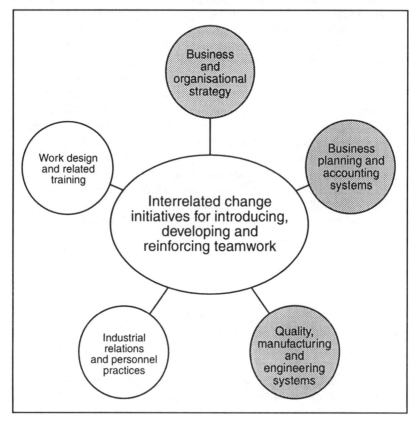

Figure 8.4. Initiative areas interconnected with company planning and accounting systems.

[194]

A Case of Relating Support Functions to Teamwork Due to Changing Company Planning and Accounting Systems

Fashionco is a US-based multinational that sells a branded luxury fashion accessory world-wide, amongst other goods. This particular product is manufactured in three different factories in a number of variants, some stable from year to year, and others more 'fashion driven'. One is a unionised, ten-year-old plant, employing about 380 people, in Northern Europe, and the other two are US sites. The corporation expects the different sites to compete with one another on production costs, redistributing production loads accordingly. Because the European plant has an average labour rate almost twice that of the Southern US plant, in recent years the management team has become extremely concerned at controlling all aspects of cost. The immediate issue is getting a share of expanded capacity in an expanding global market. In the longer run, managers are concerned at protecting the viability of their plant.

Over the last few years, they have introduced a programme of total quality management allied to a new cellular layout of the production floor and some elements of JIT production scheduling and inventory management. All of these have been intended to reduce direct manufacturing costs and improve quality. More recently, they have turned their attention to reducing 'indirect costs', given that 160 out of the 380 employees were considered 'indirect'.

The main support departments concern themselves with: designing manufacturing processes for new product variations; quality assurance for incoming materials; engineering more automated processes; financial control; materials management and purchasing; personnel and information systems. In addition, there are process engineers and quality control engineers within the manufacturing operations department.

The company hired an accountancy-based management consultancy to work with a designated two-person internal team to carry out a comprehensive activity analysis in staff areas. This analysis was to provide a basis for eliminating unnecessary activities, under the heading of activity-based management.

[195]

Further internal staff were allocated to the project, on a part-time basis. Together, over a period of three months, they identified over 400 separate activities within support departments. These were linked together in five main 'business processes', each with a number of subprocesses: 'management direction and control', 'new product evaluation', 'new product integration', 'product supply chain', and 'developing resources and infrastructure'. The last of these included 'people development'.

Each activity in each business process was costed separately. The project examined in general terms the degree of influence of nine overall cost drivers on the five business processes. The overall cost drivers were: sales forecasting, vendor performance, responsiveness cycle, new product introduction approach, unnecessarily complex systems, corporate policy, world class manufacturing initiatives, resource quality, and undisciplined culture. This led to identification of some immediate savings, particularly in the area of simplifying over-complex systems. Second, all activities were then classified as to *whether or not they added value* to the product or service, and whether they were *primary or secondary* to business objectives. The analysis showed that 40 per cent of staff activities were 'non-value-added', and 20 per cent were secondary. This led to identification of two kinds of cost saving opportunities – those that could be achieved simply by changing procedures, within the course of a few weeks or months, and those that would require some sort of process improvement or training and therefore investment taking a few months to one or two years. An important feature of this stage of implementation was a reassurance from the general manager that there would be no redundancies resulting.

Initiative Areas Interconnected with Company Planning and Accounting Systems

Executives and senior managers concerned with company systems for monitoring, controlling and developing processes will in the very nature of this activity become involved with other areas for initiative. In particular, monitoring and development systems will need to take account of changes in overall business and organisational strategy, and changes in manufacturing systems. Between them, these two areas are important in defining the critical success factors and processes to be monitored and improved.

Questions for Understanding Company Planning and Accounting Systems

- Has anyone in this organisation defined its overall critical success factors? How is to possible to measure their attainment? Which quantitative and qualitative non-financial measures are relevant? Which financial measures are relevant?
- What are the key business processes relevant to these critical success factors? What are meaningful non-financial and financial measures of their performance? What key improvements need to be made in the way these key business processes are carried out?
- How relevant and useful are cost data currently produced by the management accounting functioning for manufacturing operations? What cost data would need to be produced to increase its relevance for day-to-day management?
- Are any forms of collaboration with customers or suppliers under way in the area of joint monitoring of performance and planning improvements? What opportunities exist for creating some? What would the possible benefits be?

Further Reading

Friedmann, A. and Lyne, S. R. 1994. The organisational consequences of implementing activity-based techniques. *Research Report*. London: Chartered Institute of Management Accountants Research Foundation.

Kidd, P. T. 1994. *Agile Manufacturing, Forging New Frontiers*. Reading, Massachusetts, Addison Wesley.

9

Changing Industrial Relations and Personnel Policies

Managers and consultants concerned with the human resources and organisational development aspects of introducing change have major roles to play in the planning, sequencing and implementation of teamworking. These roles encompass both technical interventions into the human dimension – such as setting up recruitment criteria and procedures – and managing more general organisational needs for informing, consulting and involving different constituencies.

Human resources policies and practices are critical elements in any kind of major organisational change. They are expected to support the objectives of the organisation and if those objectives change, then policies and practices will need to be rethought. Behind human resource interventions, in such areas as reward systems and appraisal, are theories and views as to what kind of policies and practices are most likely to produce the greatest effort and motivation in employees in terms of the organisation's needs. Thus, an organisation which wishes to develop individual 'highflyers' is likely to have reward and

[198]

appraisal systems which emphasise and encourage the kinds of characteristics associated with this. However, these may well be at odds with the characteristics which need to be encouraged for teamwork.

Teamwork can require a great many changes to working practices. Clearly demarcated job descriptions are undermined by multi-skilling and other practices designed to increase individual and group flexibility. Existing payment and grading structures, which emphasise differentiated skill levels, then become inappropriate to support team-based work. Employees become understandably concerned that changes to these structures will affect them adversely, particularly where multi-skilling appears to threaten craft skills. For both unionised and non-unionised workforces, therefore, industrial relations issues will come to the fore when teamwork is being introduced, reinforced and developed.

In this chapter, the range of issues which human resources managers and others are particularly likely to confront, and some associated methods for handling them, are considered. Beginning with the general industrial relations framework and its impact on teamwork, the chapter goes on to cover communication and consultation processes, payment, grading and recognition, selection and appraisal of staff, and issues of management 'style' in a teamwork-based organisation.

Industrial Relations Framework

One of the compelling reasons for the introduction of teamworking is the drive for more flexible working practices. Breaking down demarcations to create much greater interchangeability among employees through multi-skilling often goes together with changes to the pattern of working time. These, together with associated payment and grading systems, are all critical issues from the point of view of industrial relations. Where unions are recognised, they will in any case be matters for collective bargaining.

Aspects of these changes – such as more direct and improved communication between management and shop floor and greater learning opportunities for semi-skilled and unskilled workers – may be considered by both management and workforce to be genuinely empowering for some employees at least. At the same time, other aspects may arouse considerable suspicion. 'Flexibility' sounds to many employees like a euphemism for getting them to take on more tasks for correspondingly less reward. Where teamwork is being introduced in a climate of recent or pending redundancies (albeit not connected directly with the introduction of teamwork), there can be a great deal of scepticism.

The industrial relations environment is thus very significant in enabling the requisite changes to take place, or in hindering them. Any organisation contemplating moving to team-working needs to consider how its own environment might facilitate or block change and assess what needs to be done to create a more constructive one. There are examples where teamwork has been introduced relatively successfully, with little or no consultation, as part of a package of urgent survival measures. But this is a high risk strategy best avoided if possible. There is a risk of storing up unresolved issues or grievances which rebound after the immediate crisis is past.

Where immediate survival is not at stake, experience shows that a more lasting settlement is best achieved through early consultation and involvement, direct and frequent communication with employees, and – where the workforce is unionised – building alliances with on-site and regional trade union representatives. Even then, it can take considerable time and effort to achieve major change.

Experience in the TIM project suggests that the history of employee relations in an organisation profoundly affects the change process. In older manufacturing sites with multiple union representation and a history of very adversarial collective bargaining, attempts to introduce teamwork will have to contend with both a high level of endemic suspicion of management motives, and with possible intra-union conflicts of interest. Teamwork cuts across what are often zealously guarded demarcations between skill levels with their associated status and payment differentials. White collar and craft unions in particular fear that their members will lose out through multi-skilling and the dilution of differentials. They may also have a more general fear that they will lose membership to other unions. In so far as the introduction of teamwork has led some UK companies to negotiate or press for single union agreements, this fear is not necessarily unfounded. In other cases, the complete derecognition of unions has accompanied comprehensive change programmes involving teamwork. This is not a path to be followed lightly, but if it is, it is important to understand that effective alternative mechanisms for consulting and negotiating with employees will have to be put into place.

What are the typical elements of an industrial relations strategy in the context of teamwork? In relation to flexible working practices and multi-skilling, an organisation is likely at minimum to need to reach a formal agreement with its employees on the ending of working practices which – while quite logical in a traditional environment – stand in the way of the kind of flexibility and upgrading of skills required in teamwork. A common first step, therefore, is to *negotiate an enabling agreement* with the union(s), removing work practices which obstruct such flexibility and putting in place certain agreed principles which facilitate teamwork.

A Case of Changing Industrial Relations and Personnel Practices Using an Enabling Agreement

Vehicle X Company, an automotive manufacturer, negotiated an enabling agreement with all its multiple recognised trade unions. The company had several aims. Facing an urgent need to improve productivity and launch a new range of products, it decided to introduce teamwork through negotiating flexible working practices and an end to craft demarcations. In association with this, it wanted to agree a new disputes procedure and negotiate local wage rates, and it wished to move to single table bargaining. Its existing recognition and procedural agreements were more than 20 years old and upheld multiple restrictions and demarcations which were based on different union spheres of influence. Further, custom and practice had developed, making shop stewards the main vehicle of communication between shop floor and management and overriding first line management in particular. The general climate of industrial relations was poor.

The resulting agreement committed the company and employees to a progressive broadening of the skills of the work-

[201]

force through training and cross-training, and committed the company to retrain and redeploy anyone whose craft or skill became obsolete. Formal distinctions between staff and manual employees were abolished. New working patterns were agreed. Communications procedures between management and shop floor were streamlined and disputes procedures greatly simplified, preventing their use as a way of blocking the introduction of new working practices.

In return, the unions received formal assurance that they would continue to be recognised for negotiating purposes. The company undertook to provide employment security through retraining and to give pay protection to anyone required to retrain. It also undertook to use natural wastage to balance labour requirements. Subsequently, the company was able to obtain agreement on harmonising union representation between shop floor employees and staff by ensuring both were represented on the senior negotiating group. It also introduced cross-union representation for each area within the site. It thus accomplished its aim to move to single table bargaining.

As this example shows, a large number of issues had to be addressed in order to create the kind of environment which would facilitate teamwork. What it also shows is that a suitable framework can be arrived at without derecognising unions and – on multi-union sites – without necessarily pressing for a single union agreement. Experience in the TIM project indicates that unions are not invariably opposed to change and, indeed, they can be important allies in the process.

Attempts to change the industrial relations environment are generally successful where negotiations are seen to be carried out in good faith and to offer benefits in return. Agreements offering protection, where possible, to employees against redundancy as a result of changes in work practices are one way of gaining cooperation. The concept of a *'new deal'* agreement, such as that implemented by Rover Group, suggests guaranteed redeployment anywhere in the plant to an employee whose job becomes surplus or redundant due to teamworking. Such an agreement offers guaranteed employment in exchange for very high levels of flexibility. Many, particularly smaller, companies are not in a position to give such firm guarantees, but it is often possible to offer at least some protection, as in the example above, as part of the necessary trade-off to achieve major changes.

Using the negotiation of an enabling agreement to change industrial relations and personnel practices

An enabling agreement is a contract negotiated between management and union(s) which commits the union(s) to the introduction of new working practices and associated organisational changes, often in exchange for an increased commitment to training and development, and guarantees to protect employees against adverse outcomes, such as compulsory

Advantages	Problems/Concerns
It clears the way for multi-skilled teamwork by removing job demarcations and other restrictive practices.	If management-union relations are poor, it can meet fierce resistance, leading to a protracted battle or pressure to derecognise.
It can be used as a basis for negotiating new bargaining arrangements, such as single table or single union recognition.	It is important to bear in mind that consulting the union does not always equate to consulting the workforce.
If handled sensitively, it can improve relations with union(s) by offering significant gains to members.	Intra-union rivalry can cause problems if new working practices are seen to disadvantage some union members more than others.
Agreements can be struck with highly skilled employees who want to retain their differentials.	Single-union deals can antagonise members of those unions which lose out.

Another important and common trade-off is that of moving towards a *single-status workforce* by harmonising conditions of service and moving to a unified payment and grading system. This may involve placing everyone on staff contracts with common terms and conditions, including monthly paid salaries, sick leave, annual leave and non-pay benefits. The advantages of single table bargaining become clear in this context.

There is also an important symbolic element to single status. Many manufacturing companies have acted to abolish visible status markers such as separate eating and washing facilities, car parking and other symbols of position, such as clocking on, for different grades of employees. Common work-wear is another way in which symbolic distance – between 'suits' and 'overalls' – can be diminished.

Communication and Consultation Processes

Good communication and consultation are essential to successful teamwork. It can be useful to think of these processes, first, in relation to the sequencing of teamwork initiatives; and second, in relation to maintaining communications after teamwork is introduced in order to develop and reinforce managers, technical specialists and team members. Companies have used four basic options for improving communication and consultation processes related to team-working:

- Communication and consultation about the introduction of teamwork
- Communication and consultation needed to maintain and develop operational and service teams
- General communication about business performance and the people in the organisation
- Electronic communication systems.

It can seem paradoxical that teamwork is so often introduced as a top down, 'survival' mechanism by senior managers, when it requires a more 'empowered' and participatory environment for the workforce. This paradox is often manifest in the industrial relations conflicts which can erupt around the introduction of teamwork. Organisational change agents may find themselves simultaneously carrying through redundancy programmes and instigating changes which require greater employee involvement and personal autonomy. However urgent the need to make changes, therefore, it is essential to *communicate and consult about the introduction of teamwork* as widely as possible beforehand. Although, in unionised organisations, union representatives will have key roles in this process, mechanisms will be needed to involve the whole workforce.

In a number of TIM companies, senior managers have had a critical input into the communications process prior to the introduction of teamwork by meeting directly with employees, either in large, specially convened forums, or by meeting section managers and employee representatives in smaller groups to explain the nature of the changes so that they, in turn, can communicate accurate information to their staff. As these companies have found, it is particularly important to explain the business context behind decisions and to make people aware of the link between what is happening in their section or part of the organisation, and the wider organisational climate. The onus for communicating major changes should not be put onto the very people who might suffer the most from them, such as supervisors whose jobs are likely to disappear.

Ideally, moving to teamworking should be a consultative and participative process. It tends to be part of the rhetoric of much teamwork-based change that a more participatory environment is being created. This is likely to be greeted with some scepticism if no attempt is made to involve employees and unions in designing teamwork or at least in communicating to them clearly how the changes are likely to affect them. Also, at this stage it may be necessary to gather data within the organisation, possibly using external consultants, on how employees feel about any proposed changes. Employee surveys can in themselves be an important tool for change, alerting employees to what is happening and enabling them to make their views known in a confidential form.

Once teamwork is in place, it will generate its own communication requirements. *Communication and consultation*

[205]

A Case of Changing Industrial Relations and Personnel Practices Using Employee Involvement

File Co, a company producing office stationery, wanted to move to cellular-based manufacturing teams. As the manufacturing site is split into two divisions based on distinct production processes, the management team set up four working groups to examine the possibilities and come up with recommendations. There were two from each side of the business and they included a mixture of production and support staff. In this way, the company involved a wide range of employees in the design process and benefited from the diversity of experience represented on the working groups.

mechanisms are needed to maintain and develop operational and service teams. Teamwork is generally premised on flatter organisational structures where the communications and decision-making lines are much shorter and responsibility for quite major decisions gets pushed much further down the organisation. This means that new mechanisms have to be created to develop the requisite communication flows and to ensure that the right information is available to the right people when they need it. This might include, for instance, information from finance, accounting and sales to production teams planning their own schedules – information that conventionally would not reach production workers.

Teams have both internal and external boundaries across which information has to flow. In terms of internal boundaries, team members need to meet with each other or have a regular contact point to coordinate tasks and generally to maintain the social dynamics of the group. There may also be key handover points where team members change. For example, production teams may need a mechanism for cross-shift communication, such as a handover meeting or information board.

Teams need to send information out and receive information in from other teams and from line managers. Team leaders may need to set up their own system of communication to manage that interface. As teams take on increasing levels of responsibility for issues such as quality improvement, they

[206]

will need regular access to information from managers and sectional heads. Regular meetings for the purpose of communication and coordination may be useful.

Much of the information a team requires to perform well can be built into performance feedback systems. But there are *communication needs about business performance and the people in the organisation* which all employees and managers need more generally. These needs encompass the wider organisation, both at site level and group level, where an organisation is part of a bigger corporate entity. Newsletters and information sheets can be a valuable way of creating inclusion and contact, as well as being a source of information. But multiple sources of face-to-face information may need to be established as well.

Team briefings have become popular in the UK as a method for authorised information to be issued from managers at every level and then to be communicated in a cascade fashion down the chain of command. In one company, team briefings were introduced primarily in response to the need to improve quality. Regular team briefings provided a way of getting information on a wide range of quality-related topics down to the shop floor. However, they also functioned as a way of creating greater involvement in the change process among operatives and moving away from a reactive, 'firefighting' style of operation to a more proactive, anticipatory one.

In order to diminish gulfs between shop floor employees and senior management, some companies have introduced regular 'meet the boss' sessions for all employees, enabling them in turn to listen to and question executives and senior managers. In order to ensure that the workforce is informed about the wider business situation of the company, quarterly or semi-annual business review meetings may be held in which the whole workforce is taken through the business plans by top managers. Cross-functional teams also provide an important way of broadening communication, particularly in a functionally based organisation.

A number of TIM companies have also begun to make extensive use of *electronic communication systems,* e.g. corporate electronic mail systems, operating over computer networks. Some of the results have been unexpected in terms of benefits to general communication. Electronic mail systems are used commonly to transmit uniform information about the state of production, problems and issues to all technical and supervisory staff. This is particularly valuable for team leaders on shifts and shift managers. One or two companies have made a point of making a personal computer connected to the company network available to operations teams. This allows access to the E-mail system, as well as software for administration and problem analysis.

Using team briefings for changing industrial relations and personnel practices

Team briefings are a regular form of communication from management to production or service teams, enabling important information to be passed on efficiently to team members. Briefings may be either in writing or in person, or a combination of the two.

Advantages	Problems/Concerns
Team briefings provide a way of getting information on a wide range of topics, such as quality, down to production or service teams.	The information must be relevant and timely or ritualisation sets in.
They can help to create greater involvement in the change process and in the aims of the organisation among team members.	They must not become the only form in which management communicates to its workforce.
They can be a vehicle for developing a more proactive, anticipatory stance among team members.	The information flow should not be one way only, encouraging passive reception, but should encourage reverse flow.
Managers support the top down approach through the chain of command.	Middle and line managers often misrepresent even the best-worded written documents; employees listen to them – not to the words.

Selection and Recruitment for Teamwork

Teamwork requires skills which may or may not be present in the existing workforce. In particular, it is likely to demand both higher levels of technical competence from all team members and social skills in managing intra-group relations. Employees in team leader roles will need also to be competent in running meetings and group activities, in assessing training and development needs, and in associated mentoring and facilitation skills. Selection and recruitment raises the question of whether to go outside the organisation or to recruit wholly or mainly from existing employees.

In practice, this decision can seldom be made without reference to the context. Only in 'greenfield' sites is it possible to base selection criteria for a whole workforce on suitability for teamwork. In existing organisations it is likely to be only selection of future employees, or of team leaders from a larger pool of candidates, which can fully incorporate such criteria. Where organisations are restructuring and shedding staff, acceptance of teamworking and willingness to adapt to it are not infrequently used as criteria for deciding on who goes, particularly at first line management level. Managers should tread very carefully here, not treating resistance to teamwork simply as something that can be eradicated by getting rid of those individuals who manifest it most prominently, or assuming that those who resist initially are incapable of change.

Underlying much thinking about recruitment and selection is something of a divide between training-based views of competence for teamwork and personality-based views. In the former view most, if not all, people can acquire the necessary skills and competences through appropriate training. This view leads to an emphasis on training and personal development after recruitment has taken place. In the latter view, some people are inherently better team workers because they are already endowed with personal traits or characteristics which match the requirements of teamworking. This leads to an emphasis on tests prior to recruitment which claim to be able to identify individuals with the appropriate traits.

This is not an absolute divide – many organisations combine the two – but it is important to be aware of the different assumptions involved. One company, involved in food processing, felt that its highly stable, traditional work-force could not change and adapt to a teamwork environment and does not expect to make progress until it can bring in new recruits. It is therefore not setting up any training initiatives for teamwork. Another company, in the automotive sector, took the opposite view that 'people will change if they have to' and is investing in a major organisation-wide training initiative to prepare for teamwork.

In most cases initial recruitment for team membership is from existing staff and this means that it is likely to be at team leader level where the problem of selection and recruitment is most commonly faced. Chapter 6 on work design and related training considers some of the issues involved in deciding what kind of team leadership to go for. From the point of view of recruitment, it should be borne in mind that the type of leadership is linked to choices about the type of team. The attributes required of the leader will vary accordingly. As the BICC case study below shows, acquiring the competences for team leadership can fruitfully be seen as a process over time, with some competences being accorded earlier priority than others.

For those wishing to use externally validated tests for recruitment purposes, there are various types available. The best known is probably *psychometric testing*. One version of testing, developed by a commercial consultant specifically for teamwork, uses information from managers talking about the kinds of characteristics they consider necessary in team-working. This was then turned into a structured interview. In the pilot project, shop floor workers were trained to administer the interview, thus enabling them to select their own team members.

A Case of Changing Industrial Relations and Personnel Practices by Selecting Team Leaders from Employees

BICC Cables at Blackley wanted to appoint 23 new team leaders to cover the whole manufacturing area. All employees on site were invited to apply for the new positions whatever their current job, and a series of information briefings were held for everyone who showed an interest, without committing them to pursue things further. At these sessions, the role of team leaders and their importance to the overall change process were explained.

All applicants were put through a comprehensive selection process involving a number of different kinds of tests. This enabled the selectors to build up a picture with maximum corroboration from the different sources. Those eventually selected came from both supervisory and nonsupervisory positions. Having recruited on the basis of a range of required attributes for the position, it was nevertheless recognised that team leaders would require a high level of training and support to implement teamwork successfully. Over the following twelve months, a series of training and development activities were set up, and a mentoring system was put in place. At the end of their first six months, based on their initial experiences, the team leaders themselves came forward with an assessment of their training needs. They went on to generate their own matrix of skill requirements which they agreed with the manufacturing management team. This then became the basis for the formal programme.

[211]

Using selection and recruitment for teams from existing staff for changing industrial relations and personnel practices

Team members and team leaders are chosen from existing staff, rather than from elsewhere in the organisation or from outside.

Advantages	Problems/Concerns
It creates minimal upheaval for the organisation and reassures existing staff that they will retain their jobs, albeit in a changed form.	It can take longer to get team-work operating effectively as old habits and ways of working have to be altered.
Most organisations have an abundance of under-used talent which can be drawn upon for new roles such as team leaders.	Organisations may not necessarily have much choice about selection, needing to find a role for almost everyone and placate the trade unions over possible casualties.
Selection from existing staff utilises people who already have experience of the organisation and the way it works.	There can be a lack of 'new blood' and fresh ways of thinking which would benefit the organisation.

Changing Payment and Grading Systems

Payment and grading systems invariably require attention where teamwork is being introduced and developed. Employees may well also demand more pay and recognition for taking on what they see as the additional responsibilities of teamwork, and this raises the question of the relationship between payment and motivation. Few would deny that payment is a critical factor in motivating employees to perform better. However, as the section below on other forms of reward and recognition suggests, it is certainly not the only factor. From the point of view of teamwork, what is important is to ensure that the payment system works with, rather than against, flexibility and collective goals.

Traditional shop floor payment systems are generally based on a close relationship between pay and a particular – usually highly specified – job. When there is a 'motivational' or 'productivity' element, it rewards individual rather than collective effort. Productivity is maintained or increased through the use of piece-rate or personal bonuses which encourage individuals to keep producing regardless of whether the pieces are piling up because of a bottleneck. This discourages employees from going to help others to clear the bottleneck. Skill hierarchies are often closed and skill and pay differentials heavily guarded by unions. Traditional grading structures link into such systems, producing or supporting hierarchies based on complex and – from a teamworking point of view – restrictive and irrational demarcations with proliferating grades. Although such systems often seem quite rational to those involved, in practice they may be based on quite irrational assumptions about, for example, the relationship between gender and skill.

There can therefore be a serious mismatch between existing payment and grading systems and what is needed to support teamworking. If some individuals gain consistently at the expense of others, collective effort will be minimised. What kind of framework is likely to be most appropriate to teamwork? There are, in general, three basic principles underlying most payment systems:

- Payment for doing a particular *job* or occupying a *position*. This is payment based on the demands of the *job* itself
- Payment based on the qualities of the *person*, in particular their skill or knowledge
- Payment for *results*, based on performance or outcomes.

Elements of each of these are relevant to, or may be combined in, setting up payment and grading systems for teamwork.

Teamwork moves organisations away from an emphasis on employees doing a tightly specified job, occupying a particular position or following a pre-set promotional path. It emphasises instead flexibility and multi-skilling. It is thus not compatible with an elaborate job-based grading system and points to the

[213]

Using payment for skills for changing industrial relations and personnel practices

Employees are paid a basic rate and then paid individually for each additional skill module for which they obtain certified competence; usually an individual payment, it can be applied to the accumulated skill profile of a team.

Advantages	Problems/Concerns
It encourages individuals to acquire multiple skills and thus increases the degree of multi-skilling in a team-based environment.	It may come into conflict with collective bargaining arrangements.
It rewards people for competence and self-improvement rather than paying them based on hierarchy.	It may encourage too much rotation which becomes inefficient.
It provides a path for advancement and can therefore be very self-motivating.	People may become over-skilled for the tasks which have to be done, and dissatisfied when they hit the top of the ladder.
It allows considerable scope in paths of advancement, offering opportunities for diverse individual needs and interest to be accommodated and made useful to the company.	It can create difficulties in controlling the total wage bill.
It can be applied to a total group's skill profile and not just to individuals; unions can still negotiate on rates of pay for skills.	Trade unions and workforces may object to differentiation in pay between different workers doing the same job.

need to simplify structures and occupational positions to no more than two or three levels. In general, this will mean some levelling up; this simplification may, however, be in some tension with the need to reward particular skills.

That said, many companies insist on retaining their job evaluation schemes. To the extent that a scheme continues to be applied to individual jobs without any group-based skill or performance element, teamwork will never achieve its potential. The one way companies have managed to get around this problem is by adding a group-based skill or performance payment for a team.

Another way is by developing *group-based job evaluation*. With a group-based job description, the team is responsible for undertaking a set of tasks for which the individuals are paid the same as others in the team. This establishes the base salary for the team and encourages cooperation. Additional elements can be added for individual skills or group performance.

Paying people for skills can be an important element of teamwork payment systems. It encourages flexibility and multi-skilling and rewards the acquisition of greater competence. It generally works by adding further individual pay as an employee successfully completes a particular skill module and requires that training opportunities are allocated on an open and fair basis.

There are dilemmas associated with payment for skills. One issue is what happens when the top of the skill ladder is reached. It may also encourage too much rotation and not enough individual specialisation within teams. 'Overskilling' for the task may occur. The wage bill may also become unsustainable if everyone attains all skill targets. In practice, companies may need to put a 'cap' on the extent to which all new skill acquisition is rewarded by a pay increase, but payment for skills can be extremely valuable in developing a more multi-skilled workforce. While pay-for-skills is usually tied to individual skill levels, some companies have chosen to reward individuals working in teams on the basis of the collective skills or competence demonstrated by the team as a whole.

Performance-related pay (PRP) can be added to other pay elements to reward employees for results. It may be individually paid or used to reward group or company performance. It is often used as a way of retaining high-performing staff and of increasing motivation. Performance-based pay can be controversial unless performance measures are seen to be fair to all concerned, and individually based merit pay does not necessarily coexist easily with teamwork. Team-based bonuses are an alternative but it is important to ensure that all teams have an equal opportunity to achieve bonuses and that the bonus scheme does not create unhelpful competition between teams which need to cooperate.

Combining the different elements to create a payment system which appears 'fair' while encouraging the appropriate motivation and behaviours to support teamwork is something of a fine balancing act. Experience of doing this is growing, however, as the Chemco example below shows.

A Case of Changing Industrial Relations and Personnel Practices by Changing the Payment and Grading System

Chemco, a UK site of a US multi-national corporation, developed a payment system to support teamwork for hourly paid workers which combined these various elements. The structure has four segments. The first segment is an 'entry' grade with a starting rate and an increased payment after basic job proficiency has been attained. The second segment is specifically team-based pay recognition; it ties pay increments for individuals in a team to a number of levels which relate to the achievement of successive degrees of flexibility and self-regulation for the team as a whole. This part of the pay system is thus a team-based pay-for-skills element. All members are put on the same basic pay grade according to how competent their team has become in task flexibility and self-regulation. Levels of development were defined using the team development grid described in the chapter on continuously developing teams. The third segment is for individual rewards for skills over and above what is required within the team. The fourth segment is a motivational element based on company-level performance.

In this design, the grading structure is simple but the payment system is able to provide a balance between simplicity and making quite fine discriminations to reward both group and individual effort.

Using performance-related pay for changing industrial relations and personnel practices

PRP provides an element of additional remuneration for performance which is based on an individual, group or company bonus.

Advantages	Problems/Concerns
It ties part of the reward system directly to the achievement of business objectives.	It can be very controversial unless the performance measurements used are seen and agreed by everyone to be fair.
Payment for contribution is often seen to be fair by employees themselves.	Individuals and groups must be able to influence the performance which is being measured.
Individual PRP can be an incentive to retain high performers.	Individual PRP may not encourage team cooperation. Group-based PRP may create unhelpful competition between teams which need to cooperate.
Base rates can be kept more equal for employees working in operational or service teams.	It needs to be at least 3 per cent of an overall package to act as an incentive.

Similar principles can be applied to payment and grading systems for salaried staff. Systems can provide for many or few levels of pay within a structure that has minimum levels of hierarchy. The main staff distinction would be between managers with authority over other staff and technical and administrative staff without supervisory responsibility. Group-based work with cross-training to acquire a wider range of competence can operate within a level of hierarchy, with associated recognition through the payment system.

[217]

The redesign of payment and grading systems does have to take account of the complexity and degree of entrenchment of existing custom and practice and consider wider issues such as the relationship between overtime and final pay packet. It also needs to take account of what employees themselves see as fair – which depends largely on their previous experience. Involving employees directly in the process of redesign can increase the likelihood of acceptance.

The importance of looking at the whole picture of rewards, including overtime, when considering a new payment system was demonstrated by a major chemicals company. The problem of overtime payments was foreseen when it redesigned its payment system to support teamwork. It used the offer of staff status and its accompanying benefits as part of a complex trade-off between gains and losses, including overtime.

Appraisal Systems for Teamwork

Performance appraisal is increasingly a feature of organisational life. As such, it raises a whole set of questions which are not specific to appraising for teamwork. Some important questions which need to be addressed in introducing any kind of appraisal system are:

- What are the objectives of appraisal?
- Are they primarily developmental or are they concerned with measuring and rewarding current performance?
- If development plans are to be the output, should the focus be on training plans for the next year, what new tasks can be taken on, or on longer-term career development?
- Who is to be appraised?
- Who does the appraising?
- How frequently is it done?
- What kind of measurement or evidence is acceptable?
- Who has access to the results?
- What 'right of response' should employees have?

Experience from the TIM project suggests that appraisal is now widely used as part of a set of human resources and organisational development activities which are put in place to support teamwork. These include training and up-skilling for opera-tives and changing management roles and attitudes among supervisory and managerial staff. Most companies have some form of appraisal system for staff levels, and *appraisal of operational teams* is increasingly being used.

In the context of teamwork, an appraisal needs to be designed so that it does actually appraise teamwork-related performance, although it may well appraise other skills and competences as well. The most common form is appraisal of more junior employees by more senior, but *peer appraisal* and *upward appraisal* can also be used effectively in assessing team-work competence.

A Case of Changing Industrial Relations and Personnel Practices Using Management Appraisal

Britax Vega wanted to appraise managers in terms of their compe-tence as managers in a 'teamworking' organisation. Directors initi-ated design of a management appraisal system as part of a key improvement area which they identified as 'people management'.

They began by setting up a task force on appraisal. The group of managers making up the task force were aware that the idea of a formalised appraisal system might arouse anxieties and resis-tance from their peers, and so set about a highly participative and consultative process for designing the system. They first held a number of workshops with managers to discuss possible purposes of appraisal, leading to a proposal that the system should focus primarily on helping managers define their development needs and achieve recognition for their performance. This would benefit indi-viduals but also the company, in that it would raise the level of professionalism of managers and provide a basis for succession planning.

After gaining approval from the company directors, the task force then turned its attention to exactly what should be appraised by whom. After further consultation with managers, the task force established a list of 28 general management competencies which all managers could be appraised on. Drawing on the standards for management competencies developed by the UK Management Charter Initiative, the competencies were grouped under four main

headings – operations management, people management, information management and resource management – and emphasised
the facilitative rather than overtly directive nature of management.

The team then drew up an appraisal system in which managers
met with their director at least once a year to discuss evidence on
strengths and weaknesses and performance with respect to each
competence, and to agree a rating and development plan. Although
carried out with full consultation, the concept of appraisal nevertheless evoked some defensiveness and resistance, and it was
decided to make a clear separation between appraisal as a developmental activity and the setting of pay levels for individual
managers.

Britax also introduced appraisal for its operators. In contrast to
the managers, this is linked directly to a new grading system introduced by the company as part of the development of team-based
skill flexibility. The grade, in turn, determines payment level. The
appraisal thus concentrates on skill attainment and associated
quality of work, and on training requirements for the following
twelve months. A combination of 'hard' and 'soft' measures is used
in appraising operators, such as absence records, skills obtained
and a qualitative assessment of attitudes to teamworking. Thus,
while the managerial appraisal system is primarily developmental
and geared to effecting a shift in the style of management, the
operators' appraisal is primarily concerned with skill acquisition and
improving flexibility.

A Case of Changing Industrial Relations and Personnel Practices Using Upward Appraisal

Leyland Trucks introduced upward appraisal of their managers
by their direct reports. This was done in the context of needing to
effect quite major changes in the management style of the
company, moving from a fairly aggressive, hierarchical, command
style to one which would encourage all employees to exercise
more autonomy and to be supported rather than disciplined for
innovation and risk-taking. Employees filled out questionnaires
anonymously as far as possible. The results were quite bruising
for some managers in the beginning but did achieve substantial
changes over time which both sides felt they benefited from.

There is no prescriptive answer as to whether appraisal should be linked to pay. It will depend on what the organisation is trying to achieve through appraisal. One company found that their linking of pay differentials directly to appraisal was potentially costing them more because their operatives were achieving very high levels of skill. This raises wider issues concerning what the organisation's needs are in terms of skill mix, and how greater skill and commitment are recognised and rewarded.

Using participative design of appraisal for changing industrial relations and personnel practices

Participative appraisal involves those who are to be appraised in the design and carrying out of the appraisal system.

Advantages	Problems/Concerns
It allows discussion of what an appraisal system is for and what should be appraised.	It may be time-consuming and bring to the fore unresolved conflicts over what managers should be doing.
It lessens resistance to appraisal once it is implemented.	The form of appraisal may be different from what executives feel comfortable with.
It can be used as a way of clarifying the nature of management in a teamworking environment.	Both appraisees and appraisers need training in all aspects of the scheme for it to work.
Participative design of an appraisal systems usually results in a good balance between self-assessment and manager-led appraisal.	There is no guarantee that employees will support the appraisal process even if they helped design it.

Self-appraisal and *peer appraisal* may also be quite appropriate to a team-based organisation where higher levels of personal autonomy and responsibility are expected of employees. In self-appraisal and peer appraisal, employees take some responsibility for identifying their own or another's strengths and weaknesses and areas for development. The role of the appraiser is to facilitate this process and to assist in the planning of remedial and developmental activity.

Employee Recognition and Reward Outside the Payment System

Employees generally expect that their efforts to increase flexibility, productivity and customer satisfaction will be recognised through appropriate salary or wage enhancements. However, there are needs for reward which go beyond the pay packet and which relate to the importance of recognition of individual and collective effort and respect for personal worth. In developing teamwork, non-pay linked rewards can be important motivators.

Suggestion schemes have proved a popular way of encouraging employees to think of cost-saving measures and improvements, such as alternative uses for waste materials. However, it is not unusual for managers to think that suggestion schemes no longer have a role to play in a teamwork environment. They reason that if making improvements is the responsibility of everyone, then why pay some people for coming up with ideas for improvements? Where there is no

---

A Case of Changing Industrial Relations and Personnel Practices Using Suggestion Schemes

Leyland Trucks' staff suggestion scheme pays a £1 voucher for every suggestion plus a chance to go into a draw for £50. The scheme is there to recognise the putting forward of ideas, not their value to the company. Nevertheless, the savings generated have been much greater than the amount which has been paid out.

---

profit-linked pay on offer, however, employees appreciate suggestion schemes as a way of getting back some of the profit they make for the company.

Regular feedback on performance is one of the most important ways of encouraging and recognising competence. Using information technology near the site of employees' work can provide routine information on results. In fact, both operational teams and service teams input their own data into some systems. But self-awareness of results is not always enough. Public recognition and some form of 'thank you' seems to be called for.

A Case of Changing Industrial Relations and Personnel Practices With Recognition

Britax Vega became concerned about the issue of non-monetary reward and recognition in the context of how to reinforce teamworking. In particular, they wanted to demonstrate the company's commitment to teamwork. They needed to encourage cooperation between teams rather than competition. They had noted a tendency for teams to be concerned only with their own internal performance, sometimes at the expense of other teams.

To find out how employees felt about it and what kinds of recognition they would like to see, a task force gathered data from employees at all levels and in all departments. A major theme which emerged was an intrinsic need to be respected and valued by the company and by their managers. From this, it appears that explicit forms of personal and public recognition are required. Employees and teams want to be commended when their performance has been particularly good, both by regular feedback from managers and others, and by public gestures such as company awards and write-ups in the house publication.

Teamworking can also produce dilemmas around rewards which cannot be accommodated within existing payment and grading systems. With the emphasis on skill up-grading, skill levels may come to outstrip the capacity of the system to pay for them as well as the operational need for them. Able staff find they cannot move further up the promotional ladder in a flat organisation. A number of organisations are beginning to offer skill and learning opportunities which are not linked to higher pay and internal career development but enable employees to pursue personal interests or catch up on education which they may have missed out on earlier. The benefits to the organisation are more indirect, assisting retention of valued staff and contributing to employees' wider developmental goals and motivation.

Using employee suggestion schemes to change industrial relations and personnel practices

Suggestion schemes are a way of encouraging all employees to contribute to the more efficient running of an organisation by posting recommendations on, for example, money-saving measures or ways of reducing waste, in return for a small financial reward or other form of recognition.

Advantages	Problems/Concerns
Encourages greater involvement by employees in business improvement activities.	Less committed employees can undermine it by trivial suggestions.
May save money in the long run.	Costs can escalate if all suggestions are rewarded.
Does not discriminate between employees on status or other formal basis.	Can discriminate informally in that some areas may be more susceptible to useful suggestions than others.
Can support a general environment of personal commitment to the organisation.	By emphasising individual solutions and rewards, does not necessarily further team-working goals.

Initiative Areas Interconnected with Industrial Relations and Personnel Practices

Executives, senior managers and other change agents involved in changing industrial relations and personnel practices in a direction complementary to teamwork may find it useful to keep in mind other interconnected change initiatives. An industrial relations framework that encourages flexibility and cross-training will only frustrate employees if corresponding changes in work design and related training developments are not forthcoming. Persisting difficulties with quality, manufacturing and engineering systems can reinforce the powerlessness of the employees and block progress on self-direction.

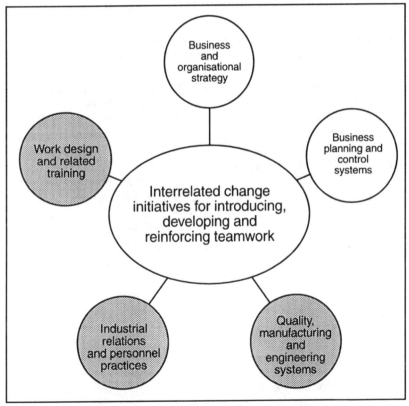

Figure 9.1. Initiative areas interconnected with industrial relations and personnel practices.

[225]

A Case of Failed Teamwork Due to Industrial Relations and Personnel Practices

Newstyle Ltd, which makes a range of fashion accessories, is a division of a US-based multi-national company with sites producing similar products in various parts of the world. It has a mainly female work force which is engaged almost exclusively in assembly operations. The site is fully unionised. In recent years the parent company changed its business strategy and moved to create global competition among the sites. This meant that each factory was required to compete for a proportion of the total business. As new lines develop, they are awarded to the site which can demonstrate the lowest costs.

In order to compete at this international level, local management has been faced with the need to cut operating costs and improve product quality, while not increasing the total wage bill. In trying to meet these needs, the company has made a number of changes to its manufacturing and engineering systems. In its assembly areas it has experimented with different layouts with team-like groupings and has increased levels of automation. It was found that by aggregating some processes and introducing a form of cellular layout with small teams, productivity improved. Job descriptions – which were based on traditional work design principles of simple mechanical tasks – became an issue for the trade union, on the basis that they believed there should be a relationship between payment grade and task. Cellular working meant that jobs became more complex and union shop stewards argued that they should be re-evaluated and rewarded accordingly.

The General Manager then authorised a redesign of the payment system but simultaneously undermined it by announcing that there would be no pay increases. He also moved ahead with the introduction of JIT and an MRPII system. These required the women operatives to take on the further responsibility for monitoring quality. The General Manager saw this technological solution, combined with teamwork, as the way to achieve increased productivity. He took the line that the site would lose business if working practices did not change. At the same time, he was not prepared to allow the payment and grading system to be redesigned for cell-based teamwork by providing the necessary funds. He informed the union that no one would get any more money until productivity was increased. The union responded by saying that he would not get the productivity increase he wanted unless he paid more for more complex and demanding jobs.

A stalemate developed between the two sides, with the General Manager unable to move forward on teamwork because he was unable to gain the cooperation of the trade union. The failure to address issues in the payment and grading systems meant that he was unable to obtain the quality and productivity gains he needed.

Questions for Understanding Industrial Relations and Personnel Practices

- To what extent do the human resource policies reinforce or discourage the motivation required for successful teamwork? Consider all aspects: planning, recruiting, selecting, compensating, training, developing (including careers), communicating and consulting.
- What factors in the company's industrial relations environment are likely to help or hinder the introduction of teamwork?
- What kinds of communications methods are being used in the organisation, how effective are they and how appropriate are they for teamwork?
- To what extent does the payment and grading system support the kinds of behaviour consistent with teamwork?
- What kind of appraisal systems are currently in place? How might they be altered, or new ones introduced, to support teamworking goals? Think about appraisal for operational teams, managers, and support functions.
- What other methods for recognition and reward are currently in use? How might they be altered, or new ones introduced, to reinforce teamworking?

[227]

Further Reading

Adams, L. 1993. Time for a change: forging labour-management partnerships. *Occasional Paper No. 52*. London: Advisory, Conciliation and Arbitration Service (ACAS).

Ford, C. 1994. Teamwork: key issues and developments. *Occasional Paper No. 54*. London: ACAS.

Gilbert, R.D. 1985. What do you know about participative management? *Chemical Engineering* , 1st April.

Incomes Data Services Ltd. 1987. Performance appraisal of manual workers. *IDS Bulletin*, Study No. 390, July.

James, G. 1988. Performance appraisal. *Occasional Paper No. 40*. London: ACAS, Work Research Unit.

Ridley, T.M. 1992. Motivating and rewarding employees: some aspects of theory and practice. *Occasional Paper No. 51*. London: ACAS.

10

Continuously Developing Teams

Executives and senior managers feel attracted to teamwork as a vision because of its potential strategic advantages in terms of cost reduction, quality enhancement and increased innovation. But the time, effort and resources necessary simply to agree an initial phase of work design and industrial relations can wear out the best of organisations. The vision of what is possible tends to diminish in the light of difficulties with implementation. Many companies settle for less than an optimal realisation of teamwork because they do not know how to develop the teams once they are formed. For some, arriving at the point where teams have been formed becomes the destination – not the starting point.

In short, it is not unusual for executives and senior managers to feel disappointed in the competence and performance demonstrated by teams. The extent that compatible changes have not been made across the organisation is the extent to which teamwork will not achieve its potential strategic advantages in terms of cost, quality and innovation. By making compatible changes within and across the following five aspects of organisation, an environment can be created in which teams develop towards ever greater self-regu-lation. These areas of change initiative have been described in detail in previous chapters of this book.

1. Business and organisational strategy
2. Work design and related training developments
3. Manufacturing and quality systems
4. Company planning and control systems
5. Industrial relations and personnel practice.

Self-regulation – a team's capacity to manage and develop itself across a range of dimensions of competence and perfor-mance – is the missing ingredient in most poorly functioning teams. This is true regardless of whether the team is an opera-tional one, a service one or a cross-functional one. Disappointments about teamworking usually are caused by disappointments in the motivation of employees to behave according to the principles of self-regulation.

Motivating with Self-Regulation

Improved motivation has been linked consistently to team-work. Indeed, improved motivation and decreased alienation stand as significant reasons for discarding Taylorism in favour of a new work design. This consistent link suggests that the role of individual motivation in teamwork is well understood and demonstrated. Unfortunately, this is not the case.

Multiple theories exist about what motivates people. Indeed, entire textbooks have been written just summarising these theories. Motivation is a complex area of human behav-iour, and individuals may act very differently in the same conditions. In other words, individuals may be motivated by different factors in their environment for different reasons.

Even so, some evidence exists for the relationship between teamwork and motivation. The few studies undertaken on indi-vidual motivation do suggest that teamwork is motivating for *some* people. One of the problems in assessing the motivational value of teamwork is that initial team membership may itself be contingent on the selection of especially motivated individ-uals.

Concerned about demonstrating rapid success, managers typically pick the 'best' operators for pilot or early phase team development. It is also not uncommon for organisations to ease out or move to other jobs those individuals who do not seem to fit the teamwork ethos. The assessment of 'fit' is made sometimes via psychometric tests or periods of probation. Sometimes, whole categories of people are assumed to be unsuitable – assumptions which do not stand up to research. For example, older employees can be prepared to work in teams as readily as younger people.

As ambiguous as the research has been on individual motivation and teamwork, it has been much less doubtful about the motivation of teams, as a team. That is, evidence for improvements in competence and performance is more consistently positive for a group of individuals working together as a team than it is for individuals. Within a team, individuals still have strengths and weaknesses, good days and bad days. Working well as a group allows one person's strengths to compensate for another person's weakness. One person's bad day can be balanced out by another person's good day. Teams tend to demand better performance from each other when team performance affects everyone. Teams have been known to insist that a consistently poor performer be removed from their team.

Successful teamwork eventually results in less emphasis on individual competence and performance and more on team competence and performance. Measuring team performance, for the most part, means measuring team results. Examining individual contribution, and the process whereby the team deals with differences in contributions, matters primarily in terms of team development, not in terms of team performance.

There are, however, issues about how to sustain the motivation of teams that have been together over a long period of time. Studies of teams over time show that productivity, effectiveness and motivation decline in the longer term unless there are intervening factors. Associated with this decline is the onset of routinisation, where groups, of necessity, settle into habitual routines.

Habitual routines help the group in that they save time and energy for non-routine activities. However, they can also be unhelpful. First, they tend to reduce innovation and continual improvement as the group settles into a comfortable routine which suppresses productive dissent about the way things are done. Second, members can cease to grow in competence or skill, thereby reducing their motivation. Third, they can stop noticing that something different is needed when the external environment changes.

What these findings suggest is that in order to continue to work well together, teams benefit from changes both within their boundaries and in their immediate external environment. This has implications for how jobs are designed and how teams are developed. One study suggests that long-term teams perform better when engaged in complex tasks requiring a high degree of interdependence and operating in an uncertain market. Changing the membership, reconfiguring the group's tasks and changing the leaders can provide a counterweight to routinisation. In terms of the environment in which the team operates, it is helpful to design teams so that they have maximum interfaces with other teams, rather than buffering them around an insulated task. This exposes them to greater environmental change.

One of the most effective ways of sustaining motivation and minimising routinisation, as the socio-technical systems perspective indicates, is to move towards self-directed or self-regulating work groups. Research generally shows such groups have better long-term prognoses than other types of long-term team. Since this type of team has been developed extensively at The Tavistock Institute, it will come as no surprise that the authors of this book advocate motivating teams through self-regulation.

This chapter offers a model for how teams might develop increased competence and performance over time. In other words, what does a reasonable job description for a self-regulating team look like at different stages in its life cycle? When it comes to operational and service teams, nearly 40 years of research and practice has been reported in the teamwork literature. This is not speculation, but experience.

Work Design and the Development of Teams over Time

Considering different supervisory arrangements for teams and different ways teams can relate to support function leads naturally to a consideration of how the design of work changes as teams develop over time. How do the tasks a team performs change as the team becomes more capable of self-direction or self-regulation?

Clearly, as it becomes more capable, a team can become less dependent on an external supervisor, manager, or coach, and also less dependent on outside service departments. The boundary of team responsibilities is likely to become wider as a team becomes more advanced. This does not mean that a self-regulating team becomes totally autonomous, totally separate from the managerial systems of the company or from the support functions – only that the degree of dependence for guidance and advice decreases over time.

In Chapter 6 on work design and related training, three aspects of team structure and boundaries were noted: job design, self-direction and leadership. Each of these aspects can be looked at developmentally. That is, as a team develops greater competence and performance, the job design becomes more complex, the self-direction more responsible and the leadership more integrated into the boundaries of the team. In Figure 10.1 this development is illustrated by a diagonal, dotted line. Moving up from a skeletal, basic level of performance and competence to an advanced one means that the team's responsibilities increase while involvement decreases from managerial and technical personnel.

A team's potential development can be charted across three dimensions of performance and competence and through five levels of competence and performance. The three dimensions of performance and competence can be understood, perhaps more simply, as the three broad categories of the group-based job description. These categories, with the relevant elements of the job listed under them, are:

1. Managing core, short-term responsibilities within the area of the team

[233]

- Basic job competence and skill profile
- Group and individual motivation
- Personnel administration
- Special competence

2. Managing wider short-term responsibilities jointly with others

- Coordination with like groups
- Coordination with unlike groups
- Setting targets for performance

3. Managing development of operational process and people

- Develop work processes
- Develop work organisation
- Develop individual people and the team as a whole.

First, the team must concern itself with performing the operational task within its immediate arena of responsibility. This will be a particular section of the production process or a product-based cell. Team members must also concern themselves with ensuring the competence of the team, both as a collection of individuals and as a functioning collective. Second, when carrying out these two tasks, there will be times when the team requires assistance from service specialists or from managers. Equally, there will be times when their cooperation will be required with technical and managerial concerns. They must manage these relationships in such a way that task performance and team competence is maintained. Third, in order to develop their competence as a team and their successful performance of the task, team members must engage in people and process improvements.

Within this basic job description, a team can be expected to achieve different levels of competence and performance over time. The levels evolve from minimal standards for performance and competence, through quite reasonable standards, to advanced achievement. Simply, the levels can be labelled as follows:

- Level I: Skeletal. Development towards self-regulation is

embryonic; only the outline shell of the team has been established.

- Level II: Dependent. The teams have begun to make progress, particularly in relation to their own internal development; however, most areas of work require significant input from managers and technical specialists.
- Level III: Limited. The teams perform quite well internally; there is a moderate degree of involvement from managers and technical specialists and the group is just starting to manage development.
- Level IV: Functional. The team is effectively self-regulating in all three categories of its job description; it manages itself but still relies on managers to take difficult decisions and to initiate significant developments.
- Level V: Advanced. The team is completely in charge of itself and its work in all three categories of its job description; managerial and technical staff only intervene when requested to do so or in exceptional circumstances.

The bulk of this chapter describes these levels in more detail. Figure 10.1 illustrates the model resulting from the placement of the three categories of job description on the horizontal, with the five levels of achievement on the vertical. Within each resulting cell, a precise description can be developed of what satisfactory performance and competence, on that particular job duty, would look like. This model has been used by several companies to write job descriptions for their teams and to link the payment system to the level of team achievement.

A Normative Model of Team Development

This model suggests a pattern of development that can be expected from a well-functioning team at different stages of its development. Achieving these possible levels of self-regulation in working groups does not just depend on how well the group develops itself: it depends very much on the degree of self-direction defined for the team by the 'powers that be' in the organisation, and the progress made by managers and technical specialists in helping teams become independent.

Dimensions of performance and competence →

	MANAGING CORE SHORT-TERM RESPONSIBILITIES WITHIN A GROUP AREA				MANAGING WIDER SHORT-TERM RESPONSIBILITIES JOINTLY WITH OTHERS			MANAGING DEVELOPMENT OF OPERATIONAL PROCESS AND PEOPLE		
	1. Basic job competence	2. Group and individual motivation	3. Personnel administration	4. Special competence	5. Coordination with like groups	6. Liaise with unlike groups	7. Setting targets for performance	8. Develop operational process	9. Develop the work organisation	10. Develop individual people
LEVEL V: ADVANCED	Total capability and versatility			Everyone with special roles			Mutual setting of targets			Career management
LEVEL IV: FUNCTIONAL						Mutual adjustment, task-sharing		Involvement in planning	Initiating development activities	Discipline, hire, fire
LEVEL III LIMITED	Effective cover				Routine and non-routine		Consultation over targets	Identify possibilities		Training some discipline
LEVEL II DEPENDENT					Routine		Knowledge of changing conditions	Problem-solving		Help plan training
LEVEL 1 SKELETAL	Minimal capability and versatility	Minimum coping with problems, changes, use skills to help group	Timekeep, overtime, holidays, safety	No special roles	Mostly done by others outside group		Received targets	Identify problems	Formal participation in delegated tasks	

Levels of competence and performance

Active Responsibility On The Part Of The Working Group

Active Involvement From Managerial & Technical Personnel

Figure 10.1. Possible levels of self-regulation in working groups.
Copyright, 1990: The Tavistock Institute

[236]

Level I: Skeletal Self-Regulation

At this level development towards self-regulation is embryonic only, but the outline shell for a team has been established. Ability to manage core short-term responsibilities within a group area is limited. Individual self-motivation is low and group members work to procedures prescribed to them by managers or technical staff, taking no further initiative beyond the specified procedure. Their ability to manage their internal relationships is low. Conflicts arising from interpersonal differences and from, for instance, perceived inequalities in rewards and grading systems cannot be resolved within the group. This leads to decreased effectiveness and the need for external intervention to resolve problems.

Multi-skilling is minimal, with no one member being able to perform all the basic tasks of the group. They are therefore unable to cover for each other in the event of absenteeism or holidays, having to rely on resources from outside the group. There are no specialities within the group other than the basic job competencies. In order to meet specialist needs, they have to rely on people from outside the group, or else attempt the task collectively rather than trusting individual members to manage it.

Ability to manage wider short-term responsibilities jointly with others is similarly undeveloped. The group is distinctly separate from other groups which are also significant for maintaining operating standards. Task coordination with other groups is done by referring them upwards through the organisational hierarchy. Individuals may initiate ideas themselves, but lack ability, authority or suitable mechanisms for coordinating tasks across groups. As a consequence, there are some problems with quality and maintaining performance levels.

The level I group can carry out some basic tasks of administration and coordination, but managerial and technical staff mainly carry responsibility for ensuring they are carried out. If these staff do not develop procedures to enable team members to take on responsibility for such tasks, they do not get done and a backlog builds up.

Group members are heavily reliant on extensive routine support from technical staff in order to carry out basic tasks and maintain standards. Technical staff themselves may maintain close involvement with basic task performance in order to monitor it. Group members, in turn, may not be clear about their own technical capacities and fail to ask for help, resulting in technical mistakes.

Ability to manage the development of operational processes and of people is limited at this level. Group members tend to be far too caught up in learning basic tasks and in understanding how to work as part of a group to begin developing innovative work methods. Both innovations and implementation plans will originate wholly with managerial and technical staff. Similarly, these staff will tend to act as a buffer against external changes, interpreting the impact of these changes in terms of local requirements (such as alterations in production schedules) to the group, but not involving the group in decisions in the wider organisation.

Inter-group and cross-functional cooperation are generally lacking. There may be evidence of conflicts and poor coordination across the various organisational boundaries, including across shifts. Consultation processes are insufficient and mechanisms for communicating across the organisation are inadequate.

Level II: Dependent Self-Regulation

Groups have begun to make progress, particularly in relation to the internal development of the group. The main areas of dependency are in the need to involve managerial and technical staff in interfacing with other groups and with the wider organisation.

In terms of managing core short-term responsibilities within the group, most group members are adequately self-motivated and responsible, although those who are not are still being tolerated. Basic task performance is satisfactory. Some capacity to identify problems has developed, but group members do not yet take responsibility for working through solutions. They suffer from a lack of clarity about the extent and limits of their own authority.

There is still a clear division of labour with limited duplication of skills, but it is adequate to allow for some cover for absences. Cross-training is taking place. A few group members are developing greater competencies in three main areas – a particular basic task which enables them to train others, an administrative task, and expertise in a non-routine job which is essential to group performance. However, the majority have yet to develop a speciality. Confidence in delegation within the group has yet to develop and specialists from outside continue to be needed.

Generally, the group is working effectively, without major conflict or inequities, but is still reliant on managerial and technical staff for help in maintaining or developing its working relationships. Members may deny that there are any problems in the internal relationships of the group, while those outside may be more aware of blocks to effectiveness.

In relation to managing wider short-term responsibilities jointly with others, there is still significant separation between the group and like groups. Coordination between groups has developed thorough formal, lateral channels, enabling the managerial hierarchy to be bypassed, but resort to that hierarchy is still needed to sort out conflicts over, or lack of recognition of, areas of responsibility.

The group can perform all administrative and coordination activities for routine, same-shift management as well as for cross-shift coordination. It coordinates satisfactorily with groups of a like kind (e.g. production to production to production, service to service groups). Managerial and technical staff still have major influence over these activities between unlike groups (e.g. production to service) and over wider organisational issues.

Technical competence levels within the group have increased and operating standards are generally maintained, with fewer mistakes. There is more internal reliance before assistance is requested from technical staff, but resort to them remains fairly frequent.

In managing the development of operational processes and of people, group members are now working together with technical staff to identify improvements in working methods, but technical and managerial staff tend to plan and implement the changes themselves.

There is increasing awareness at this level of the impact of changes in the wider environment on the group's work. Such changes are communicated to the group by managers but they retain the role of translating the implications into, for instance, changes in work schedules. Meanwhile, at least one group member participates in department or section-wide administrative and coordination forums, but the majority are not informed or consulted about department or section-wide issues and take no initiative themselves to find out about them. Thus organisation-wide involvement at this level is low.

Level III: Limited Self-Regulation

At this level, the group performs quite well internally. Involvement by managerial and technical staff in interface activities between like groups continues to a moderate degree. The group is beginning to develop responsibility for managing interfaces with the wider organisation, but managers retain a primary involvement with this.

In terms of managing core short-term responsibilities within a group area, all group members are now showing self-motivation and responsibility to the group. Basic task performance is good. Problems are identified and some group members now take responsibility for resolving them through consultation with the group. However, they will also need to consult outside the group in order to implement solutions.

At least half of the group members have basic competence in multiple jobs within the group's remit and they can cover for all absences within the group. Job rotation is in progress and cross-training continues. At least half of the members have developed specialities necessary to the group and the possibility of delegation of certain tasks to individuals frees the group to concentrate collectively on issues which actually require the whole group to be involved. There remains an absence of competence in many specialities, necessitating referral to managerial or technical staff.

The group is able to take responsibility for managing its own internal difficulties and can assess, realistically, its own performance as a group and act upon that assessment. Managerial and technical staff are called in to assist only rarely.

In managing wider short-term responsibilities jointly with others, some breakdown of the distinct separations between groups is now apparent and cooperation between groups is strong, with some sharing of tasks. While clear demarcations of task responsibilities are still apparent, the use of formal channels of communication between groups has lessened. In addition to its routine administrative and coordination tasks, the group is able to manage some non-routine activities, such as discipline, itself. It is also able to cooperate across group boundaries in managing certain of these tasks, although managers still need to oversee the process. At this point, integration of other disciplines into the group is possible. The group is technically self-reliant, makes no technical errors and rarely requires support from technical staff.

In managing the development of operational processes and of people, members are able to discuss, under managerial leadership, the implications of environmental changes for their work schedules and task performance. They are consulted by managers in setting targets but target-setting remains the responsibility of managers.

Increased involvement in non-routine administration and coordination with unlike groups produces a new kind of intergroup conflict as earlier competencies developed by the group are challenged. Group members show ability to sort out these more complex relationships with other groups. At the same time, a greater number of members are involved in departmental or section administration and at least one member is involved in organisation-wide coordination.

Level IV: Functional Self-Regulation

This corresponds to self-regulation proper. The group can manage itself effectively internally and in relation to other like groups. Such groups are well able to manage interfaces with the rest of the organisation but still rely on managers to take the lead in these areas of decision-making.

In terms of managing core short-term responsibilities within a group area, the group continues to show a high level of self-motivation and responsibility to the group. Problem identification and resolution enables operating standards not only to be maintained but produces steady, small improvements. Some issues about full commitment to the group remain and the resulting inequities may cause problems for the group.

All members are cross-trained on multiple basic tasks and at least a third of the group is trained on all basic tasks. The group can now take responsibility for all intra-group cross-

[241]

training and a small number of members now start cross-training in relevant basic tasks within other groups significant for maintaining operating standards.

All members have now developed a speciality necessary to the overall functioning of the group and some are developing additional ones. Specialists are beginning to train others and there is general acknowledgement and encouragement of further specialist learning within the group. The group continues to take responsibility for its own internal development and for finding creative solutions to intra-group problems.

In managing wider short-term responsibilities jointly with others, groups continue to operate a high level of integration with other groups and to refine their intergroup relationships. They continue to carry out all routine administrative and coordination tasks satisfactorily and take on, in addition to existing ones, the non-routine tasks of selection, dismissal and training.

Backup from technical staff is needed only in exceptional circumstances and when invoked is given in the form of coaching, with the group taking responsibility to work out solutions.

In managing the development of operational processes and of people, group members share equal responsibility with managerial and technical staff for identifying improvements in working methods. Technical staff function as guides and monitors, involving group members in the planning and implementation of changes.

Group members set their own targets and plan short and long-term tasks based on information provided by managers. They discuss progress with managers and do their own planning of any adjustments necessary. Managerial and technical staff similarly function as monitors, assisting where needed. Groups continue to operate effectively in relation to other groups and the wider organisation. Groups encourage each other to develop further involvement in departmental, sectional and wider organisational issues.

Level V: Advanced Self-Regulation

At this level, the group is completely in charge of itself and its work. It manages its relationships throughout the organisation effectively and creatively, operating in partnership mode. Management and technical staff intervene only when requested to do so and in exceptional circumstances.

In relation to managing core short-term responsibilities within a group area, the ideal of highly self-motivated individuals taking responsibility for their own group's performance is fully realised. Task performance is invariably excellent. Technical problems are identified and resolved, both within the group and across group boundaries.

All group members can carry out all basic tasks within the group. They do all the training of incoming members and also cross-train members of other groups that are significant for maintaining operating standards. All group members are trained in several areas of speciality necessary for the functioning of the group and participate in continuing learning and training among themselves.

In managing wider short-term responsibilities jointly with others, the effective performance reached at level IV in administrative and coordination activities is maintained at a high level. At the same time, the group is completely technically self-reliant and members are invited into other parts of the organisation to help in resolving technical problems which relate to similar operational standards.

In managing the development of operational processes and of people, the group is able, technically and administratively, to identify, plan and implement improvements to working methods. They inform managers and technical staff of these plans and receive approval for capital expenditure over a specified limit. They communicate their findings to other groups and cooperate as necessary with those groups affected by the plans.

The group was already able to respond appropriately to changes in the external environment. At this level of self-regulation, group members are actively involved in identifying such potential changes and initiating ideas for dealing with them without recourse to managers. At the same time, they cooperate to a high level with managerial and technical staff. Group members continue to resolve conflicts, facilitate communication with other parts of the organisation and to encourage other groups to be involved in organisation-wide matters.

Development towards Self-Regulation

The process of development towards self-regulation is likely to be uneven. Experience suggests that aspects of development relating to the first of the categories – that of internal functioning – are likely to progress more rapidly than the other two categories. This is because teams have more direct control over their internal functioning than they do over other teams or managerial and technical personnel.

However, progress in all the aspects of the first category will, in turn, produce development in the group's ability to manage its relationships with other like groups. That, in turn, will increase the group's ability to address issues in the wider organisation. The developmental process outlined here can be used as a basis for bringing in a group-based payment system, making further reward contingent on the achievement of all aspects of self-regulation at a particular level.

This model of the development of self-regulation should not be taken as a blueprint which must be followed in every particular. In practice, organisations have to take decisions based on their own needs and capacities. There may be compelling technical, administrative or market reasons to limit the degree of autonomy available to production or service teams in certain spheres of their operation.

Self-regulating behaviour on the part of individual members and the team as a whole results from a combination of:

- The personalities and capabilities of the individuals
- The culture and capabilities of the group, and
- The environment surrounding the team.

All three of these characteristics of self-regulation require compatible change initiatives across all five aspects of organisation. Teams fail to achieve their potential because executives and senior managers lack awareness of this fact, or refuse to make changes necessary for reinforcing and developing individual and group capabilities and the environment in which those capabilities can be exercised. For example, some executives refuse to alter the payment system so it rewards behaviours consistent with teamwork. They hope for teamwork while they continue to pay for individual performance. Another example: operational teams frequently flounder because they can not procure the services necessary for taking responsibility for their product or process – changes in the structure and purposes of service departments need to be made. If a company would like their teams to achieve more than skeletal self-regulation, comprehensive change is required.

Further Reading

Neumann, J.E. and Holti, R.W. 1990. Possible levels of self-regulation in working groups. Working paper. London: The Tavistock Institute.

11

The TIM Methodology for Planning and Sequencing Comprehensive Change

In researching the challenges of reinforcing and developing teamworking in manufacturing, we have found that executives and senior managers tend to identify three types of situation during a comprehensive change programme when issues of planning and sequencing are especially difficult. In the first instance, an overall business strategy has been outlined and the decisions and changes necessary for implementing that strategy need to be agreed, with a corresponding plan for sequencing and relating various strands of implementation. In the second instance, responsible people in the organisation, already involved in implementing comprehensive changes, are experiencing difficulties of the sort where developments in one function or aspect of organisation – or lack thereof – are blocking developments in another. The third instance arises when the organisation has completed a programme of fairly satisfactory changes and the next stage of development needs to be identified.

Interconnections between change initiatives in the five basic areas of organisational change relevant to teamwork - and uncertainty in how to manage the whole picture - are fundamental characteristics of all three of these situations. They make planning and sequencing difficult. This chapter presents a practical framework that people in organisations can use to guide themselves in making planning and sequencing decisions, taking account of interconnections and uncertainties. The methodology draws heavily on an approach to decision-making first developed at The Tavistock Institute during the 1970s, and further elaborated by Friend and Hickling (1988), known as 'strategic choice'.

From here, the chapter first briefly introduces some ways of thinking about interconnections between change initiatives and uncertainties in carrying them out. It then offers an overview of the five-step methodology, before presenting a more detailed guide to each one. This detail is illustrated with a case. The final section reviews the overall purpose of the Methodology, and describes a number of ways and formats in which it may be put to practical use.

Interconnections and Uncertainties in Comprehensive Change

This interconnected nature of change initiatives is one source of uncertainty in planning and managing comprehensive change in general and managing teamwork-related changes, in particular. There is uncertainty because change initiatives depend on one another. From the perspective of the main decision-takers in an organisation, a planning and sequencing methodology is needed which assists them in:

- Deciding which aspect of organisation to change in what order
- Dealing thoughtfully with the complicated relationships between interrelated aspects of organisation
- Facilitating cross-functional cooperation between those middle managers and technical specialists charged with the task of implementing changes
- Managing the tensions and competing pressures and conflicts of interest inevitable in comprehensive change.

However, even within the boundaries of a particular change initiative, it is difficult to predict at the outset precisely what will work, because not all the information is available at the outset. There are sources of uncertainty in addition to those stemming from the interconnected nature of change initiatives, which on the face of it make planning and sequencing changes even more daunting.

The idea of planning in the face of multiple forms of uncertainty is central to the 'strategic choice' approach to decision-making developed by Friend and Hickling (1988). They identify three broad classes of uncertainty which are readily applicable to analysing the situations faced by those responsible for planning organisational changes associated with teamworking:

- Uncertainties in the working environment, requiring some form of data gathering or investigation to resolve them (UE)
- Uncertainties about guiding values calling for some sort of values clarification process (UV)
- Uncertainties about related choices or developments requiring interactions with those outside the area being addressed (UR).

The concepts and techniques of strategic choice offer an approach to planning and sequencing interrelated change activities which focuses above all on the management of these different varieties of uncertainty. Friend and Hickling speak of finding a balance along five dimensions which characterise the basic 'dilemmas of practice' in planning in situations where there are many interconnected interests and decisions. There are balances to be struck between adopting:

- A more focused or synoptic treatment of the scope of issues addressed
- A simplifying or a more elaborating treatment of complexity
- A more reactive or a more interactive treatment of conflict
- A more reducing or a more accommodating treatment of uncertainty
- A more exploratory or more decisive treatment of progress through time

[248]

The Five Basic Steps

The TIM Methodology draws on the concepts and techniques of strategic choice, as well as large group and inter-group intervention techniques. It offers a framework that people responsible for managing changes in organisations can use to guide them in finding an appropriate balance in their solutions to the dilemmas of practice in planning and sequencing changes that are both interdependent and uncertain in their precise effects.

There are five basic steps in the methodology, although in actual use there may need to be several iterations through two or more steps, as some uncertainties are removed and new ones emerge. These five steps, summarised below, offer a structure for a large-group planning and sequencing workshop, attended by all those in an organisation who have a significant role in leading or facilitating organisational or technical change initiatives, drawn from all departments or functions. For a 400-person manufacturing organisation, with perhaps seven or eight main departments, between 20 and 40 people would need to be involved in the workshop, with between three and five attending from each department, in addition to senior management with plant or enterprise-wide responsibilities.

The five steps move through a quite straightforward sequence of pencil and paper activities which start with a simple form of mapping of issues and end with a set of commitments from the participants. Participants should be drawn from as wide a constituency as possible in order to attract people likely to be involved in changes in all the five areas, as well as those who may have an interest in interconnections specifically. Also, participants need to reflect the real decision-makers in the company (be they top managers and/or employee representatives and/or significant technical specialists and managers) so that they have direct access to the information likely to emerge from the workshop.

In **step 1** all the members of the workshop are together in a large group with a facilitator. The aim of the first step is to map what people consider to be the important issues in planning and sequencing for teamwork, using the brainstorming technique. The idea is then to group these into areas from which *initiatives for change* can be identified. Everyone then tries to agree on what are the two most important and/or urgent initiative areas to be given priority. These are what will be taken forward to work on for step 2. At the end of this process, the whole group splits up into smaller groups which will have members from all the functions or departments present at the workshop. Each small group takes away its copy of the materials produced in step one.

Step 1: Map issues and identify broad areas for initiatives

Key concepts ◆ Brainstorming issues or problems which give rise to the *need for planned change*
◆ Grouping them into a number of broad areas for initiatives
◆ Considering *importance* and *urgency* in order to select up to two broad areas for priority atten-

---

In **step 2** the aim is to identify, from the areas chosen, which initiatives are likely to be needed to move forward on teamworking. In this step, the smaller group asks itself a series of questions to clarify what these initiatives should be, what dilemmas attached to them, how they are connected, whether they are compatible or incompatible with each other, and whether there are other initiative areas not already considered which might affect them. These small groups then dissolve and the members reform into different small groups consisting of people from the same function or department, or working area, again taking their materials from the cross-functional groups with them.

Step 2: Identify a set of interconnected and compatible initiatives for more detailed planning and sequencing

Key concepts ◆ Identifying possible *initiatives*
◆ Exploring possible *interconnections* and *incompatibilities*

In **step 3** the aim is to start moving towards identifying what *actions* can begin to be taken. This will involve deciding which are the initiatives where actions should be taken first. The group then identifies what are the dilemmas and uncertainties it will have to consider or choices it will have to make in order to make any progress. It then proceeds to chart possible actions that could be taken in the light of these dilemmas and choices, and further work or explorations that could be done to make actions possible. The functional groups then dissolve and all the members come back together into a large group with their charts.

Step 3: Clarify initial actions to be taken, uncertainties that make action difficult and explorations to address them

Key concepts   ◆ Selecting *focal initiatives*
                ◆ Identifying the main *dilemmas* or *areas of choice* in making progress with these
                ◆ Categorising the *uncertainties* that make choosing difficult
                ◆ Identifying *actions* and *explorations* that make progress possible

---

In **step 4** the aim is to try to agree on what actions and explorations can be taken. All the small groups' charts are put up for everyone to see and their differences and compatibilities are discussed. With the help of a facilitator, the whole group negotiates a consensus, as far as it can, on what *immediate* actions and explorations it will undertake and what actions and explorations it identifies for the *future*. Convenors are appointed for each action or exploration and participants then go back into their functional groups.

Step 4: Agree a 'progress package' of actions and explorations across the whole organisation

Key concepts   ◆ Agreeing *immediate* actions and explorations
                ◆ Identifying *future* actions and explorations that can be considered once the immediate ones are completed

---

In **step 5** the members of the functional groups sort out among themselves what their roles are in carrying forward the agreed actions and explorations. Representatives then go out into other groups and give their views on these roles. Convenors organise meetings with representatives from all the functions who have a role to play in the action or exploration and agree an agenda for moving forward. All participants then come back together and the convenors report on what has been agreed. Everyone decides on when a follow-up meeting will be needed.

> **Step 5: Make commitments across departments**
>
> Key concepts   ◆ Setting up *cross-departmental working groups* for carrying out actions and explorations
> ◆ Agreeing the *next point at which large-group review* will be needed

These are the basic steps of the methodology. They can be repeated as necessary in future meetings – or only the later steps can be repeated – depending on the large group's assessment of its progress.

Guide to the Five Steps of the TIM Methodology

What follows outlines the procedures employed within each step of the methodology, including some case material. Guidelines for each step of the Methodology appear in shaded boxes. The case material is based on a one-and-a-half day workshop involving 25 managers from a vehicles components firm, Carco, with a total workforce of 350.

The context of the workshop was that Carco was concerned about maintaining a traditional strong position in supplying a range of machined components to most of the UK vehicle assemblers. The company was facing increased competition, mainly from oversees suppliers, and was at the same time particularly concerned to win more business with the newer Japanese 'transplant' UK assembly plants. Over the last few years, Carco has introduced new production technologies, particularly computer-numerically controlled (CNC) machine tools, encouraged flexibility amongst shop floor operatives within manufacturing cells, and holds operators responsible for their own quality inspection. Senior management are now concerned that operators within the cells need to become 'teams in the true sense of the word'. They feel that greater flexibility and more concern with waste could increase productivity markedly. At the same time others in the company feel that the whole manufacturing strategy needs looking at, including changing the design of some products to make them easier to manufacture.

The following functions within Carco were represented by the following people at the workshop, in addition to the Managing Director: Quality – 1 director, 1 manager, 1 support specialist; Information Systems – 1 manager, one senior analyst; Finance – 1 director, 1 manager; Commercial – 1 director, 4 managers; Human Resources – 1 director, 1 manager, 2 support specialists; Manufacturing – 1 director, 4 operations managers and 3 engineering managers.

Step 1: Mapping issues and identifying broad areas for initiatives

Configuration: The entire membership of the workshop, working as a large group

(a) Individual participants brainstorm, one thought per card, written as a complete sentence, those issues which they think need to be tackled in introducing, developing or reinforcing teamwork in the company or plant.

(b) The facilitator gathers all the cards together and helps the whole group cluster issues into a set of broad 'initiative areas' using some sort of visual display.

(c) The group agrees labels for the set of initiative areas.

(d) As a basis for grouping decision-making on which of these initiative areas should receive priority for further planning and sequencing, each participant first decides on their own a score for the importance and the urgency of each initiative area. They use the same five-point scale for each score:

1	2	3	4	5
None at all	Minor	Moderate	Considerable	Extreme

The facilitator displays to the group the average and range of the scores for urgency and importance for each broad initiative area.

(e) The group discusses the scores displayed and decides on two broad initiative areas to be given priority. These will probably be one that the group as a whole sees as the most urgent, and another that the group sees as most important. In some cases, high levels of urgency in two or more areas may win out over considerations of impor- tance, or vice versa. As will emerge in Step 2, committing to two initiative areas at this point does not rule out consideration of the effect of other initiative areas on what needs to be done within the selected two areas. The purpose is simply to agree an initial focus for planning and sequencing work to take forward into Step 2.

(f) The whole group prepares to split into a small number, typically three to five, of cross-functional subgroups, with three to eight members each. Each subgroup should have representatives of the main functional groupings present. Each subgroup takes away a record of the two chosen broad initiative areas, and the original lists of issues grouped together during activity (b) under each of the two headings.

Case illustration of Carco: Step 1

Figure 11.1 shows how the issues produced by the group of 25 from Carco were clustered into a number of broad areas for initiative, with some overlaps. The following two pages list the organisational and technical change issues that were grouped

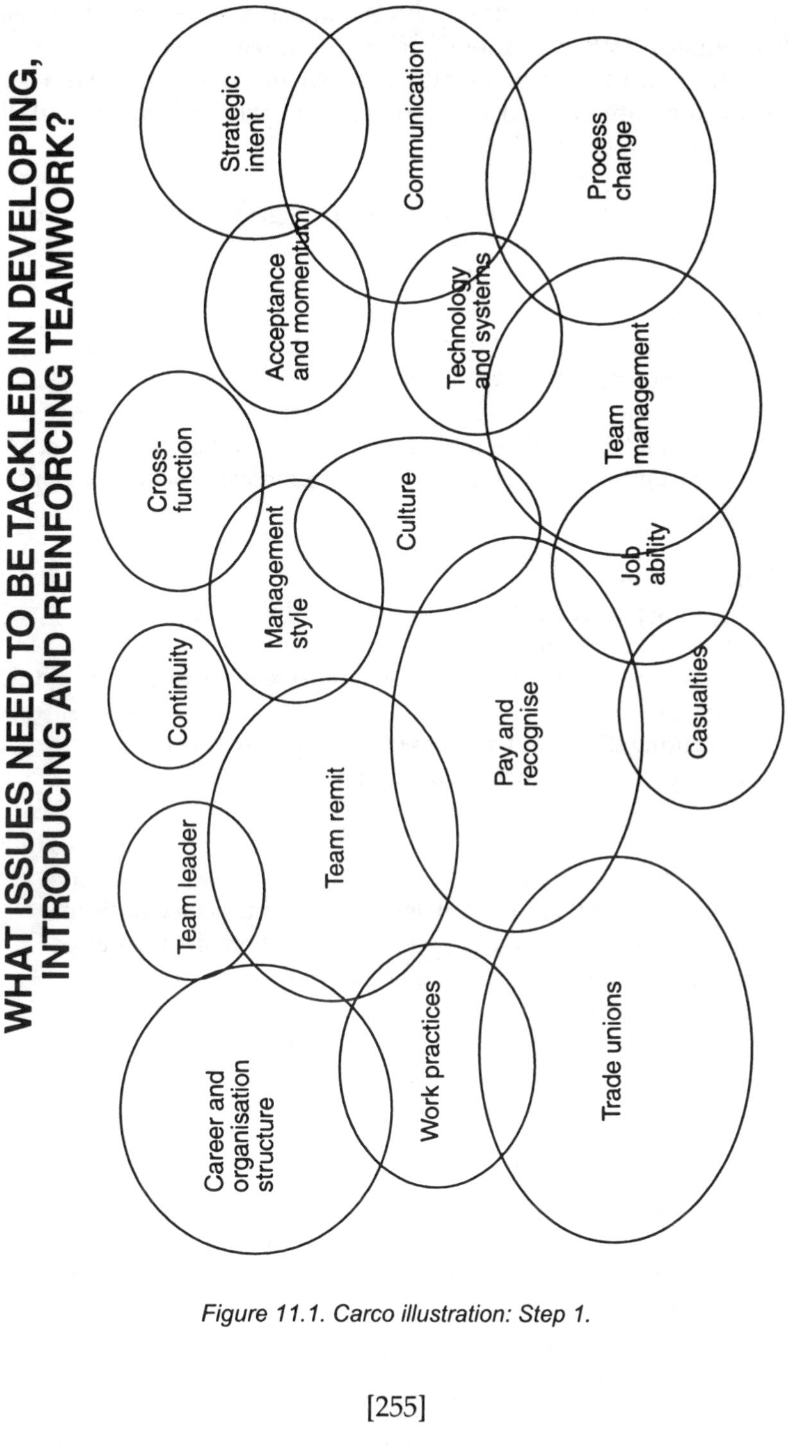

WHAT ISSUES NEED TO BE TACKLED IN DEVELOPING, INTRODUCING AND REINFORCING TEAMWORK?

Figure 11.1. Carco illustration: Step 1.

[255]

together within each of the broad areas. Of the broad areas, 'Strategic Intent' was identified as the most urgent for further attention, and 'Team Remit' as most important. These two were therefore carried forward as the foci for more detailed consideration in Step 2.

What issues need to be takcled in developing, introducing and reinforcing teamwork?

Career and organisation structure
Enhancing career opportunities where 'flatter' structures exist
Career prospects limited by flatter structures
Reduce the number of levels of management
Developing a replacement for hierarchical promotion
Training required for operators to accept increased skills/responsibilities

Work practices
Redesigning jobs for shop floor self-directed work teams
Introduce flexible working skills
Increased job rotation and multi-skilling from operators to middle managers
Implementing different ways of working: review existing practices
Integrating 'service' function into manufacturing teams

Team remit
Establish clear objectives
Providing information mechanisms for the team to take decisions
Determine who the team customer really is: internal/external
Defining boundaries/limitations of the team
Define team roles
Given the widening of existing role boundaries, how do you manage uncertainty? (my role to our role)
How much detail to have prepared at the initiation of the change

Team leader
How to establish team leaders
Deciding remit of, selecting and recruiting team leaders
Changing traditional supervisors into either managers or team leaders
Change the role of 'supervision'

[256]

Trade unions

Revisit IR agreements from the point of view of their compatibilities with teamwork

Gain the support of the unions

Gain the support of trade unions, both full time and operators

Pay and recognition

Implement an employee appraisal scheme

How to design an appraisal and payment system that increases team-working

Change the payment system so it is compatible with teamworking

Elimination of individual bonus payments

Redesigning payment and grading systems to support multi-skilled teams

Incentives rewards need to reinforce collective (team) contribution

Agreeing/shaping reward mechanisms seen as reflecting performance

Develop reward system to reinforce the 'right' kind of behaviour

Eliminate and replace individual reward systems

Finding a method of rewarding good teamworking

How to reward individual performance and team efforts

How to align the reward and recognition process to the new business expectations

Changing 'reward' systems so that they complement rather than contradict team ethos

Rewards should reflect organisational objectives

Continuity

How many changes can the organisation cope with at one time?

What will be the implications on output during transition?

How do we keep the business running while making change at same time?

Casualties

Have clear vision of what happens to casualties

What action needs to be taken in case of redundancy?

What plans do we have to encourage initially those who resist team-work and those who persist to resist?

Remove people from the organisation who do not share team-working values and beliefs

[257]

Cross-function
Reluctance to impart specialist knowledge to team members
Elimination of staff status
How can we have teamworking when, currently, we have process, craft, staff – all on different grading and payment systems?

Management style
Introduce participative management style
Management preparedness to really delegate authority and decision-making
Changing management behaviour to support teamworking
Ensuring management style enables development
Improve the leadership skills of managers
Do we have the right leadership in place to make change happen?
Preparation of middle managers/supervisors for the change in roles on implementing teamwork

Culture
Create environment where individuals and teams can 'take risks'
Change the culture to cooperation
How to identify, support and project role models for the new organisation
Change trusting respecting environment

Job ability
Carrying out assessment of training needs for teamwork and planning training programme
Selection of the team in terms of – size, skills, resources
Team member selection v. targets
Building teams that have the best 'role' profile as well as skill profile
Recognition and planning/training resources to raise awareness/capabilities
Building team/organisation skills
Developing 'teamworking' skills within the team members

Acceptance and momentum
For change there needs to be a perceived gain for individuals to become committed
What security can we provide during change process?
Have we confirmed all the benefits and loss of change process?
Understand and forecast the reaction to change

[258]

What training is required to introduce change?
When change is continuous, how do you keep the initiative going when people want a rest?
Give people time to accept change: moderate pace
How do we generate and maintain interest and enthusiasm?

Process change
How do we introduce people to teamwork? – cascade?
Do we pilot the new structures in one area first of all?
Method of involving teams in decision process (for implementation)

Technology and systems
Clearance of 'blocking' organisational policies and procedure
Simplify company systems
Fear of the introduction of new technology
Influence of technological change
Create systems that help continuous improvement flourish

Team management
How to break up a successful team, when the project ends or objective achieved, without demotivating the individuals
Management and coordination of cross-functional teams

Strategic intent
What if the process fails? – have we an alternative/faceback strategy?
Which areas of the business do we include/exclude in the change process?
Really understanding the stakeholders' objectives
Do we need consensus among top managers before we introduce teamwork?
Establish the business reason for the introduction of teamworking
Do we all have the same view of what we mean by 'teamworking'?
Clear communication of strategy
How to convince senior people that the functional system that made them successful is wrong
How can we convince people that this isn't simply a de-manning or cost-cutting exercise?
The organisation requires alignment to common objectives
The establishment of a business imperative is necessary in most cases

[259]

Communication

Taking people with the change, e.g. culture

Have we communicated to employees why we need to change in order to get cooperation?

Identify and communicate benefits to all concerned

How to communicate plans to the people affected

Teamworking between shift and day environments

Creating environment where team fulfils role within larger team (team ↔ team dialogue)

How to involve a large group in a change that affects them all.

Need three-way communication channels that work

Step 2: Identifying a set of interconnected and compatible initiatives for more detailed planning and sequencing

Configuration: Small groups with cross-departmental membership

Working in parallel, each group does the following:

(a) Using a flip chart and markers, the group begins to produce a diagram of possible initiatives by first drawing two large circles near the centre of the page, representing the two broad initiative areas chosen at the end of Step 1.

(b) Within each broad area for initiatives, the group brainstorms issues where *initiatives* are likely to be needed, i.e. aspects of the organisation where there is a need for some sort of decision about whether or how to carry out planned change. If the group finds it difficult to agree what exactly is an issue or aspect of organisation, members can simply be asked to produce questions in any or all of the three forms below, prompted by their consideration of the two broad areas for initiative:

- What do we do about _____?
- How do we do _____?
- Do we do _____ or not?

[260]

The words used to fill in the blanks can then be listed and, with some grouping to avoid repetition, will form a list of more detailed initiatives or aspects of organisation where change is needed within each of the two broad areas for initiative.

(c) The group then assigns labels to each of these initiatives or aspects of organisation where decisions about how to proceed with planned change are needed. To remind everyone that there is some sort of dilemma associated with each initiative, each label should finish with a question mark, e.g. PAY SYSTEM? BOUNDARIES?

The group then attaches each initiative label to a small bubble within the larger circle representing the corresponding broad area for initiatives. If there are more than five bubbles within each circle, the group will need to eliminate some, based on lesser importance or urgency.

(d) With a red marker, someone connects those initiative bubbles where making progress would appear to be incompatible, in the sense that making progress with one initiative would make it virtually impossible to proceed with the other. With a blue marker, someone connects the initiative bubbles where there are clear interconnections, in the sense that making progress with either depends on progress being made with the other, and so there is likely to be mutual influence between the form that progress takes across the two.

(e) The group considers whether there are other possible initiatives outside the two broad areas for initiatives chosen at the end of Step 1 which might affect the course of initiatives within these two broad areas. The initiative bubbles currently on the diagram may need to be connected to some additional initiative bubbles stemming from a consideration of the larger issue map produced during Step 1. If so, mark these bubbles, together with appropriate initiative labels (ending with question marks) on the diagram, showing them outside

[261]

the two larger circles, but with blue lines showing how they are connected to the initiatives under consideration within the two broad areas for initiatives.

(f) Finally, members produce a number of copies of the diagram showing a web of interconnected possible initiatives, to take with them into the new functionally-based small groups responsible for Step 3.

Case illustration of Carco: Step 2

The next two figures show the diagram the group produced indicating how the different possible initiatives are interconnected and a set of interconnected change initiatives identified by one of Carco's cross-functional groups.

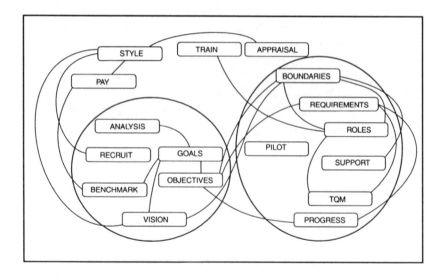

Broad Area	Initiative Label	Description
STRATEGIC INTENT	Analysis?	Undertake strategic analysis of the business, against its markets and competitors
	Benchmark?	Compare overall performance with key aspects of comparable leading organisations
	Goals?	Set key business goals, and clarify broad product strategy
	Vision?	Define overall vision and values for the organisation
	Recruit?	Review top team membership and recruit or select to fill gaps
	Objectives?	Set operational objectives and measures
TEAM REMIT	Boundaries?	Define boundaries of team responsibilities
	Roles?	Define jobs within teams and competences required
	Support?	Set up supports for team development, e.g. facilitation, coaching
	Progress?	Define measures of team performance and ways of establishing progress
	Requirements?	Establish customer requirements for teams
	TQM?	Provide TQM education and training
	Pilot?	Set up team pilot
OTHER RELATED INITIATIVES	Style?	Identify appropriate management style and behaviours and communicate them
	Train?	Train managers for appropriate skills, including leadership
	Pay?	Review pay systems and adapt to reward new behaviours and remove demarcations between groups
	Appraisal?	Set up system for assessing current skills and development needs

[263]

Step 3: Clarifying initial actions to be taken, uncertainties that make action difficult and explorations to address them

Configuration: Small groups composed of all participants from the same department. For many organisations these will be function-based groups, e.g. operations, human resources, manufacturing services, commercial. For organisations with product-based structures, some groups will be product-centred.

(a) Each new group considers the diagrams of interconnected possible initiatives produced by each of the cross-functional groups. From the perspective of the new group's functional area, it discusses which two to four *focal initiatives* are the ones where activity should be undertaken first. This may involve grouping some overlapping initiative labels used by the different groups during Stage 2 into new initiative labels. If it is immediately clear where priorities should lie, the group can undertake a more or less structured comparison of priorities between a larger number of possible initiatives. Considerations of urgency, importance, the extent to which a possible initiative is connected to others, or is in some other sense controversial, are all relevant criteria that offer reasons why a particular initiative should be prioritised.

(b) The group discusses what making progress would look like for each of these two to four focal initiatives. The group should go as far as identifying the first major point of choice or dilemma they would encounter in carrying the initiative forward. The dilemma or choice may, for example, be whether or not to proceed with the initiative at all, whether to go with one particular type of solution as opposed to another, or whether to use one particular method or approach for arriving at a solution as opposed to another. Once this choice point has been identified, the group identifies the broad options that its members see themselves as facing – probably two, but possibly three or more.

(c) For each focal initiative, the group produces on a flip chart a simple balance sheet of advantages and/or disadvantages for the options just identified. Once advantages and disadvantages have been listed for the different options, it may #be useful to summarise the group's thinking on the options for each focal initiative in terms of their scores on a number of comparison areas, which summarise the advantages and disadvantages taken into account. With this accomplished, the group may be in a position to agree a firm recommendation for action along the lines of a particular option for one or more of the focal initiatives. If agreement is not easy, the group should not force a consensus.

(d) Whether or not agreement has been reached on how to proceed with the focal initiatives, the listing during (c) of the advantages of different options under each one can lead to clarification as to the nature of uncertainties that make deciding how to proceed difficult. The group looks at the flip charts just produced for each focal initiative and considers the question:

What makes it difficult to decide?

Answers can be displayed listed on a new flip chart headed 'Uncertainties'. If there is time, the group can consider each uncertainty to decide if it predominantly stems from:

- Lack of knowledge of the environment (UE)
- Lack of agreement between the different stakeholders about values or policy direction, or general lack of clarity (UV), or
- The need to wait for a related decision to be made or initiative carried out (UR).

(e) The group considers the list of uncertainties that make decision or further action with the focal initiatives difficult, and identifies the ones which are most important –

probably between one or three. This provides a basis for considering the kind of exploration which will reduce uncertainty sufficiently for progress to be made. Explorations may take the form of :

- Some form of empirical investigation, i.e. gathering some data to reduce UE
- Convening a policy-making session with relevant to decision-makers to clarify values or policy directions, or requesting clarification from decision-makers to reduce UV

or

- Encouraging progress with a related decision area, or a decision to wait until progress has been made elsewhere, to reduce UR.

(f) If there are a number of possible explorations put forward for each focal initiative, the group may need to compare their potential benefits in terms of increasing confidence to choose one or other course of action against the cost of carrying them out and the delay involved. This will provide a basis for judging trade-offs in terms of selecting the most effective exploration to make progress with each focal initiative.

(g)Having considered possible actions and explorations needed for the identified focal initiatives, the group can now give some consideration to the kinds of things that might be done once the first round of actions and explorations have been completed. The group can record its discussions in the form of a short list of future or deferred actions and explorations. It may also be possible to list some options for each of these, and to note how the choice to be made will depend on what emerges from the first round of explorations.

(h)The group summarises its deliberations in terms of preparing a flip chart describing:

> - The *focal initiatives* its members see themselves as being involved in
> - Any *actions* they consider need to be taken immediately
> - The *explorations* that should be put in hand immediately
>
> and
>
> - The second round of *future actions* and *future explorations* that may then be relevant

Case study of Carco: Step 3

Four department-based groups worked in parallel. They labelled themselves as:

1. *Overall business strategy,* consisting of the managing director, finance, manufacturing, and commercial directors
2. *Human resources,* including personnel, training and organisational development
3. *Manufacturing and engineering,* including operations and manufacturing engineering,
   and
4. *Manufacturing support services,* including quality assurance, quality systems, and accounting.

The following pages illustrate the work produced by each of the four groups. For each group, there is first of all a chart where the group noted its proposed focal initiatives, the choices associated with them, the uncertainties underlying the choices, and the explorations they see as reducing the uncertainties. This is followed by the group's proposed 'progress package'.

[267]

GROUP: Overall Business Strategy

Focal initiatives	Key choices or dilemmas	Uncertainties that make choosing difficult	Possible explorations
Produce strategic analysis and business objectives	Which strategic process to use – more or less structured, more or less detailed?	Experiences of different approaches on board (UE) Other available approaches (UE) Cost and time scales for different approaches (UE)	Investigate different strategic approaches, assign someone to do this
Clarify and communicate organisational vision	Should it be put together participatively or not?	How will people react to different ways of formulating the vision? (UV) How detailed or open should a vision be? (UE)	Carry out discussions with different groups and departments to establish levels of interest in being involved in formulating the vision Find other examples of organisational visions

GROUP: Overall Business Strategy

Initiatives	Now		Future	
	Actions	Explorations	Actions	Explorations
Produce strategic analysis and business objectives	Initiate business strategy process	Investigate different strategic processes	Decide strategic process to use	Undertake market analysis Undertake competitive analysis Identify competitive advantage and clarify business direction Set business objectives and time scales Assign resources – people, money, facilities
Clarify and communicate organisation vision	Initiate process for defining vision	Sound out views of department managers on process to be used Explore what needs to go into a vision – what headings should we use?	Decide vision process and headings	Carry out consultations with departments according to the process

GROUP: Manufacturing and Engineering

Focal initiatives	Key choices or dilemmas	Uncertainties that make choosing difficult	Possible explorations
Develop operational plan for manufacturing	Improve quality and reduce waste with current processes and products vs. Design new processes around a smaller number of simpler products	Willingness of customers to accept easier to make parts (UE) Need to fit with strategic objectives and product strategy defined by top team (UR) Lack of knowledge of implications of technological developments for costs and skills (UE)	Market research – sensitivity analysis 'Would you accept a substitute?' Seek to influence product strategy and marketing strategy to minimise manufacturing hassle Undertake technological forecasting and evaluation Undertake skill audit of total workforce
Define management behaviour and attitudes	Build on current strengths vs. Define what is needed and change people if necessary	Lack of knowledge of what managers and employees currently want (UV/UE) Lack of knowledge of implications of new strategies for required behaviour and attitudes	Carry out job analysis and focus groups to find out what managers and employees want

GROUP: Manufacturing and Engineering

Initiatives	Now		Future	
	Actions	Explorations	Actions	Explorations
Develop operational plan for manufacturing	Request involvement in overall strategy formulation process, particularly concerning product strategy	Undertake technological forecasting and evaluation for new production technology. Market research implication of easier-to-make products. Carry out skill audit of total workforce	Develop operational plan strategic cost objectives	Investigate effective cost management techniques e.g. Activity Based Costing (ABC)
Define management behaviours and attitudes		Carry out job analysis and focus groups to find out what managers and employees are looking for in their jobs	Define management behaviours needed to see through the new strategy	

GROUP: Human Resources

Focal initiatives	Key choices or dilemmas	Uncertainties that make choosing difficult	Possible explorations
Identify company objectives and mission	Market shaped vs. Human resources shaped strategy	Lack of knowledge of how well top team really understand HR issues (UV) Willingness of top team to involve HR at an early stage (UV)	Identify key players on the top team and their human resources views Explore different ways HR can be involved in strategy formulation
Determine management style for the teamworking organisation	Stay within current strong hierarchical style vs. Encourage much greater autonomy and less hierarchical direction	Lack of knowledge as to how much resistance or cooperation there will be with attempts to change style (UV) Lack of knowledge as to how competent existing managers will be with a new style (UE) Lack of knowledge of costs to moving to new style (UE) Uncertainty about styles that will be appropriate (UE/UR)	Consult managers about what they see as appropriate management styles Benchmark management practices against other forms Undertake attitude analysis and psychological testing of managers Liaise with top team to determine required style

GROUP: Human Resources

Initiatives	Now			Future		
	Actions	Explorations		Actions	Explorations	
Identify company objective and mission	Request involvement in overall strategy process	Explore different ways HR function can be involved in strategy process		Translate overall strategy into a form others can understand		
Determine management style for the teamworking organisation	Initiate consideration of new management style	Liaise with top team/other departments to determine required style Undertake attitude analysis and psychological testing of existing managers		Define most viable and appropriate management style	Consult managers as to best way to support continuous development of new style	

GROUP: Manufacturing Support Services

Focal initiatives	Key choices or dilemmas	Uncertainties that make choosing difficult	Possible explorations
Determine business rationale for teamwork in support functions	Relative emphasis to be placed on: reducing costs and increasing quality in operational departments vs. reducing costs in support services	Lack of knowledge of current costs of quality, e.g. waste, customer returns (UE) Lack of clarity about group financial expectations (UR) Lack of knowledge about potential IT to central service functions (UE)	Compile data on waste and customer returns Clarify group financial expectations Survey use of IT in service functions with similar processes
Identify appropriate management structures and styles for support services	Relative emphasis to be placed on hierarchical control of own staff providing services versus facilitating manufacturing staff providing own services	Lack of knowledge of views of senior managers in manufacturing (UV) Lack of knowledge of ways of structuring services activities (UE)	Ask or facilitate top team for clarification of views Investigate how support functions are organised in other companies

GROUP: Manufacturing Support Services

Initiatives	Now		Future	
	Actions	Explorations	Actions	Explorations
Determine business rationale for teamwork in support functions	Take part in determining business rationale for teamworking. Request clarity on financial expectation of group	Compile data on waste and customer returns. Survey use of IT in service functions in other companies		
Identify appropriate management structures and styles for support services	Request top team clarification of views on management and organisation of service functions	Benchmark against organisation of support functions in leading companies	Select management structures and styles for support functions appropriate for teamworking organisations	

Step 4: Agreeing a 'Progress Package' across the whole organisation

Configuration: All participants as one large group

(a) Each group from Step 3 puts up its summary flip chart in a 'poster gallery' and all participants take time to assimilate each poster. The whole group discusses the compatibility or otherwise of each group's proposals for:

- Focal initiatives
- Immediate actions and explorations
- Future actions and explorations.

Where there are conflicts or clashes of priorities, the Step 3 groups are asked to put their cases and decisions made by the whole group, voting if necessary. Solutions may also be sought in terms of combining and re-labelling initiatives, actions and explorations so that they become more strongly cross-functional in character.

(b) The whole group produces a summary of its proposals in terms of a flip chart listing focal initiatives, actions and explorations for the next round of activity, and noting some future actions and explorations that will be reviewed once the coming round is completed. It may also be useful to note any consensus that certain time-consuming and expensive initiatives should be consigned to the 'backburner'.

(c) The group as whole agrees which person or department is going to take a lead in convening activity concerning each of the coming round of actions and explorations.

Case study of Carco: Step 4

The next page shows the Commitment Package agreed by the 25 Carco managers. This illustrates a number of the benefits stemming from the way that the methodology allows several

[276]

Overall Progress Package

Initiatives	Now		Future	
	Actions	Explorations	Actions	Explorations
Clarify business strategy and objectives		→ Analyse firm's strengths and weakness in its product markets (B) → Undertake market research concerning viability of easier-to-make products (B,O) → Forecast and evaluate available manufacturing technologies (O) → Compile data on waste and customer returns (O, S)	→ Identify strategic goals for business, with time scales (B, S, O, H) → Develop a manufacturing operations plan, with strategic cost objectives (O, B)	→ Investigate Activity Based Costings (S)
Define 'organisational vision' – the type of organisation and management style we need		→ Benchmark ourselves against leading manufacturing companies, in particular concerning: (H, S, O) – use of IT in support functions, e.g. finance, quality systems – organisation of support functions – management practices and styles in general → Carry out focus groups with managers and employees to find out what they see as important in their jobs (H)	→ Identify management behaviours and skills needed to support new strategy (B, S, O, H) → Select management structures for support functions (B, S, O, H) → Communicate new thinking on management styles (B,H)	→ Undertake skills audit of work force (H)

Deferred initiatives important for consideration at next overall planning and sequencing sessions: Redesigning team boundaries, Shop floor training

Key: B = Business Strategy Team; S = Manufacturing Support Services; M = Manufacturing and Engineering; H = Human Resources

[277]

different possible inter-related initiatives to be considered jointly by different stakeholders, compared with a more conventional linear planning process.

The overall business strategy group, in their deliberation during Step 3, were concerned with finding the most effective strategic process to use, with a degree of participation by other stakeholders in the organisation informed by what such people saw as appropriate for them. The commitment packages proposed by the other three groups in fact indicated that each group had well formed ideas as to how it needed to be involved in the determination of the overall strategy and organisational vision, effectively short-circuiting the first round of explorations that the Overall Business Strategy group had seen as necessary.

The upshot was an Overall Commitment Package where there are a number of explorations underway in a first round of activity, with a variety of stakeholders responsible for them, and all feeding into a future definition of business strategy and organisational vision, to be led by the Overall Business Strategy group, but with clearly defined roles for other stakeholders. This process is more effective than a conventional, linear and top down strategic planning process in two respects. First, it leads to quicker formulation of strategy, based on accurate information, since the stakeholders best placed to carry out relevant explorations are authorised to do so and can proceed simultaneously. Second, these stakeholders can then act with an awareness of how their responsibilities are to feed into an overall process, making it more likely that they will understand, accept and act on the basis of the outcomes of strategy making.

Step 5: Making commitments across departments

Configuration: Participants begin within department-based groups, but take part in cross-departmental meetings to make arrangements for making progress

(a) Each department group considers the actions and explorations proposed or agreed for the organisation as a

---

whole, and what they see as being their role in carrying them out. They identify who else from which other departments would need to be involved.

(b) Groups send out representatives with their views on their role to the designated convenors for each action or exploration. Each convenor chairs an initial meeting of representatives of all departments who feel they have a role, with an agenda of clarifying who needs to be involved in what kind of a way for making progress with the action or exploration.

(c) In a final plenary reporting session, the group convenors report on progress made in establishing who needs to be involved in what, and what next steps are. The whole group discusses any immediate problems or conflicts.

(d) Finally, participants discuss when it will next be useful to have a follow-up large group planning and sequencing workshop. Usually, this will make most sense when the initial round of actions and explorations have been completed. Depending on how many unexpected things have happened, or the amount of time that has elapsed, the next workshop may at one extreme repeat the whole process described from Step 1 onwards. At the other extreme, if those planning the next workshop feel that the basic situation has not changed a great deal, the event may profitably begin with a brief review of the 'Progress Package' agreed at the end of Step 4 of the current workshop and then move straight to Step 3, with department based groups considering the implications of explorations they have been involved in for the next round of actions and explorations.

Case study of Carco: Step 5

The precise arrangements for cross-functional groups to be set up within Carco, to carry out the round of explorations needed prior to strategy-making, do not contribute much to this general overview of the TIM Planning and Sequencing Methodology. More relevant is that participants agreed to convene again two months ahead to consider the situation created by the explorations agreed.

Using the TIM Planning and Sequencing Methodology

This TIM methodology is applicable to those situations in which multiple aspects of organisation are being changed simultaneously and in overlapping sequence. Of special relevance are those situations in which changes, or lack thereof, in one aspect of organisation affect progress in another. While the methodology recognises an overall motive for such comprehensive changes, special attention is paid to competing pressures and conflicts of interest experienced by those responsible for implementing changes while also managing the needs for continuity – individual, group and organisational – basic to daily operations.

The Tavistock Institute recommends participation of all those responsible for implementing organisational changes and technological innovations. If all the key actors – or, at minimum, a significant quorum of those in positions of formal authority and informal influence – are not present, then achievement of the purposes of the methodology will be weakened. Depending on the size of the organisation, as few as 12 and as many as 50 can be accommodated.

Numbers should be determined by adequate representation to make the methodology successful. Based on the Institute's research into comprehensive change, the following aspects of organisation need to be represented, with possible involvement along any other geographical and hierarchical identity groups relevant to the particular organisation:

- Business strategy and overall organisational design
- Finance and accounting systems
- Information technology systems
- Operational systems (e.g. production, engineering, service management)
- Employee relations, industrial relations and personnel

- Job design and related developments of individuals, groups or organisation
- Technical quality systems.

Although the method might be of interest to external management and organisational consultants, it has been designed primarily for those working inside organisations who have responsibility for implementing organisational and technological changes.

The Tavistock Institute offers three versions of this methodology for planning and sequencing complex organisational and technological changes: a one-day working session; a three-month series of activities; and an on-going, longer-term process. The first version – the short working session – has been spelled out in detail, along with the case study of Carco, above. All versions share one element in common. Those responsible for implementing changes engage in activities (which differ in frequency, duration, and type depending on the version) designed for the purposes of:

- Developing their capabilities to review, plan and sequence those change initiatives which constitute the comprehensive changes necessary within the organisation
- Increasing awareness of the challenges and opportunities for organisational change and technological innovation facing them both individually and collectively
- Undertaking a decision-making process that accommodates changes in the problem itself over time, handles management of complexity, and deals with management of multiple uncertainties
- Making commitments to each other for implementing change initiatives in a way that takes cognisance of inter-related changes developing simultaneously and sequentially.

Someone considering using the planning and sequencing methodology needs to study these purposes carefully both to understand what the methodology can do and, perhaps more importantly, what it cannot do. The methodology cannot help executives and managers undertake a top-down, linear, problem-free strategic planning process in which planning is followed by implementation, followed by evaluation. It is the

[281]

bias of the creators of this methodology that such an approach is inappropriate and ineffective for comprehensive changes.

Comprehensive changes require cycles of review, planning and sequencing in which each cycle changes the conditions in which successive cycles take place. As multiple change projects, with multiple initiatives (some incremental and some more dramatic) being undertaken simultaneously throughout the organisation are required, no one executive or manager can be in a position to plan, monitor and adjust to outcomes of change efforts. Addressing unintended consequences, unpredictable events, partial successes, competing pressures and conflicts of interests must be a part of managing such change. Such messiness and confusion (and the resulting anxiety) is a characteristic of comprehensive change, not a failure on the part of managers, method, or consultants. Therefore, this methodology can not promise conflict-free, neatly controlled solutions to the challenges of interrelated decisions.

Nonetheless, the creators of the methodology are confident the above purposes can be achieved to varying degrees depending on the version of the methodology being used. Good progress can be made towards the purposes with the short working session. The shortest version of the methodology can be used effectively for building a common awareness and understanding of the opportunities and challenges facing the organisation overall and its relevant parts. The short working session can make a contribution to those organisational development goals typical of a team building or cultural change intervention.

Significant progress can be made towards the purposes with the quarterly activities. This second version of the methodology has the advantages of the short working session with the addition of more in-depth work on interrelated decision areas and examination of the uncertainties once additional information is collected. The quarter-long activity can make a contribution to some of those organisational development goals typical of data feedback, team-building, cultural change, problem-solving and conflict resolution interventions.

[282]

The continuing, longer-term process engages the organisation in developing as a learning organisation, in which cultural resistance to achieving the purposes can be worked through. Therefore, the greatest achievement of the purposes is likely with this version; however, an organisation would be advised to commit to the quarter-long activity before committing to a lengthier involvement. The longer-term process can make a contribution to those organisational development goals typical of action research, self-directed job and organisational design, and cultural change interventions.

In summary then, what happens in the short working session described in detail in this chapter? Those people responsible for implementing organisational changes and technological innovations gather together for one day of uninterrupted thinking and talking. The only topic or issue under consideration is planning and sequencing multiple, interrelated change initiatives necessary for bringing about effective development and change. During the day, participants meet in the following configurations around steps in the 'strategic choice' methodology:

• As a large group, to identify opportunities or challenges facing the organisation as regards planning and sequencing multiple developments and changes
• In small groups across functions or products/processes, to explore interrelated decision areas or change initiatives
• In small groups by function or products/process, to study their particular implications for both the overall comprehensive changes and the interrelated decisions
• As a large group, to identify promising areas for simultaneous progress throughout the organisation
• In inter-groups by interrelated change initiative, to examine more fully the nature of relationship and to consider commitments for mutual cooperation and compromise.

Prior to the short working session, executives and senior managers meet to agree the guidelines for the meeting, the boundaries for decision-making, the selection of people to participate, and the content and process for invitation and communication related to the working session. After the short working session, executives and senior managers meet to

[283]

evaluate the day and to discuss their role in leading the changes.

A minimum of three days is involved in the short working session: one day during which the executives and senior managers prepare for the day-long event (agree guidelines, boundaries, selection, communication, and logistics); one day for the event itself; and one day during which executives and senior managers evaluate the outcomes and consider their role in the changes.

As an uninterrupted day is required for the success of this short working session, a location needs to be chosen away from the demands and pressures of the office or shop floor. In addition to a room large enough to hold the number of participants meeting as a large group, small seminar rooms or spaces with sufficient privacy will be needed equivalent to the number of groups which will be meeting separately and then together. These logistical arrangements may be worked out during preparation discussions.

Further Reading

Friend, J. and Hickling, A. 1987. *Planning under Pressure: the strategic choice approach.* Oxford: Pergamon Press.

12

Concluding Thoughts

Four important messages in this book merit summarising here. The first concerns the *nature of teamwork* and its development. Arrangements labelled 'teamwork' take many different forms. Those that people in manufacturing companies regard as successful do, however, share a basic social attribute – they demonstrate a renegotiation of boundaries of authority and control linked with development of individual and group competence. This occurs in a number of ways. Teams usually exhibit variety in terms of the knowledge and experience brought to bear, and fluidity in terms of who is taking a lead at a particular point in time. There is an underlying assumption that a group of people can together take authority to accomplish a task, which, if not actively agreed to, is implicitly accepted and pursued. This provides a basis for the development of group competence.

Teams are not devoid of conflict or competition, but offer a potentially more fluid pattern as to which perspective dominates, as to who takes what authority and who controls. All members do not usually have an exactly similar view on the value of the task, or on the best means of tackling it. Rather, they tend to see the task through the particular framework of values and assumptions which guided their previous organisational lives, often associated with their occupation. In successful team arrangements, people show a willingness to tolerate these conflicts in the interests of moving the task forward. Teamwork also does not mean absence of external controls. Teams of all kinds are generally set up within an increasingly tight and explicit system of overall company measurement and control, and have to justify their actions with respect to this. Part of functioning successfully as a team is learning to manage the constraints placed upon the team's authority.

The overall dynamic of teamworking arrangements then is one of opening up entrenched patterns of authority and control to release collective competence. Once established patterns have been challenged successfully, it is very difficult for these challenges not to continue, particularly as teams gain greater and greater competence. Hence the importance placed in this book on reinforcing and developing teamworking. Teamworking will either develop further or degenerate back into previous patterns of authority and control under a different name.

The second conclusion concerns the *role of teamwork in comprehensive organisational and technological changes occurring* within Western manufacturing. This book has painted a picture where teamwork sits at the nexus of a wide range of change initiatives which together amount to a realignment of manufacturing. This realignment is needed to respond to the competitive success of 'lean manufacturing' systems in Japan, where the implementation of new quality, manufacturing and engineering techniques has been facilitated by a very particular type of organisational culture. This culture apparently manages to combine immense respect for rules and authority with the bringing of initiative and critical faculties to bear in analysing processes and making improvements. Given that Western industrial culture seems to see these two elements as contradictory rather than complementary, the types of teamwork described in this book in a sense stand as a Western answer to the question of organisational culture. More fluid patterns of authority and control and the collective expertise liberated by them offer a different route for implementing the same quality, manufacturing and engineering techniques. In particular, they address the need for an integrated cross-functional approach to planning, monitoring and developing manufacturing processes. At the same time, they raise unresolved issues about where the boundaries of authority and control should lie. Are they really being pushed back, so that the authority of the shop floor is increasing? If so, at whose expense? And where does the process stop?

The third conclusion stems from the first two. The fact that *teamworking both unfreezes authority issues and brings them more to the surface* and the fact that it is so central to new manufacturing priorities and techniques together mean that the management of change is a bewilderingly complex matter.

Much of this book has been devoted to conveying the interconnected nature of the many change initiatives in different parts of a manufacturing organisation that interact with the development of various kinds of teamworking. Either they require some form of teamworking in order to proceed, or else teamwork in one arena becomes stalled unless a particular change is made in another. Reinforcing and developing teamworking to meet competitive challenges will almost inevitably involve significant changes at some point in each of the five main areas: business and organisational strategy; work design and related training; quality, manufacturing and engineering systems; company planning and control systems; and industrial relations and personnel policies.

Progress through these areas, however, is not easy to chart in advance, or even to describe. While the detailed patterns of movement around the five areas seem to depend very much on particular company circumstances, and are difficult to predict, it is possible to identify some very broad patterns. In the 1980s and 1990s, changes have predominantly started from considerations of business and organisational strategy and quality, manufacturing and engineering systems. Issues of work design, industrial relations and personnel practices almost always take on a central role sooner or later, but are often encountered only once the programme of change is well underway. This is almost the opposite emphasis of the Quality of Work Life movement of the 1960s and 1970s.

At best change takes a directed but iterative course, as

unanticipated blockages and interconnections are discovered, and various groups' reactions to change emerge. One group may become much more defensive when its members realise that those in other groups are questioning the continued relevance of their expertise, or when they hear new proposals as to where authority to make decisions should lie. No simple formula exists as to how organisational leaders should navigate through this sea of change initiatives – there is no one obvious linear progression route through the five main areas, rather a need to revisit different aspects of each many times over. The metaphor of areas of change moving from 'ground' to 'figure' and back again, as issues emerge and are dealt with, is a useful one. It is vital to think of managing teamwork-related change in terms of regularly reviewing possible areas for initiative and their interrelationships, rather than drawing up a master plan of several years' work and ploughing through it regardless.

The fourth message concerns the *importance of recognising that worries about job security and threats to people's work identities* often play a fundamental role in teamwork-related change programmes. Mature and declining markets and more efficient forms of organisation have led to marked falls in levels of employment in practically all sectors of UK manufacturing in the last fifteen years. Very few companies have been able to sustain growth in employment numbers, and most medium-sized and large companies have been managing decline. In such circumstances, recent experiences of seeing colleagues made redundant are very much part of the experience of employees as they encounter changes associated with teamwork. Further, organisational leaders often present these changes as necessary because of difficult business conditions and as giving rise to a still more efficient organisation, and hence quite possibly a 'leaner' one. In the current national climate of high unemployment, threats to job security and people facing choices as to how to respond to them lie at the heart of teamwork-related change programmes.

This is the part of teamwork change that is fundamentally political. In any successful transition to teamwork there is usually a stage where in some forum or other employee representatives and managers negotiate a new balance or trade-off of interests. Employees accept that new working practices are needed to ensure the survival of the company and their jobs, and senior managers accept that employees will perform more effectively in some ways, but will continue to reserve their creativity and energy in others. In renegotiating what is really an informal contract, employees continue to be aware that their employers' interest in them is inevitably limited – if market conditions become difficult, there will be a parting of the ways. Likewise, organisational leaders are unwise if they imagine that they have a right to total commitment and unlimited effort from employees, who inevitably continue to make calculations about just how much they owe their employer and how much they need to invest in other areas of their lives. The terms of an agreement to cooperate on a new basis are crafted in the best traditions of political compromise, without denying divergence of interests.

New political settlements need to be crafted not only between managers and blue-collar workers. Teamwork and related changes in manufacturing and engineering systems profoundly question the continued relevance of many traditional engineering occupations – such as work study – as well as traditional supervisory and middle management competencies concerned with directing the work of others and maintaining work discipline in the form of adherence to detailed procedures. Managing change involves allowing space for threatened groups, such as supervisors and middle managers, to identify elements of their old job that can be built on in the new circumstances. They can then begin to craft a new work identity for themselves. In the process, there are once more elements of loss and of gain.

Index

cellular production 25, 36-7, 152, 157-64, 174
centralised processing functions 83, 86
Chaney, Brian 11
change
    and disruption 60-1, 62-3
    agents 35, 53, 54, 55, 56, 57, 58, 80-1, 108, 205
    comprehensive, and teamwork 9-10, 50-69
    contradictions in 62-3
    'cooker' metaphor 64-6
    employee attitudes to 60-1
    fear of 159-162
    initiatives 51-4
        identification 250
        interconnected 52, 102-3, 138-40,168, 170, 194, 196-7, 225, 246-8
coaching 131,135
coal mining (UK) 20
collective bargaining 199, 200
commitment *see* motivation
communication 58, 259-60
    across functions 87-8
    processes 204-7
company redirection methods 73-4
    see also organisational restructuring
competition, global 23-4
competitive advantage 72
computer aided production management (CAPM) 151
computerisation *see* information technology
computerised accounting systems 154-5
conformance quality 144, 147-8
consultants, external 81, 131, 134, 137, 205
consultation 58, 204-7
'cooker' metaphor 64-6
cost accounting 182-9
counselling 133, 136
craft demarcations 201
critical success factors 176-9
cross-functional task teams 30, 31, 45-8, 72, 115, 175, 207, 258
cross-training 37, 39, 116, 131 *see also* multi-skilling

customer 143, 176
    relationships 54, 74, 97-102

Dale 144
Davis, Lou 110
dedicated service team. 42, 44
Department of Employment 21
Department of Trade and Industry (DTI) 11
'dependent' level of self-regulation 235, 238-40
design for manufacture 164-70
design quality 143, 147
developing teams 229-45
disruption 60-1, 62-3
dominant coalition 66-8

electronic communications systems 204, 207-8
employee
    attitude 60-2, 90-1
    fears 159-62, 199
    involvement 206
    needs 106-7
    recognition 222-3
enabling agreement 201-3
engineering
    simultaneous 164-8
    systems 55-6
engineering manufacturing systems 142-71
Europe 19, 22, 23
European Committee for Standardisation 146

failure mode and effect analysis (FMEA) 147
feedback on performance 223
figure (concept in organisational change) 50-69,
    shifting 63-8
financial decision-making 182-9
flexibility 199-200, 202
    in job design 110
flattened hierarchies *see* hierarchies, flattened
Ford, Campbell 11
Foster, Michael 110
Francis 165
Friedmann, Andrew 67, 183, 186, 188, 197

Team Management
Practical New Approaches
Charles Margerison and Dick McCann

(PB, £9.99, 176pp, 229 x 145mm, 1-85252-114-7)

Team Management presents a new set of techniques developed by two influential thinkers and consultants, Dr Charles Margerison and Dr Dick McCann. These techniques will improve team performance and increase your business success.

Margerison and McCann have drawn on the original findings of psychologist Carl Jung and adapted his concepts to the workplace. The heart of their techniques is the Team Management Wheel - a management tool to aid self-understanding, teamwork, career development, communication and leadership.

'This book provides a new insight into understanding how people work together and is an essential handbook for managers who wish to improve cooperation and commitment within teams.'
Journal of Management Psychology

'The springboard for a radical reappraisal of the way work teams do business in your organisation.'
Quality Newsletter

Dr Margerison and Dr McCann are co-founders of the international consultancy, Team Management Systems, which promotes and supports the techniques and principles outlined in this book. Before founding TMS, Dr Margerison spent a number of years working in industry, government and education. He has been a Professor of Management at Cranfield in the UK and the University of Queensland in Australia. Dr McCann's previous experience was as a chemical engineer and in project management for the alternative energy business.

The Quality Revolution
Best Practice from the World's Leading Companies
Steve Smith

(HC, £19.95, 400pp, 234 x 156mm, 1-85251-113-3)

Total Quality has caused one of the biggest shake-ups ever in western management practice. Today, Quality in business is a pre-requisite for success. *The Quality Revolution* looks at how successful companies have transformed their businesses with Quality and how they have obtained major benefits as a result.

The Quality Revolution identifies lessons for all managers. Anyone with vision and determination can lead their own Quality revolution. *The Quality Revolution* shows how.

Steve Smith has been learning about revolutionary change for twenty years. In that time he has helped over a hundred and fifty organisations, including many blue chip names, to manage change more effectively and positively. He is chairman of Quest Quality, an international management consultancy which focuses on transforming organisations.

Dr Smith is one of the pioneers of the Quality movement in Europe. Before forming Quest Quality in 1988, he was a director of PA Consulting Services, where he set up the TQM division in the early '80s. Prior to that he was a lecturer at the University of Aston in Birmingham for two years and a manager with Chrysler for eight years.

'Books about TQM and quality have poured out of publishers in recent years. But few are as practical or valuable as *The Quality Revolution*. This book is packed with the kind of hands-on detail which brings a quality programme to life.'
Executive Management

Global Quality
The New Management Culture
John Macdonald & John Piggott

(HB, £16.95, 22~pp, 234mm x 156mm, ISBN~ 5251-039-0)

Global Quality is an established guide to the principles and practices of quality management.

ABOUT THE AUTHORS

John Macdonald is recognised as a pioneer in bringing the quality revolution to Britain. He is a frequent contributor to the national and business press, TV and radio and is a well-known speaker on quality. Having joined forces with Philip Crosby in 1983, he left Crosby Associates in 1988 to write this book and to develop his concepts with consultants Resource Evaluation Ltd.

John Piggott is a member of the Board of Management of the British Quality Association and a member of the Institution of Production Engineers Quality Management Activity Group. In 1989 he helped form the Total Quality Management group of Resource Evaluation Ltd.

'An easy-to-read introduction to TQM...accessible to the typical British manager in a way that some other summaries of this topic are not' *Financial Times*

'An excellent introduction to the theories and practice of TQM' *Virginia Bottomley*

'For those interested in implementing Global Quality this book provides an excellent background' *Total Quality Management*

But We Are Different!
Quality For the Service Sector
John Macdonald

(HB, £16.95, 224pp, 229mm x 148mm, ISBN: 1-85251-131-1)

A new guide from the authors of *Global Quality*, applying the pioneering principles of TQM to the service sector.

This book highlights the desperate need for quality improvement in a variety of service organisations. Experience and research shows that the waste of resources in the service sector amounts to more than 30% of operating costs. Additionally the customer is not getting the service he demands. However, a major barrier to progress lies in the service perception that the lessons of quality management only have practical application in manufacturing.

But We Are Different (subtitled *Quality Sells Services*) recognises the differences in the service sector and explains them in a wide range of areas. It demonstrates that the principles of TQM are common principles which apply to all organisations. The book describes these principles and then provides a practical guide to their implementation in each area.

ABOUT THE AUTHOR

John Macdonald is recognised as a pioneer in bringing the quality revolution to Britain. He is a frequent contributor to the national and business press, TV and radio and is a well-known speaker on quality. Having joined forces with Philip Crosby in 1983, he left Crosby Associates in 1988 to develop his concepts with consultants Resource Evaluation Limited. He is co-author of *Global Quality*, also available from Management Books 2000.

The Quality Makers
The Leaders and Shapers of Europe's Quality Revolution
Robert Heller

(HB, £25.00, 272pp, 270mm x 195mm, ISBN: 3-907150-47-3)

Robert Heller charts the development of TQM in Europe with in-depth studies of 20 European organisations that are at the vanguard of the total quality revolution. Companies studied include world-class multi-nationals like Ciba, Rank-Xerox, SGS-Thomson, Groupe Bull, British Telecom, Volkswagen and Societe Generale: divisions or affiliates of leading corporations like Honeywell, British Airways, and American Express; national champions like Italy's Alenia and Britain's Post Office.

ABOUT THE AUTHOR

Robert Heller was the founding editor of *Management Today*, now Britain's leading monthly business magazine. He has written many books, including most recently The Superchiefs (also available from Management Books 2000) and continues to write regularly for a number of leading periodicals.

Guides to W Edwards Deming's Quality Theories

W Edwards Deming was arguably the founder of Total Quality Management. His pioneering approach first came into public acclaim when he was employed by the Japanese to assist in their corporate reconstruction following the Second World War. Honoured by the Japanese for his remarkable success, Deming went on to become the recognised master of Quality.

Management Books 2000 publishes a unique collection of guides to Deming's theories and principles, as set out below.

The Deming Management Method
Mary Walton
(HB, £16.95, PB, £9.99, 256pp, 234mm x 156mm)

The definitive basic guide, reprinted several times since publication in1989. Recommended by the British Deming Association as an introduction to the Deming's theories and principles.

'Lucid, practical and thoroughly convincing' *Business*

Deming Management At Work
Mary Walton
(HB, £16.95, 256pp, 234mm x 156mm)

A companion volume to *The Deming Management Method* this book is a review of Deming's theory *in practice*, taking a detailed look at six successful companies which have followed the Deming methods. It explains both theory and application.

'A useful, easy-to-read guide for employing the master's methods.' *Los Angeles Times*

Guides to W Edwards Deming's Quality Theories (contd)

Dr Deming – The Man Who Taught the Japanese About Quality
Rafael Aguayo
(HB, £25.00, 304pp, 234mm x 156mm)

'Dr Deming has become synonymous with quality. But the essence of his masterly teaching, excellently expounded in this book, is that quality is synonymous with everything that makes the difference between bad management and very good'
Robert Heller

The Deming Route To Quality and Productivity
William W Scherkenbach
(HB, £14.95, 176pp, 234mm x 156mm)

In 1982, at the recommendation of Dr Deming, William Scherkenbach joined Ford Motor Company with responsibility for guiding the implementation of Deming's philosophies throughout the company. Based on his success at Ford he is now helping General Motors implement the Deming philosophy.

The Keys To Excellence - The Deming Philosophy
Nancy R Mann
(HB, £12.95, 156pp, 216mm x 138mm)

A concise guide, written by the former Vice President of the American Statistical Association.

'A rattling good read...As clear a message as you're likely to find anywhere' *Executive Development*